Getting the Max from Your Graphics Computer

Lisa Walker and Steve Blount

NORTH LIGHT BOOKS

Cincinnati, Ohio

95 94 93 92 91   5 4 3 2 1

The permissions on page 160 constitute an extension of this copyright page.

Library of Congress Cataloging-In-Publication Data

Blount, Steve
      Getting the max from your graphics computer / Steve Blount and Lisa Walker
      p.   cm.
      Includes index.
      ISBN 0-89134-392-S
      1. Computer graphics.   I. Walker, Lisa.   II. Title.
   T385.B6 1991   91-6809
   006.6—dc20   CIP

Produced for North Light Books, an imprint of F & W Publications, Inc., 1507 Dana Avenue, Cincinnati, Ohio 45207 by Blount & Walker Visual Communications, Inc., 136 Buckskin Way, Winter Springs, Florida 32708.

Edited by: Mary Cropper
Interior designed by: Sandy Conopeotis

. . .

WHAT THE WORLD HAS COME TO

The burning question is not <u>whether</u> to use design computers, but <u>how</u>

There's nothing automatic about art. A technology is only as good as its end product. For working designers, that means not only the *design* that results from a process, but also the *profit* it generates. To be good, a technology not only has to work, it has to work economically. As you'll see from the case studies presented here, the desktop graphics computer is a very good technology indeed. But while graphics computers have been promoted as the answer to all of our needs, they are, in fact, the *best* solution to only some of them. We wanted to know how design studios are using these computers in the real world and how the myths stack up against the day-to-day reality of producing real work for real clients with real deadlines.

We talked to studios large and small, to desktop publishers, service bureaus, pre-press shops, publishers, and printers.

ROLE MODELS

Graphics computers play some role—often a major one—in the work done by the vast majority of mid to large-sized studios. They play a role in a large number of small studios as well. Regardless of their size, studios with well-established computer operations have gone far beyond the basics of electronic cut-and-paste and are heavily into experimentation with multimedia, color separations, three-dimensional imaging, and other "advanced" uses.

In addition to using graphics computers to speed up traditional processes—such as illustration and creating mechanicals—many designers have used their computers as a springboard to launch themselves into businesses ranging from animation to retouching. And while some have opted for the seemingly far-out, others have focused on using their computers to garner new clients and new projects, and realizing new profits from existing clients.

In this book, they tell you how they did it: how they have integrated desktop computers into their studios, what kinds of hardware they use, what services they offer, how they price their work, how they sell their work to clients, and how the results compare—in quality and in terms of profit—to similar work done by traditional means.

Their experiences offer a roadmap to the full variety of destinations open to designers who embrace the computer as a partner as well as a tool.

THANKS A MILLION

We're deeply indebted to the many people who shared their hard-won knowledge with us. The studios listed on the contents page are only the tip of the iceberg; for every case study we selected, there were many others who gave generously of their time and experience to help us with this project. The hardware manufacturers and software developers answered endless technical questions and were instrumental in steering us to the latest and best uses for their goods. In particular, Derek White and Jay Williams at Graphic Connexions in Cranbury, New Jersey, have been a great help to us for several years, serving up both output for our projects and technical expertise on demand. Mark Crumpacker at Landor Associates and Sanjay Sakhuja at Digital Prepress, both in San Francisco, were especially generous with their time and their knowledge as were Brian O'Neill at Hornall Anderson Design Works and Tom Harper at Peterson & Blyth. Special thanks are due Doug Howe at Nikon for opening his Rolodex to us and to Alan Darling at QuadText and Brian Blackwelder at Rapid Lasergraphics.

We're also deeply indebted to our publisher, F+W Publications, for its support and especially for the help afforded us by David Lewis, Diana Martin, Mary Cropper, Sandy Conopeotis, and Lynn Perrigo in getting this book into print.

We only hope that you'll find these studies half as engaging and helpful as we did.

— Steve Blount and Lisa Walker

CONTENTS

• • •

Depending on your point of view, graphics computers may be the best, or the worst, thing that's happened in the graphics field in the past decade. No matter how you feel, the genie is out of the bottle and designers who've learned to use computers wisely—to lower prices, raise profits, and create new services—have a tremendous advantage.

• • •

Studios are learning how to maximize their investment in computers by using them on high-volume, high-profile publishing assignments that would have been beyond their reach using conventional means. The mouse's roar has been heard on Madison Avenue, too; advertising agencies have integrated graphics computers into their operations.

• • •

Yes, you can do professional color from the desktop. Desktop equipment is capable of making commercial-grade continuous-tone separations. Studios are using this capability in many ways: Some boost revenues and profits by providing pre-press to their clients while others have focused on retouching and electronic collage.

• • •

The most aggressive typographers have become service bureaus, offering a buffet of high-tech production services from PostScript separations to slide imaging to full pre-press functions. Savvy studios exploit these new services, letting service bureaus carry the burden of buying and maintaining high-priced equipment.

• • •

Clear, dynamic, convincing composites can make a sale more quickly than any other single tool. The key is in choosing the right tool for the right job, and while color comping gear is pricey, it's proven to be cost-effective by reducing client uncertainty and shortening production times.

• • •

Graphics computers have helped spark a renaissance in typography by putting the means of producing fonts in the hands of thousands of designers, making each studio a potential type foundry. A few have seized this potential, creating type for electronic media and even whole alphabets for commercial distribution.

New markets—for business presentations, training programs, and educational materials—have opened to studios that have branched out into multimedia. While interactive technology is still far from being mature, it's being used more frequently for commercial applications in advertising and promotion.

.   .   .

The videocassette recorder is now found everywhere, vastly expanding the demand for electronic graphics. With powerful animation and video-editing capabilities available for desktop graphics computers, some designers have found animation a lively and profitable new niche for their talents

.   .   .

The pressure to move, respond, and create faster affects everyone. A few studios have leveraged their graphics computers to give them more time to design, while telecommunications links with clients' computers have proved a boon to some, giving them a toehold inside the client's own marketing department.

.   .   .

Just as the airbrush and technical pen spawned designers who specialized in their use, the graphics computer has given rise to a new category of designer: the designer/technologist. Well-paid either as freelancers or part of a permanent studio staff, they act as technical gurus, teaching others and keeping the computers running smoothly.

.   .   .

Few small and mid-sized studios have fully transferred their business controls—estimating, cost tracking, billing—to computers. Those who have describe the new perspectives afforded by having instant access to estimates, costs, and hours as "essential." Two studios demonstrate bare-bones tracking systems that have helped them increase profits.

.   .   .

The large size of graphics files has made networking impractical or uneconomical for many studios. However, high-speed network protocols and the ability to integrate a variety of computers and peripherals is making an effective network a basic tool rather than a luxury.

. . .

CHAPTER 1

FUTURE PRESENT

Meeting challenges is opening new doors for designers

When our editors at North Light Books asked us to check up on how designers are using computers, we found a lot of contentment, shops where a Macintosh or two is being used for page layout with no firm plans for upgrading equipment and skills. But we also found plenty of curiosity: Can graphics computers be used in ways other than as a substitute for the drafting board? Do those uses make sense for designers? How much does the extra hardware cost? How much time is needed to learn advanced software? The questions are good ones. And some answers are starting to emerge.

Clearly, there's nothing wrong with sticking to the knitting, maximizing your use of graphics computers for print production. You will get the highest percentage return per dollar invested by buying a single computer and using it in place of outside typesetting services. That approach makes all kinds of sense in the short term. Your monetary investment in equipment is low. The amount of time invested is small. The savings are proportionally large.

However, the designers we chose to interview for this book have gone beyond using graphics computers to replicate traditional graphics processes. They're exploring the application of computers to making good communications and making money in the most varied, and most creative, ways they can.

While most admit their aggressive use of technology has sometimes created frustrations, they've also found opportunities for growth. Growth of revenues through new products created with the aid of a computer. Growth of profit margins through increasing automation. Growth in skills. These designers are engaged in a bewildering diversity of pursuits. But they have one thing in common: Enthusiasm. Enthusiasm for the technology, and most of all, enthusiasm for their craft.

Remember the thrill you got the first time you revised a layout, reset the type, and printed it out in under an hour? These designers have made that thrill a regular part of their work by challenging their technical skills every day. They've challenged themselves to learn and challenged themselves to *market* their knowledge, finding new clients and pulling profits from businesses that were unknown a few years ago. They've broken a lot of ice for the rest of us. And they're surprisingly eager to share what they've learned.

"I don't think you profit much by keeping new knowledge to yourself," one said. "If I discover how to do something with a computer, chances are someone else can figure it out, too. So I don't gain anything by hiding my skills. If I share information with other designers, maybe we'll all learn faster. We'll stay in front of the curve."

Design studios, advertising agencies, and publishers make money by doing things their clients can't or don't want to do for themselves. Because the technology of mass communications is getting easier to use month by month, staying "in front of the curve"— finding new services to offer and new ways to wring higher profits from existing services—will become increasingly important.

Some businesses are moving communications tasks—especially routine print communications— from outside suppliers to in-house departments. Whether or not the average retailer will be able to create an effective ad using an in-house desktop publishing system is a moot point. He may save enough on your fee to buy twice as much space. Even if the ad is only half as effective, he may feel he's broken even. And he was able to control the whole process. In businesses where the only measure of success is dollars and cents, clients are often more concerned with the cost of their communications than with their effectiveness. And since many clients drastically underestimate the true costs of producing communications in-house (not adding in the cost of employee labor, for example), professional design services begin to look pricey

SNAPSHOT: WHO'S GOING DIGITAL?

In the U.S., six out of ten businesses that employ artists use, or will buy, design computers...

40.1% don't use computers

37.4% own computers

14.5% intend to buy computers

8% use outside computer services

...but ad agencies lag behind design studios

Ad Agencies

43% own computers

34% intend to buy

23% use outside computer services

Design Studios

68% own computers

24% intend to buy

8% use outside computer services

Data courtesy of Hunt Manufacturing and the National Art Materials Trade Association. Source: Research, Inc.

Studios need to go beyond the basics to continue reaping economic benefits from computerization. That's one conclusion that could be drawn from the first comprehensive survey of the use of graphics computers by businesses that employ artists. The survey indicated that more than 50 percent of these businesses will have installed graphics computers by the end of 1990. The survey was conducted in late 1989 for Hunt Manufacturing and released by the National Art Materials Trade Association in 1990. Researchers polled advertising agencies, graphic design studios, and major corporations with art departments. Seventy-six percent of the corporations reported they already owned graphics computers. This suggests designers may be a little behind the clients in the installation of graphics computers. The survey didn't probe the power of those computers, however; designers who buy more powerful workstations can probably hold onto their technological edge over their clients for a few more years.

---

compared to what a secretary can do with Windows® and PageMaker® on an IBM clone.

BEYOND THE COST CURVE

Many of the "dumb" print production tasks designers rely on to boost billings can be automated and done by clients. Even if your clients know they're buying a brain and expertise when they hire you to create a piece or a campaign, how much of your profit comes from design and how much from production services? Could your business survive on design fees alone?

You have to continue to offer services that clients can't, or don't want to, to do for themselves. Most clients' desire is closely linked to their pocketbooks. If they know they need it and can't do it themselves, you get the business. If they need it but can't do it at a lower cost than you can, you get the business. What clients *can* do for themselves has been expanded and its cost cut dramatically by the proliferation of easy-to-use graphics software.

Some designers have found graphics computers to

be a valuable tool in keeping themselves on the front side of that all-important curve: The cost curve.

Because of its ability to output video, film, lithographic negatives, and sound, the graphics computer gives even solo practitioners the kind of media capabilities that were once the province of specialized, highly capitalized studios. As they used to say about the man who designed the Colt .45-caliber Peacemaker (the gun that won the West), "God created all men equal, and Sam Colt made them the same size." Graphics computers are something of an equalizer and can be used to catapult a studio into new, profitable ventures. Some of the strategies used by businesses we interviewed are:

Advanced print production: Simple layout tasks are the ones most likely to be taken in-house by clients. Services that require an in-depth knowledge of printing, more specialized equipment, and expertise with complex software (such as integrating process color or database publishing) can't be done by a secretary with an IBM clone.

Multimedia: Most clients won't want to tackle complex color slide presentations, video, or hypermedia projects. As presentation technology improves, video and slides are being used more frequently. While there are multimedia studios serving this market, the use of a graphics computer may give you a cost advantage. Having both print and multimedia work done in the same studio can save clients money in administrative and design costs. And the convenience factor shouldn't be underestimated. From the studio's point of view, it usually costs less to sell a new service to an existing client than it does to sell to a new client.

New communications vehicles and products: Some studios have become suppliers, selling digital type fonts and clip art, or acting as technology consultants to corporate clients. Others have diversified into interactive software programming, producing sales presentations, catalogs, animation, and educational or training materials.

New and higher revenues are one part of the equation. The other side is profit margin.

Greater efficiency: Graphics computers can help wring more profit from each dollar of revenue. They can do this by increasing your output per hour for items that are billed per unit produced, especially for repetitive production work.

They can also improve cash flow by shortening the amount of time between beginning a job and completing and billing it. The old adage "I'd rather have a quick nickel than a slow dime" is still valid. Computers can make those nickels come in as well as in greater numbers.

Computers count nickels faster, too. Untended, all businesses tend to "leak" money through hundreds of procedural loopholes. There are bills not paid on time that incur finance charges, bills paid too early, unprofitable projects, potential clients not pursued. Comprehensive software for running a design studio—time and billing, purchase orders, invoicing, and marketing—is now available. It's helping studios earn more, and to keep more of what they earn.

DESIGN ADVANTAGE

Who among us hasn't thought, "If I just had another day to really fine-tune this project...." That's the other important plus that computers are bringing to studios. By automating routine tasks and making it possible to handle complex jobs with less administrative oversight, computers leave more time to think. Think about the client's message. Think about how to get it across. Think of visuals that communicate the point.

In the context of what we have to sell—things the client can't or won't do for himself—this may be your most important advantage. The client does not have your training in how people react to communications, he does not have your skill in formulating messages, and he does not have your talent for creating attractive and effective images.

COMMUNICATIONS BREAKDOWN

This brings us to a vital point of philosophy. For a communication to be maximally effective, there has to be a link between the context of a communication and its presentation, between its content and its form. To paraphrase Marshal McLuhan's famous aphorism, the medium *does* greatly influence how well the message registers and is understood, but it is *not* the entire message; the message is the message.

When the work at hand is a piece of communications, designers are communicators first, visual artists second. That ranking is the foundation for the successes profiled in this book, enabling designers to effectively convert new skills and new technologies into cash.

It's unfortunate that interior designers are often called interior decorators. It creates a false equation: Design and decoration are not synonymous; they're two very different things. Too many people believe a designer's function is to make communications visually compelling. It's too easy to get caught up in perfecting the *skin* without considering the *substance* of a project. Too often, the search for visuals that appeal to us as designers creates a gap between content and appearance. Decoration is about appearance. Design is about content.

Ironically, the graphics computer has acquired a taint. A few have found in the computer's ability to tilt and compress images a mandate to do so, whether there was a reason or not. We're not against visual experimentation. Experiments, even overexuberant ones, are part of the lifeblood of the profession. Neo-Dadaism may occasionally be the right stylistic expression for a particular communication, but as an overarching design philosophy, it's a dead end.

One of the stalwarts who helped make mega-agency Ogilvy & Mather such a powerhouse in the 1970s and 1980s was a gentleman named Francis X. Houghton. "X" had only one rule to follow in the pursuit of creative excellence: Be clear and then be clever—but for Christ's sake, at *least* be clear. He was also fond of saying he'd much rather show a client a piece that was mundane but which projected the right strategic message than one that was extremely creative but off-target.

As the projects covered in this book demonstrate, the computer is equally a vehicle for excellent designs as it has occasionally been for bad ones. Though its repertoire of image-manipulation techniques can be seductive, the graphics computer is as value-neutral as a hobby knife. It's value is in how *you* choose to use it.

TOOLS, NOT TOYS

Designers who use their computers as more than electronic drawing boards have found that it is substance, not a pretty skin, that sells their new services. Their experience is underscored by communications buyers such as Lincoln Colby. Colby was for many years the director of field communications and development for international pharmaceutical maker Merck Sharp & Dhome. During his career, Colby has seen business communications advance from no-tech to low-tech to lasers and satellite hook-ups. By itself, he said, technology is never the right answer.

"I look for designers who ask about our communications objectives," Colby said. "You can't sell a canned media program; it has to fit the client's needs. What doesn't work is trying to force-fit a technology to a problem. When a technology is new, people are excited by it. They think, 'I've got to use this for my next project.' It may not be the most effective way of communicating the message. If you're called on to create the media for a business meeting, for example, staging a laser show at the main session will be just that—a laser show, rather than a meeting, which connotes an exchange of ideas.

"Designers need to think of themselves as communicators—visual communicators. They need to think about *what* they're being asked to communicate. As a meeting planner, I have an obligation to my clients. If someone asks me to set up a meeting, I need to ask if a meeting is the most effective way to get the information across. Could it be done with a letter and a stamp instead of a computer presentation in a meeting hall? Designers need to ask those questions, too. What's the purpose of the communication? What kinds of media are appropriate?"

Graphics computers can expand the time available to think about design and expand the variety of creative and production techniques a studio can exploit. They can lower the capital and operating costs associated with color, video, animation, and other media. With this widening capability comes greater choice, and, hopefully, better fit of message with medium. The case studies in this book illustrate how designers are using the capabilities of graphics computers to match new technologies to client needs in a way that is both appropriate and profitable.

CHAPTER 2

PAGE LAYOUT

Small shops lead the way as major players struggle to catch up

Ironically, it's not the mega-buck studios or wealthy advertising agencies that are wringing new profits from desktop publishing. They aren't leading the parade in terms of technology, either. The action in producing printed materials using computers is largely in small, profit-driven design shops and, to a lesser extent, with midsized traditional publishers.

There's a kind of inverse law at work here: With some notable exceptions, the bigger the organization, the more enmeshed it is in traditional production techniques and the greater the inertia that must be overcome in making the switch to desktop publishing. That inertia exists both in the bureaucracy that approves the purchase of graphics computers and among the artists who use them.

The real innovations are coming from firms in the middle of the pyramid, not those at the apex. However, companies that occupy the rarefied atmosphere at the pinnacle of publishing and advertising do know what they're missing and their production managers are quick to admit that digital processes will be the norm very soon. Those who don't convert, they say, will suffer a competitive disadvantage.

DO YOU BELIEVE IN MAGIC?

Whereas enthusiasm and expanding profits are the chief motivations for small- and medium-sized organizations to adopt desktop publishing, fear seems to be the common denominator among larger ones. Is the fear that others will outflank them if they don't adopt the technology justified? Probably. Has this created an opportunity for small- and midsized shops to compete toe-to-toe with the big guys on some business? Definitely.

Client demand for desktop publishing services is growing. There is a widespread perception that digital production is somehow more efficient and therefore less expensive. Apple Computer has done its utmost to foster that impression. Whether digital production is really more cost-effective depends on the task at hand. But clients are beginning to see other benefits of digital production that are very real indeed. These include greater control over the end product by both the client and the producer; the ability to make revisions later in the process and at lower cost; and the ability to archive the bits and pieces of a job, reusing them later and amortizing their cost over two or more projects. Producers, too, are finding that reusing templates, drawings, charts, and clip art is an easy way to squeeze extra profit from each job.

In one instance, a design studio provided its client with both a catalog on film ready to print and with the electronic template used to create the catalog. After the catalog was printed, the client used the template to produce updates for the catalog on a laser printer as new products were released. Previously, the client had created these update pages using a typewriter and clip art. The studio was paid extra for the product update template and the client was pleased by way the laser-printed pages looked. The client's overall cost to produce the catalog didn't increase, yet it got more for its money. The studio's profits didn't decline and it gave the client an obvious reason to consider them for future projects.

This is the genie that studios and publishers are finding in the graphics computer. While they may initially be attracted by the economics, it is the ability to render better service that provides a platform for growth in volume and profits. And this is the bit of magic that makes the largest studios, agencies, and publishers nervous.

CAPITAL CONCERNS

If they're nervous, you ask, why don't they just buy some Macintosh stations and have at it?

Aside from the bureaucratic inertia, the figures just don't add up on a balance sheet for large organizations. Not yet, anyway.

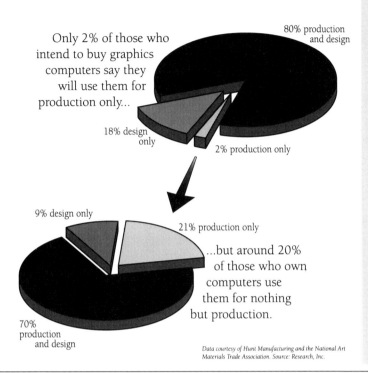

SNAPSHOT: INTENT VS. REALITY—WINDOW OF OPPORTUNITY?

Only 2% of those who intend to buy graphics computers say they will use them for production only...

80% production and design

18% design only

2% production only

9% design only

21% production only

...but around 20% of those who own computers use them for nothing but production.

70% production and design

Data courtesy of Hunt Manufacturing and the National Art Materials Trade Association. Source: Research, Inc.

The study of the use of design computers conducted by Hunt Manufacturing in 1989 contained both good news and bad news for designers. First the bad news: A higher percentage of corporate users have desktop computers used for graphics (76 percent) than do either design studios (68 percent) or advertising agencies (43 percent). The good news: A large number of them are only using the computers for cut-and-paste.

The reasons given for not moving into design and other advanced applications include the high cost of specialized hardware (scanners, imagesetters, film recorders) and the time required to learn the software.

Just as typographic suppliers have had a large chunk of their billings cut by studios who now do their own electronic page files, studios may eventually lose billings from production work as clients move simple jobs in-house. For studios, there are opportunities in offering the advanced services clients can't, or don't want to, bring in-house and in concentrating on electronic design.

Smaller studios, agencies, and publishers who buy their type from outside vendors can use the money saved on typesetting to offset the cost of the equipment. A large organization that already owns typesetting equipment and employs typesetters can't do that.

The more repetition there is, the more money is saved by digital production. Advertising agencies, for example, do a lot of one-off work. While the various executions for a print campaign may contain common elements, the time saved by reusing a template is a small fraction of the billable time required to produce the ad. Creating the concept for the ad and getting it approved take far more time than executing the mechanical.

Graphics computers can produce superb comps, of course. Where they are used in large agencies today, this is their predominant role. But for the senior art director who can produce a marker rendering worthy of Chagall with one hand while re-leading a type galley with the other and negotiating with a freelancer on the phone, the computer offers very little creative leverage. That may change as the "downstream" production processes of the agency are computerized; especially those used for typesetting, to create new business pitches, and gain client approval. The art director's tissues will then be of less use than an electronic concept file that can be quickly merged into an account executive's slide presentation.

In large organizations, the number of workstations required to significantly reduce the reliance on traditional production methods is very large. The total cost, therefore, is high. You could computerize a shop employing ten designers for less than $75,000. If purchases from outside vendors dropped by $25,000 a year, in three years the gear would pay for itself. A shop with one hundred designers would have to lay out $750,000 for the gear, then recoup $250,000 a year in expenses to pay for it. Outside vendors are generally a smaller proportion of the overhead for these companies. The bulk of their overhead is in management and account service. In most cases, neither of these is made drastically more productive by the introduction of graphics computers.

In the world of print advertising, graphics computers can't do anything that can't be done with an airbrush, a Quantel Paintbox®, or a Scitex®. They *can do* them in less time and at a lower cost, neither of which is terribly important to agencies working on large national accounts. In the agency business, the client pays for airbrushing or Scitex time (plus a nice service surcharge levied by the agency) over and above the base cost of the advertising. If there's a rush charge, the client pays that too (along with the service charge on the rush charge). In large agencies, therefore, graphics computers can reduce billings without creating new billings or profits to offset these losses.

For many agencies, the incentives to control expenses are not yet strong enough to make graphics computers mandatory. However, advertisers have begun to pressure agencies to change the way they bill. They're moving away from paying production costs plus a percentage of the media cost to flat-fee arrangements. These pressures will intensify and many large agencies may find the motivation to go digital—at least for their production functions—as they reach the end of the depreciation schedules on current equipment.

BUSINESS OPPORTUNITIES

This time lag between capability and exploitation has opened a window of opportunity.

When it comes to traditional, two-dimensional print production, computers are largely a replacement for the art table, waxer, and photostat camera. Computers contain no intrinsic magic. But, combined with a keen sense of what clients will pay for—effective communications that increase their profits—and a nose for packaging information in novel ways, they have lead some to discover new opportunities. Specific examples are in the case studies that follow, but there are some common themes.

High-volume production: The efficiency of a publishing operation can be increased tremendously using graphics computers. The time not wasted waiting for photostats and galley type adds up quickly; the more pages that are produced, the more time is saved. Large projects, therefore, produce the largest benefits. Catalogs, technical materials, and long proposals, traditionally handled in-house by many clients, can be handled effectively by even a small studio. The client benefits because the material is *designed* rather than merely pasted up. If the design is good, the communication will be more *effective;* easier to read and use.

Complex projects: Generally, the more complex a project, the more elements to be integrated, the more useful a graphics computer. While it does take time to convert the elements—drawings, illustrations, photographs, words—into a form the computer can use, electronic paste-up and the ability to make revisions usually save time in the long run.

Combining technology with design skills: In this world of visual clutter, clients are always looking for ways to "cut through," to make customers pay attention to their message. One way to do that is to have a message that derives its impact from being visually clear; one where the content and the design are synonymous, with graphics used to *clarify* and *communicate* rather than to *decorate.* Graphics can have a powerful impact on how quickly information is communicated. The faster the client's message is delivered, the more likely it is to fit into the customer's attention span and the more impact it will have.

By reducing the hours of labor and materials cost for a project, the computer allows more time to think about what the message should be and to experiment with ways to present it visually. This increases the odds of hitting upon an effective presentation of the client's message. Clients can bring desktop production services in-house, but hiring designers who can create effective communications is much harder.

THE UNDERSTANDING BUSINESS

High-volume, high-touch products combine with full-color PostScript for this San Francisco studio

Although our subhead suggests The Understanding Business is a studio, the folks who work there would probably bridle at that suggestion. It's a lot more than a place where clients come to have some clever graphics done or to find a new name and a well-made package for a consumer product. The Understanding Business, founded by designer Richard Saul Wurman, is about creating, well, *understanding*.

If you accept the notion that the purpose of the visual arts is to render information and emotions in a visual form, then you'll have no trouble understanding what Wurman et al. mean when they say they create *understanding*. They take *data* supplied by clients and publish it in a way that is easy to understand—turn it into *information* that can be used and acted on. That means more than designing clean layouts and catchy decorative elements. It means rolling up the sleeves and wading into the marketing equation, comprehending what the client wants to communicate, anticipating how readers will want to receive that information, and then designing products that transmit the message cleanly and clearly.

"We often deal with projects where the amount of data is totally overwhelming," explained Nathan Shedroff, senior designer. "For example, how can you understand everything that's in a telephone book? Our job is to make the information accessible and useful."

While their design process is as much a question of mental acuity as it is of artistry with type and graphics, the graphics computer plays a central role in the shop's philosophy. Control of the process, reduction in the number of different workers needed to complete large projects, and the flexibility to economically update and revise projects right up until final film is created—abilities supported by computers—have been key components in many TUB projects.

BELLWETHER BUSINESS

There are two modes for integrating computers: "gradual" and "trial by fire." TUB chose the latter method, bringing in Macintosh workstations to help complete a project begun for Pacific Bell in 1987. The project was about as complex as publishing gets—revising all 103 local editions of the Pacific Bell Yellow Pages.

Feeling the oncoming challenge from competitors such as R.R. Donnelly's Donnelley Directory, Pacific Bell was looking for a way to make its yellow pages more useful to consumers and more attractive to advertisers.

"We analyzed the content of the yellow pages, trying to find ways to organize the information that would make sense to users," Shedroff recalled. That meant doing things like adding maps of the local areas, seating charts for arenas and stadiums, indexing restaurants by category and location, and creating "subject search" indexes.

The result of the analysis was the SMART YELLOW PAGES® that are becoming standard issue for telephone companies across the country. If you've ever photocopied a seating chart out of a phone book before going to buy concert tickets, you owe TUB a nod.

"The idea of the subject search came to us because we went through the yellow pages and found, for example, that only ten percent of the headings that had to do with automobiles actually started with 'auto.'

SNAPSHOT: THE UNDERSTANDING BUSINESS

The Understanding Business
101 Spear Street, San Francisco, CA 94105
TEL: (415) 543-5673
FAX: (415) 543-5994

Equipment: (30) Macintosh II-family design/production workstations with 24-bit Supermac displays or Apple 13-inch color monitors; (5) Macintosh SEs for editorial stations; (5) Apple IINT laser printers; (1) Apple IINTX laser printer.

Staff: (35) designers and production artists, (2) computer technicians.

Typical clients: Communications or marketing departments of large corporations, and publishers.

The rest started with other letters. The subject search is a spread in each directory where all of the yellow-page headings that pertain to one subject, such as autos, are grouped together."

Sounds simple enough. But yellow pages had been published for the greater part of a century before anyone thought of it.

TUB started revising Pacific Bell's books beginning with the greater Los Angeles area directories in 1987. The project was done in phases, and TUB completed the redesign of all 103 directories with the release of the 1990-1991 editions.

"There was a great deal of graphic design involved," Shedroff said, and TUB handled the project right through to mechanical boards: design, typesetting, paste-up, and post-production.

"At first, we were doing everything traditionally. At the height of the project there were about sixty-five people involved," Shedroff recalled. That's when the Macintosh hit the beach.

"We brought the computers into the project as we felt they could contribute and as we felt comfortable using them," he said. Their impact was enormous.

In the first few editions done by hand, the maps had been drawn conventionally and colors separated using rubylith overlays. One issue TUB faced was in making sure that maps of adjoining areas were drawn so that they fit together correctly. Using the computers, designers were able to create large master maps. Because PostScript® drawings can be enlarged to any size without losing resolution, these master area maps could be easily divided into subsections, enlarged as needed, and printed. The designers no longer had to worry about whether roads and boundaries would align from map to map because they were all sections of the master map.

"Overall, the computers reduced our need for personnel on the project, which dropped by a quarter to a third. The time needed to make corrections dropped dramatically," Shedroff said. "But the real benefit was that we had much better control of the project. Working traditionally, we were handing things off to typesetters or stat houses, then having to track the pieces and check them for accuracy when they were returned. Using the computers, we created the editorial matter and illustrations on Macs and flowed it into page layouts. When the files were ready, we sent out for film, then checked the negatives before sending them on to the client."

There were some learning curves to get up, as well, Shedroff admitted. Not all of the time formerly spent managing outside suppliers was saved, because the designers had to spec the type and ensure its accuracy. "The computers give you the capability of doing many things, but the knowledge needed to do them correctly doesn't come automatically. You have to train people, especially with the color image processing that's now becoming available. The equipment will let you do separations in-house, but you have to *learn* how to do them well.

"The big benefit of that knowledge is to demystify the whole production process. Because you know how to do this work yourself, if you do contract work out to a typesetter or a conventional separation house, you now know what it is that they do, and whether they're doing it well," Shedroff said.

TUB handled the design and production of the smart sections for all 103 guides for two cycles, then turned it over to Pacific Bell.

"We gave them the templates and trained their people how to use the Macintosh to produce these sections," Shedroff explained. "The production of the directories is spread out over twelve months. As the directories came up for revision, we phased ourselves out and they began handling them."

In all, the project lasted for the better part of three years, with TUB going through two complete revision cycles on all 103 directories.

DRAW ME A MAP

An even flashier project, and one no less complex than redefining the yellow pages, was the creation of *The U.S. Atlas*, published by Prentice-Hall in 1989.

The atlas is a fundamental rethinking of the way geographic data is displayed, in the same spirit as the work done by Herbert Bayer—who introduced such notions as the demographic map—in the 1950s.

Designed by Wurman, the atlas threw away one of the fundamental precepts of twentieth-century mapmaking: that maps should fit on the page they're printed on, regardless of the scale required. If you look at a conventional atlas, you'll find that each state map fills one or perhaps two pages. That's fine. It fills up the pages nicely. But it's confusing as heck if you try to compare one area to another. In our office atlas, for example, Rhode Island and Connecticut are drawn so that they fill the same-sized page that Florida is on. The only problem is that, in reality, Florida is 400 miles by 350 miles while Rhode Island is only fifty by thirty miles. You can drive from one end of Rhode Island to the other, from Woonsocket to Westerley (four inches on the map), in under an hour. Driving the territory covered by that same four inches on the Florida map would keep you on the road for more than four hours.

TUB broke the U.S. up into grids. Each grid is the same size and drawn to exactly the same scale. Each grid takes up one spread. The spreads are organized geographically instead of alphabetically, so Alabama falls next to Georgia, rather than Alaska. Looking at this atlas, you can see at a glance that the distance between Boston and Brattleboro is eighty-five miles, about the same as the distance between Bangor and Brunswick in Maine. Maps of larger scale are used to show downtown areas or points of special interest.

Despite the experience TUB had gained working on the Pacific Bell project, Shedroff admitted "we had a lot of learning to do about color, trapping, and print-

ing. Those are things you really don't get a chance to experiment with working on two-color jobs."

The maps, which are printed in five colors, were drawn in Adobe Illustrator®, separated on the Macintosh, and provided to the printer as composite negatives. The cover, created in Aldus Freehand®, was also provided as composite film.

Just getting reference for the maps was a chore. At first, TUB tried converting computerized map files obtained from the U.S. Geological Survey. When that turned out to be impractical, they traced over map references provided by Gousha, a sister company of publisher Prentice-Hall.

These reference materials were scanned in and used as a template for the Illustrator drawings. After the drawings were made, further work was required to provide adequate trapping for the color elements, to surprint type, and to ensure that the negatives would contain the correct color tints.

"We had problems with the printers at first, too," Shedroff pointed out. "They said [our technology] wouldn't work, that the negatives weren't the same as those made by conventional pre-press equipment, that the density wasn't controllable. But it worked. It was a headache at times, but it did work."

When doing a full-color job like the atlas, Shedroff contended that "there's no substitute for experience. The problem is that you don't know what you don't know. No one tells you to bring your own screen fonts when you take the file to the service bureau. No one tells you when you need a trap or how to build a choke and a spread into a file.

"Whether you get help by bouncing ideas off of someone who's knowledgeable about computer color or hiring someone to come in as a consultant, there's no substitute for experience."

Shedroff added that it helps if your color guru can also work with the printer. "We went through a real hand-holding process with the printers to gain their respect. We had to absolve them of all responsibility and offer to pay for test runs.

"There are a lot of people out there using Macintoshes, but they don't necessarily know much about the printing process. Printers are wary of working with people who don't know printing. Designers may have learned a lot of the skills of the typesetter, but many are still not up to speed on color pre-press. A good printer, however, will work with you. In the case of the atlas, the printer became very enthusiastic about the project, and the people in the plant became very proud of their work on it."

While atlases have been around for centuries, this one owes more than its artwork to new-fangled computer technology. The deadline for the project was just six months from start to finish. It would have required a large group of artists to complete the maps and separations in that short a time using traditional methods.

After their experience with Pacific Bell and other projects, the group at TUB was confident they could find a way to create quality color files on the Macintosh. But because of the short deadline, they had to begin the maps before they had all the technical answers in hand.

Flying by the seat of your pants a bit is a common and recurring theme among studios and publishers who are pushing the limits of the technology in order to reap bigger rewards. Predictably, there are downsides, too.

"During the first two months, we were drawing maps even though we didn't know specifically what kinds of trapping and overprinting techniques we'd ultimately use in the files," Shedroff explained. These details were worked out by experimenting with files and with printing while the maps were being drawn.

"Designers need to find out what questions to ask about color," Shedroff said. The dangers lie more in being blind-sided by a technical concern you aren't aware of than in any inadequacy of the technology.

This danger does put a lot of pressure on designers. So far, desktop technology has given us the designer as typesetter and the designer as computer jock. Because of the need to control the process from inside the studio, rather than rely on outside suppliers, we now have the designer as production manager.

"We pulled a Matchprint® color proof for every page of the atlas," Shedroff said. "The proofs were very expensive, but we caught a lot of things in the proofs that, had we tried to correct them on press, would have cost a bundle. If you're doing black and white or spot color, you can get away with a few small errors. Some designers may not think to spend the money up front for color proofs, but tying up a four-color run while you fix something on the plates is very, very expensive."

TOOLS OF THE TRADE

Experiences with the electronics aside, Shedroff was quick to point out that the main business of TUB is not desktop publishing; it is the design of information. The design—how easy it is to see, to read, to grasp, to understand—is what makes the information work and makes it valuable.

TUB imparts value to information by processing and refining it. Graphics computers allow them to do that in ways that may not be economically feasible using traditional methods, or which might not otherwise fit the ever-shrinking timetables that clients desire. "We're able to work faster because we don't have to send out for type or stats, and sometimes that translates into working less expensively," Shedroff said.

Philosophically, TUB hasn't made a business of simply exploiting the computer as a tool—almost anyone can learn desktop publishing. But the design of information is a precise, and valuable, skill. TUB has exploited the computer's ability to enhance and extend the mental skills that it brings to bear on the problems of effective mass communication.

16 · · ·

PLAYBOY MAGAZINE

Proving premium pre-press is possible with PostScript

Whatever your feelings about *Playboy* as a magazine, there's no denying that its color reproduction is in a class that includes a small and select group of publications. This may be the last place you'd expect desktop computers to turn up. After all, flesh tones are among the hardest colors to print. And if there's a magazine that requires good flesh tones, it's *Playboy*.

Actually, *Playboy* has been experimenting with desktop technology since 1987. The initial purchase of a Lightspeed® design station has evolved into a large-scale Macintosh installation. In 1990, the magazine made the decision to go to completely digital production, with at least two-thirds of it being done on the desktop. The reason, for the most part, is the same every other publisher gives: Dollars. Computers save lots of them. But especially for *Playboy*, quality control and profits are just two sides of the same coin.

"Initially, we wanted to save money laying out the magazine. We were using a lot of photostats and galley type," said Eric Shropshire, assistant design director. "I knew that graphics computers would save money, but I also felt they would smooth out the operations in the art department."

Most magazine art departments operate under conditions that are frenetic in the best of times. Publishers aren't known for overstaffing art depart-

ments. And, because the actual number and sizes of ads for any given issue isn't known until shortly before mechanicals are due at the printer, the designers have to work "blind." When the ad count is known, it's a race to the finish to sequence the pages and mold the editorial so that it fits together with the advertising properly. It's kind of like assembling a giant jigsaw puzzle without having the benefit of the photo on the front of the box showing how the thing's supposed to go together.

Playboy has long used its cartoons as "zippers," putting one in to fill a hole, enlarging or reducing them to fit, or dropping them to accommodate late ads. Still, when done manually, this process was tedious and time consuming.

"The computers have made this work faster and more interactive," Shropshire said. "The cartoons can be scanned, then sized to fit. As each section of the magazine is laid out, the production person responsible for that section comes to the art department and sits at a terminal, plugging in the ads."

Most of the changes to the art department's existing layouts are to the cartoons, rarely to the layout of text or to color art. The designers can work freely on editorial material without fear of having to tear it up later. Color art is scanned on one of several color scanners: a Howtek Scanmaster®, a Barneyscan® 35mm scanner, or a video camera. The art is sized and placed in page files created in Quark XPress®. When the advertising and editorial have been merged, the files and the original color art are sent to the service bureau for separation and printing.

As of the summer of 1990, *Playboy* was being separated and printed by Quad Graphics (*see* Chapter Four: Service Bureaus). Using its high-resolution Scitex scanners, Quad scans the color art and substitutes its high-resolution scans for the low-resolution ones in the page files, picking up sizing and positioning from the Quark files. The files are then run through a

---

SNAPSHOT: PLAYBOY MAGAZINE

Playboy Magazine
680 N. Lakeshore Drive, Chicago, IL 60611
TEL: (312) 751-8000
FAX: (312) 751-8252

Equipment: (14) Macintosh IIci workstations with 8-bit or 24-bit RasterOps 19-inch displays, 8 mb RAM, 100 mb hard drives; (1)Barneyscan 35mm scanner; (1) Howtek Scanmaster; (1) video camera and frame grabber; (1) QMS Colorscript color printer.

Staff: (8) designers, (6) computer production artists.

Typical clients: The department designs and produces *Playboy* magazine.

Hyphen® raster image processor running on a Digital Equipment VAX® and sent to a Scitex plotter to be output as composite film. This hybrid of desktop and high-end digital technology has allowed *Playboy* to move into the world of digital production without skipping a beat quality-wise.

Asked whether graphics computers have made the magazine better, Shropshire responded, "It certainly doesn't look any worse. The computers have allowed us to design more, to spend more time on details, and to experiment more freely with typefaces and illustrations. But *Playboy* has always put a great deal of emphasis on design, so whether all of that makes it look better, that's subjective.

"It's given all of us more time to work out our designs, and also a better and faster way of getting work designed, reviewed, revised, and approved. We get a much clearer picture of what the magazine is going to look like at an early stage.

"*Playboy* was a very difficult place to integrate graphics computers because no compromises were made. We weren't going to limit designers to a few typefaces or to the kinds of effects that could be produced easily. We bought a lot of typefaces and a lot of fast Macintoshes. We realized that we weren't going to get what we wanted buying low-end Macs."

The integration took time to accomplish. There were concerns that the boundaries between departments would be blurred. And, there were natural concerns that some jobs might be at stake.

"We had to be sensitive to that," Shropshire said. "We used to have a fair-sized photostat department, but there are only two people left now. That work is being done using scanners now, but someone still has to run the scanner. The people in stat department were transferred into other areas of production; no one has been laid off because of the computers."

The computers were brought in slowly, first in typesetting, then gradually moved into other departments over a period of months.

One would think that converting a premier magazine to digital production would be enough of a laurel to rest on, if only briefly. But Shropshire has loftier goals: proficiency and progress.

"Training is something I'm very concerned about, the thing we're doing least well," Shropshire said. "Unfortunately you can't stop publishing the magazine or pull people out of their jobs to train them. Our people are learning as they're doing things live. That's not the way I would want it, but it's the only way we can do it efficiently."

Shropshire believes *Playboy* will soon be doing high-resolution continuous-tone scanning in-house. "That's the next step: to scan our art here and create files that are ready to be run to film," he said. "High-resolution desktop drum scanners are what we're waiting for. Color separation programs are getting better. By the end of 1990, we expect to be using one of the existing scanners, perhaps the Nikon LS-3500, on a trial basis. We're using the scanners for position images, but we've not yet done any continuous-tone separations that have been printed in the magazine.

"The scanners are only part of the equation. We're also concerned about being able to handle the large files that high-resolution color scanners generate."

Shropshire is investigating an Ethernet® network that would allow the designers to pull images from a central repository. There's also the question of manpower: "We'll need a color person to pull this off. By the time we get through buying the equipment, hiring, and training, I don't know where we'll be. We think it will save us money compared to current pre-press costs, but we haven't done a complete analysis."

Shropshire estimated the magazine's investment in graphics computers at $350,000. That's nothing to sneeze at, but the savings—in type, in stats, and especially in time—have convinced *Playboy's* management it's money well spent.

• • •

BBDO WORLDWIDE

Will Madison Avenue adopt the Mac?

Back in the days chronicled in *The Man in the Gray Flannel Suit* and *Confessions of an Ad Man*, it was known as Batton, Barton, Durstine & Osborne. This is the agency that created the expression "necktie products" to describe the proclivity of Americans to use certain brands to express their status. It fired that memorable salvo in the cola wars sometimes called the "pop heard around the world" by signing Michael Jackson to moonwalk for Pepsi-Cola®. Today, it's known acronymically as BBDO Worldwide, part of the mega-agency Omnicom Group. The structure has changed, but its tradition of breaking new ground remains.

While a plethora of smaller agencies use graphics computers, the sheer size of BBDO's installation is staggering. According to Stuart Levine, manager of computer services, there are approximately 500 workstations manned by the 800-odd employees at BBDO New York alone. At BBDO Atlanta, BBDO Los Angeles, BBDO London, BBDO Detroit, and other offices, hundreds more monitors flicker daily, displaying everything from print ads to media schedules. The desktop units wear the familiar six-color logo belonging to Apple Computer. That's not surprising since BBDO is the agency of record for Apple. But BBDO began installing the machines more than a year before getting the Apple account. The Macs are in every department, from account service to media to creative. While its use of the most advanced capabilities of graphics computers may lag behind smaller, less conventional shops, it's likely BBDO will become a familiar pattern as the other mega-agencies adopt desktop technology. The message? If you aspire to work in an agency, learn computer graphics. And if you own an agency, be prepared to compete head to head with the big guys in a digital environment.

THE BACK DOOR APPROACH

Ironically, BBDO's road to computerization is just about opposite the route taken by many design studios. The first people to get Macintoshes were not in the creative department. They were in account service, research, and media.

"The idea was to get the productivity of the machines not just for one department, but for the entire agency," Levine explained. The tradition of using computers has a much longer history in the other departments, especially media and research, so the new machines were installed there first, with account service not far behind.

"The account executives and their secretaries use the Macs to create new business pitches right on the desktop in Cricket Presents®," he said. "In the four years since we began installing Macintosh, they've spread into every department."

That includes creative. Levine runs a novel training program in the New York office. A training room equipped with twelve Mac II-family computers, a scanner, and printers is used to provide instruction in the whole range of software programs in use at the agency: Microsoft Word®, Excel®, Quark XPress, Macromind Director®, Illustrator, and more. Although the training isn't mandatory, Levine said department managers are in charge of scheduling their staffs for the classes. Depending on the subject, sessions vary in length from a few hours to several days.

SNAPSHOT: BBDO WORLDWIDE

BBDO Worldwide
1285 Avenue of the Americas, New York, NY 10019
TEL: (212) 459-6645
FAX: (212) 459-5000

Equipment: More than 1,000 Macintosh stations ranging from the Mac Plus up to the IIfx; Linotronic imagesetters; Supermac 24-bit color monitors; Laserwriter IINTX laser printers.

Staff: 2,200.

Typical clients: Large national and multi-national advertisers such as Pepsi-Cola, Polaroid Corp., Sizzler restaurants, Delta Airlines, and Apple Computer.

The productivity gains, Levine said, are very real. Presentations—complete with photo-maps generated in the research department if need be—can be created quickly and revised until the last minute.

BBDO has also instituted a company-wide electronic mail system using Quikmail® to cut down on telephone tag and boost productivity among the offices, which are spread over a dozen time zones. A company-wide user's group has been established on DialCom, a bulletin-board service. One of the agency's California clients, Worldwide Church of God, participates as well. Through DialCom, offices can exchange memos and reports as well as complex data files.

Despite some initial reluctance, the agency's creatives have been affected by the pervasiveness of desktop computers. Levine set up a graphics room in New York complete with scanners and large-screen monitors to provide high-quality graphics tools to workers who ordinarily work with SEs. Slowly, the creatives have come around. A CAD department provides three-dimensional drawings. Body copy and logotypes are now commonly done on Macintosh. And, Levine said, the creatives in New York are being spurred on by the fact that other regional offices have gone even further. Two of those offices, Atlanta and Detroit, have their own Linotronic® imagesetters.

DESKTOP DELUXE

One of the reasons Atlanta has its own Linotronic is that, compared to the New York office, a much higher percentage of its work is print, rather than television. A large part of that print is newspaper advertising for clients such as Delta Airlines. Retail ads, with their need for weekly or daily updates, fit perfectly with the capabilities of the Macintosh.

According to Hank Corriher, manager of information systems for BBDO Atlanta, there are 115 Macs in that office. About two-thirds are SEs while the others are a mixture of SE 30s, Mac IIs, and Mac IIcxs.

"I would never have gotten 115 people in an ad agency to use a computer if that computer was something other than a Macintosh," he said. "Advertising tends to be a nontechnical field. The people are mostly creative. To try to talk them into sitting down at a DOS machine every day, I can't see it happening. There's too much inconsistency between the applications. And it doesn't have the same esthetic feel as a Macintosh. People overlook that sometimes. The friendliness of being able to put customized start-up screens and sounds on your computer, to personalize it, is important. Certainly DOS machines have gotten to that point, but they're playing catch-up."

When Corriher arrived at BBDO Atlanta in mid-1984, there were no computers. He soon changed that.

"I started in the media department," he recalled. "One of my first jobs was to add up this enormous table of figures, the yearly media budget for one of our clients. After a couple of hours I said to myself, 'There has to be a better way.' My father had an IBM-PC at home, so I brought it into the office and began putting the numbers into a spreadsheet. Some other people in the office thought that was pretty terrific."

Shortly thereafter, Corriher was exposed to the Macintosh through the New York office and began pushing the machines in Atlanta.

"We started in account services and media, where we felt we could handle the machines easily until we got some experience with them," he explained.

With the release of the Mac II in 1987, Corriher began fishing for creatives. A Mac II was set up in the creative area "just to see who'd be attracted to it" he recalled. One of the office's paste-up artists began using the machine frequently and spent time after business hours experimenting and learning the software. The Mac II ended up on his desk.

"We tried giving a Mac II to a senior art director, but he was so fast doing roughs by hand that he felt it slowed him down," Corriher recalled. "But he's come to love the machine for administrative tasks and especially for inter-office mail."

The company's E-mail system has eased the burden of being a branch office of a national agency.

"We have three people in this office who actually work for BBDO Los Angeles," Corriher explained. "They're working on the Sizzler restaurant account, handling the Southeast region. With E-mail, they're able to interact with the other people working on the Sizzler account in Los Angeles quite handily despite the time difference."

BBDO's E-mail has even leaked outside of its own walls: the agency's main contact at Delta can access the system as well to send or receive messages.

"It's a tremendous help," acknowledged Judy Jordan, assistant vice-president of advertising and sales promotion for Delta. "Instead of playing telephone tag, I can write out a question or answer one, then have my computer call their computer. It's great." While everyone knows how fickle the winds of advertising can be, Jordan did say that, personally, she'd have hard time switching to another agency that didn't offer E-mail.

As of fall 1990, BBDO Atlanta had nine Macs in its creative department. Three of those, all IIcxs, were being used for electronic paste-up.

"Right now, about 70 percent of what can be done on the Macintosh is done that way," Corriher estimated. "By this time next year, that figure should be 100 percent.

"You have to understand the investment to payback ratio for an agency of our size," he pointed out. "One workstation can give you a quick payback if you do all of your work on it. We have to put in fifty machines before we start to reduce outside costs."

Since those outside costs are fully covered by the agency's clients (with a nice service charge tacked on), BBDO is staring at a tough trade-off.

"Let's say 40 percent of our business is black and white ads that we've been billing so many dollars an hour for," Corriher observed. "If we begin doing those on Macintosh, and doing them more quickly, our commission and our margins go down because we're doing the same amount of work for less money. We're looking at that very carefully. Maybe we'll tell the client that the money will be saved and suggest they reinvest the savings in some other area, such as media. Of course, they might not choose to do that."

Despite the economic peril, Corriher said BBDO Atlanta is moving ahead aggressively with desktop publishing. To help breach the inner sanctum of the creative department, he helped set up a working group to make suggestions as to how graphics computers should be implemented. That group included people from creative, production, and computer services.

"We still do thumbnails by hand. When two or three of those have been chosen, they're scanned into the Mac and worked up to full scale using a DTP package. Those are printed and sent to the client for approval. The elements, meanwhile, are stored in a file on the network server. When the client's approval is received, the production department accesses that folder and puts the file in final form. It's output on RC paper and sent out for engravings. Instead of having six to seven people involved, the job can be done by two or three people," Corriher said. The agency's most experienced typographers and art directors keep an eye on the output to ensure quality.

In the Detroit office, which handles the Dodge account, Corriher noted that a complete set of scanned photos of the entire Dodge product line is kept on-line using an optical drive. As new ads are produced, the artists can simply call up the correct model and drop it into a page layout, saving the time and expense of making a photostat and halftone.

"Five years ago, we didn't have a desktop computer in this office," Corriher said. "Today, I don't think you can get into the agency without already knowing how to use one."

CHAPTER 3

IMAGING & PRE-PRESS

Believe it: Desktop color production is for real

L et's get the headline right up front: It is now possible to create high-quality composite film for lithography with type, screens, and *separated four-color photographs in place* using desktop graphics hardware. "Now" means the fall of 1990, when this book was written. By the time you read this, the italics in the preceding sentence probably won't be necessary; further significant advances will have been made in manipulating and outputting color images from the desktop and everyone will likely have been convinced that desktop color works. As of now, not only is end-to-end color production possible, it is being done—by our studio and by others. Scitex-like color manipulation, photo-illustration, composite color seps, and high-resolution images on photographic film are now available directly from desktop equipment, and at a cost undreamed of just two years ago.

Of course, desktop color production is not new; it's been around in various incipient forms since the mid-1980s. The Macintosh-to-Scitex link and links to other high-end systems such as Hell® and Crossfield®, have been used by an increasing number of studios since 1988.

Now for the news: For many jobs, the quality of desktop color—scanned, manipulated, separated, and plotted in PostScript with no Scitex equipment involved—is now indistinguishable from that of a dedicated high-end separation system.

High-end systems still have some advantages. There are very few things you can imagine that can't be done on them, and they'll give you maximum quality for almost any job. You will pay handsomely for that power and flexibility. By contrast, not every color job is best done on a desktop computer, but the advantages to studios using desktop machines to produce color separations—lower costs, higher profits, faster turnaround, increased control—are enormous.

Like most print designers, we've lived for years with the joys and terrors of pre-press: a photo that's wonderfully composed but right on that borderline where a good scan will save it and a mediocre one will kill it; choosing which shades of subtle coloration you're willing to sacrifice to get a pleasing separation without breaking the bank with retouching and overtime; choosing between a design you're in love with and one that will be easier and more foolproof for the strippers; sacrificing color quality to meet a deadline; or sacrificing a deadline to buy the time for another round of proofs. Bringing some of our color work inhouse has been a refreshing, and confidence-building, change. We get to make the choices, rather than having them forced on us by a supplier.

DESKTOP COLOR COMES OF AGE

The year 1987 is remembered as the year the Macintosh grew up. The Macintosh II, with its modular design and brawny CPU, put to rest the notion that the Mac was a toy rather than a serious production tool. In the same way, 1990 will be remembered as the year that color output made it to the desktop.

Of course, it's been possible to make separation film of color illustrations created in Illustrator, Freehand, Canvas®, and other programs since 1987. Separations from photographs, however, have remained a tantalizing chimera. Various patchwork solutions for creating color litho film from IBM-PCs and Macs have been around since the mid-1980s, but seamless end-to-end integration of color production based on standardized products from major suppliers arrived in 1990. The availability and capabilities of the Nikon LS-3500, Array AS-1, and Microtek MTS-1850 transparency scanners combined with ColorStudio®, Adobe PhotoShop®, and upgrades to Linotronic and Agfa® imagesetters have confirmed it.

FILM STARS

Color separations from desktop files are aces if you're doing everything from design to composite film in

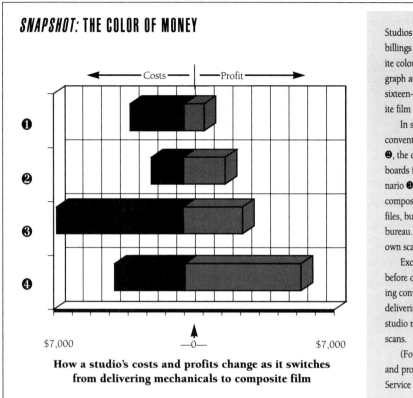

SNAPSHOT: THE COLOR OF MONEY

❶
❷
❸
❹

← Costs ——— | ——— Profit →

$7,000   —0— $7,000

**How a studio's costs and profits change as it switches
from delivering mechanicals to composite film**

Studios can substantially increase both billings and net profits by creating composite color film. In the example shown by the graph at left, the client's total cost to get a sixteen-page catalog from design to composite film is $9,950.

In scenario ❶, the design studio creates conventional mechanical boards. In scenario ❷, the design studio creates mechanical boards from electronic page layouts. In scenario ❸, the design studio sells the client composite color film made from electronic files, but buys the scans from a service bureau. In scenario ❹, the studio uses its own scanner and delivers composite film.

Exclusive of capital costs, net profits before overhead rise from $1,057 for delivering conventional mechanicals, to $3,150 for delivering composite film, to $6,190 if the studio makes composite film from its own scans.

(For a complete breakdown of expenses and profits for this job, *see* Chapter Four: Service Bureaus.)

your own studio. However, for illustrators, getting images out of their computers and into a form their clients can use has been problematic.

Fortunately, there is now a link between PostScript and high-resolution film recorders. PostScript files can be output on four-by-five inch transparencies at a resolution equal to a conventional photograph made with a high-quality view camera. The recorders write up to 3,000 pixels per linear inch in each direction (length *and* width), which exceeds the maximum resolution of four-by-five inch Ektachrome film (*see* Chapter Four: Service Bureaus).

This capability is a spot-illustrator's dream. You can start with a drawing or a photograph, apply any number of airbrush or Scitex-like effects, and output a four-by-five transparency that can be sent to the client for conventional separation.

BENEFIT PACKAGE

For anyone who's enviously watched the majority of the profits from a job go to a film house or who has

sweated last-minute corrections, commercial quality desktop separations and color images are a godsend. Like most digital processes, they're a mixed blessing, bringing with them more responsibility and requiring more hardware. But on balance, we'd still rather have them as our primary product and save the conventional separation process as a backup.

Many of the advantages will be familiar, as they're the same as the benefits of converting from conventional to digital production of mechanicals. But, because you're now following through right to the press, you save even more dollars and more time. The services you can offer are more extensive. And your control over the product—quality and schedule—is much greater.

CREATIVE CONTROL

At every step in the production of print graphics, there are choices to be made. You create (and the client approves) a budget, design, and mechanicals or electronic files. If the client's budget is lean, you sacrifice an extra color for more separations. You made the choice. When you send out for separations, however, your ability to choose is limited by the graciousness, and usually the price schedule, of the color separator. Flexibility and control cost money. Budget-priced film houses usually give you one correction cycle on the color. If they still didn't get it quite right, you either accept it or pay for additional corrections.

By bringing the separation of photographs and creation of composite film in-house, you broaden your choices. Within the limits of the accuracy of your monitor, you can see on your own screen that, when the red is punched up, the yellows are going orange. You can choose to accept that or spend the time to mask the red out of the yellow. You make the choice, not a film-house technician. You're also able—within the limits of your original material and the limits of the technology—to ensure the separations are of optimum quality given the schedule and budget for the project.

Communication: It's much easier to guide a mouse around a desk than it is to guide a technician. You can see, on the screen, what's working and what isn't. You can experiment with colors, silhouettes, effects, and then output them quickly in final film without having your ideas "translated" by a film house.

Creativity: Things that cost big money to buy from film houses such as complex drop shadows, silhouettes, or montaging of images can be handled on the desktop. You will be less limited by budgets.

This also dispenses with the quandary of deciding whether to ask for an expensive effect that may or may not work. There's still a cost for hardware and labor to create the effects. But their cost to you is less than what you would pay a film house. The difference can go in your pocket as extra profit or you can use the effects as a "sweetener," giving the client better-looking work at the same price.

Some studios use this as a way to build their portfolios, adding complex effects to jobs without charging the client. In return, they get a finished piece from which to sell the effects to subsequent clients.

PROFIT CENTER

Even without factoring in the time and labor saved by not having to deal with a film house, desktop separations just plain cost less than conventional separations. This opens up new avenues: retaining the difference between desktop and conventional separations as extra profit; bidding jobs with low design fees but hefty production budgets; convincing clients to move ahead with projects that might otherwise be too expensive.

Without doubt, the highest *percentage* profits come from using a computer to create mechanicals. Still, with the exception of a few types of design-intensive projects (such as packaging and corporate identity), your *revenues* and *total profits* from color jobs will soar if you deliver them as composite film rather than mechanicals.

For the catalog described on page 43, total profits are nearly doubled by delivering the job as composite film rather than mechanicals. If you delivered the job as mechanicals, the billing would be $3,950, the net before overhead would be $2,222, and the profit percentage a healthy 56 percent. If you delivered the job as composite film, the profit percentage drops to 32 percent, but total billings climb to $9,950, resulting in a total profit before overhead of $3,150. This calculation doesn't take into account the cost of sales. Obviously, more than doubling your billing from one job drastically reduces your marketing cost as a percentage of revenues.

REVISED TOTAL

Sure, clients like to make changes in color proofs. But so do designers. Graphics computers give you the ability to alter type and design before making final mechanicals. They can also give you that same flexibility—albeit at a higher cost in time and materials—for color separations. Still, the costs of revising and rerunning a desktop color file are far lower than what you might expect to pay a conventional separation house to reseparate, restrip, and reproof a job.

When accurate digital proofing printers are available, which will probably be by the end of 1991, those costs will drop even more. You might then expect to pay ten dollars or less per page for full-color proofs before you make the film. Changing everything on a page—new photos, new type, new seps—will then cost you the price of a proof, ten bucks, and the labor required to make the change. The going price for a new Chromalin®-type proof is about twenty-five dollars per letter-sized page, not including the cost of corrections to the film.

VIDEO REPLAY

Film, processing, and scanning are major costs in any project involving a large number of photographs. Combining still video cameras and graphics computers can eliminate these costs entirely. Still video cameras work like a regular camera except they record their images electronically on a small disk instead of on conventional film. Using a digitizer, these can be imported directly into electronic page layout files and separated using a separation program.

The advantages are obvious: no bias or "cast" from the film emulsion, no waiting for processing to check the day's shoot, no film to buy, no scans to pay for. The Canon still video and Sony Mavica systems can't match the resolution of a Sinar studio camera or even a Nikon 35mm yet, but for direct-mail catalogs, reports, and other projects, their quality is ample.

Still video has one other important advantage over conventional photography. When you separate a photograph, by the time you get to the printed piece, the image has been copied five times: from live image to film, from film to an electronic scan file, from scan file to separation film, from film to plate, from plate to

paper. Since a graphics computer can read still video directly, a still video image is only copied four times: from live image to video, from video to separation film, from film to plate, from plate to paper. The step it saves—scanning—is the one most apt to go awry. It also prevents mishaps with exposures and processing since the video shot can be checked immediately and its contours reshaped at will afterwards using a desktop separation program. Unfortunately, high-quality still video equipment is very pricey; you could pay as much for the highest-grade gear as you would for a commercial-grade desktop transparency scanner.

FLEX TIME

PostScript is a more flexible language than the proprietary languages used by conventional separation systems. The Scitex language is a raster, or bit-map, format while PostScript is an outline, or vector, language. PostScript handles electronically generated text better. It allows powerful drawing tools, such as the Bezier curves used in Illustrator and Freehand. It's also size-independent. Once an image is sized in a Scitex system, it has to be resampled and reconstructed to be output at a different size. Using PostScript, you can enlarge or reduce individual images or entire pages from a single dialog box without reprocessing the whole file.

Since PostScript can be written to videotape and film recorders as well, you can use the same color files for separations, slides, laser prints, and videotape. This ability to readily transport images and pieces between media can save clients time and money. It can also create extra profits. Savvy designers archive everything. They reuse bits and pieces of jobs, or whole jobs, wherever they can. Once you have a library of color blends, for example, every time you pick one up and reuse it, you're making extra profit. A presentation originally created for a slide show can be delivered again later as handouts.

If desktop color seems like every designer's dream come true, maybe it is—almost. There are some definite downsides. Some are the natural by-products of the process of making composite film while others are the kinds of surprises you might expect from a developing technology.

PRIME TARGET

This is a big one: Do you really want to be responsible for making the color right? Film houses exist for a reason—they know how to put the dots on film in a way that printers can use them. Putting yourself in that role presumes you either know a good bit about color reproduction—what color is supposed to look like and what to do if it doesn't—or that you'll hire someone who does. Service bureaus can be a tremendous help, lending expertise and assisting you in working through the inevitable rough spots of your first few projects.

Making four-color film is more than four times as complex as making one-color film. Again, a good service bureau is a necessity. Many traditional pre-press houses have incorporated Macintosh or IBM-compatible workstations into their operations. A number of type houses have added outputting separation film to their buffet of services. And there are some entirely "new breed" operations created solely to image PostScript files (*see* Chapter Four: Service Bureaus). Before plunging into desktop color, find a service bureau that has experience with totally PostScript color and access to high-end tools such as drum scanners and Scitex plotters. Have them demonstrate their process for you. Talk to them about what brands of hardware they've used and how well they work. Find out what system they use and what they recommend.

It also helps if someone in your shop has a firm grasp of four-color lithography and a sharp eye for color originals, separations, and proofs.

Designers who are handling four-color process say never buy hardware or software before you try it under "field conditions" (less-than-perfect originals, short deadline, demanding client). And *never* try out a new process on a client's job. Always experiment first with files of the same kind and size as you'll be working with on the project.

PAYING THE PIPER

There are big bucks to be made creating composite film. And there are big costs as well. A minimum configuration for doing serious color work would be a Mac IIci, 8 mb RAM, 24-bit monitor, 24-bit card, a 300 mb hard drive, a 45 mb removable cartridge drive, PhotoShop or ColorStudio, Quark or PageMaker, and Illustrator or Freehand. If you had to buy the whole package, you're looking at about $9,500 at 1990 prices, and that's with a thirteen-inch monitor and no scanner. A two-page color display and a flatbed color scanner would add almost $5,000; a high-resolution transparency scanner would kick it up another $10,000. Upgrading an existing monochrome Mac II station to color capability would run about $4,000 with a thirteen-inch monitor and flat-bed scanner.

And there are other costs. Archiving jobs, which you probably do using floppy disks or tape, is much more costly when you add color. The separation files for a letter-sized photo can weigh in at better than 25 mb. There are the peripheral files to consider, too: color Illustrator or Freehand images, your working files, the pages themselves. A direct-mail catalog containing a hundred photos could easily set you back a gigabyte or more. You either buy a lot of 45 mb cartridges at seventy dollars a pop, or you buy an optical drive, which will run upwards of $3,500.

There is also the labor cost to consider. Do you know enough about color reproduction to handle PostScript separations? Can you learn? How much will that time cost? Or will you hire someone who already knows process color? It takes more time to scan, separate, integrate, and format four-color art than one-color art. With the tools available in 1990, you can expect to spend twenty minutes to make a high-resolution scan. If you're already dealing with film houses and printers, the labor needed to follow the composite film through the process may not increase your work load noticeably. But if you're currently just turning in boards to the client, coordinating the production and delivery of film will add labor.

The good news is there's room to recover both the capital costs and extra labor because PostScript film is relatively low in cost: about eighty dollars for a composite set of four negatives. Even if you pay a service bureau to scan the art (at about twenty dollars per scan), you can price PostScript separations below those of conventional film houses and tack on a small profit.

CONSISTENCY COUNTS

For every area where desktop computers exceed high-end systems, there are two where they fall short. At the time of this writing, the most bedeviling seems to be maintaining color consistency throughout a project—from original art, through the computer, through interim proofs, and into final film.

Solutions are in sight. It's only been in the past few years that advanced color monitors have given operators of high-end systems an accurate representation of their files. That technology is now trickling down to the desktop. Various calibration devices appeared in 1990, and RasterOps released a color monitor with a built-in microprocessor to keep the color from drifting. Married to an inexpensive digital proofing system, say an accurate color laser or improved versions of the DuPont 4Cast® or Kodak's XL7700® printer, these monitors will help make separating color a certainty rather than a crapshoot.

Remember that color reproduction is never guaranteed. Unless you're using a well-equipped color house with diligent, well-trained operators (translate: expensive), you won't get perfect consistency from a high-end system either. Too many operators have a habit of dialing up the colors to suit their own tastes. This can play hob with any project, but especially with large ones where consistent negatives are needed to ensure the best result during the press run. Whether you get consistent results from a trade film house can depend on who's running the scanner when your job comes in, how recently they changed the chemicals in the processor, and how well adjusted their consoles and imagesetters are.

It's possible to eliminate all but a tiny fraction of inconsistency in a high-end system. At this time, you can't do that with a desktop system because some of the inconsistencies are technological in nature. But, designers say, you can *reduce* the amount of inconsistency in a desktop system by being methodical.

All of the designers we spoke with who have done photographic separations using desktop equipment agreed that the inconsistencies are no worse—and oftentimes less—than seen in the work of the average trade separator. Their comments perfectly reflect our own experience.

THE TECHNO-BABBLE

Graphics computers—including the Scitex—work with color based on a digital model that breaks down all colors into percentages of red, green, and blue (RGB). Breaking color into its red, green, and blue components is the standard for video equipment as well. Video monitor screens are coated with dots of phosphorescent material that glow red, green, or blue.

Computers, therefore, have to generate RGB signals so that images can be sent to a video monitor.

The printing press, of course, reproduces color by building it up using cyan, yellow, magenta, and black (CYMK). These colors have no direct relationship to the red-green-blue model. For practical purposes, the computer is speaking French (RGB) and the press is talking Farsi (CYMK).

When a color is specified in the computer, it exists as a signal composed of various amounts of red, green, and blue. In order to be output as a color separation for a printing press, the RGB signal has to be converted to CYMK. This is done automatically by the computer using a color look-up table (KLUT). The KLUT tells the software how to blend CYMK to match the RGB values in the file.

Anytime you translate information from one language or one theoretical model to another, something gets lost or changed. Oil paintings can't be reproduced with exact fidelity on photographic film because the film does not exactly mimic the way your eyes perceive the light reflected by the pigments in the oil.

The number of "translations" is increased if we want to reproduce the oil painting using a lithographic press. In getting from a live image to a piece of printed paper through a graphics computer, the image has to be put on photographic film (unless you can somehow scan directly from the oil painting). Photographic film does not record colors with complete accuracy. Next, the photo has to be scanned, and scanners are not completely accurate in picking apart the dyes used in photographic materials and translating them into an RGB signal. Then, the operator has to view the image on a monitor; monitors are not wholly accurate in reproducing the information in the computer file. Also, monitors operate at a lower color temperature than the standard "daylight" frequency of 5000° Kelvin used to calibrate photo materials. This causes some bias in the image. Finally, the image has to be translated from RGB to CYMK through the KLUT. If the KLUT is not built correctly by the software manufacturer, more inaccuracies will creep in.

Given all the translation needed to get from a live image to a piece of printed paper, it's a wonder that color can be reproduced even approximately, much less precisely. Scitex is still better than desktop machines at doing that, but desktop technology is catching up fast. In 1990 Kodak announced it was working on a color standard for all digital color processes, including graphics computers. If adopted by hardware and software manufacturers, it could give the same kind of assurance and accuracy that Kodak's test strips and density standards provide for photographers and prep houses using photographic materials.

PROOF IMPERFECT

Part of the consistency problem lies in the lack of an accurate interim proof, something you can look at while correcting a color file. Currently, there's no foolproof way of proofing color PostScript files without running film on an imagesetter and making a color key or chromalin-type proof. If corrections are needed, you've blown eighty bucks for each page of film and twenty-five or thirty for the proof.

That will change in 1991 since a number of heavyweight players—Canon, Kodak, DuPont—have made digital proofing a priority. As of fall 1990, they had all released or demonstrated technology that was extremely close to providing accurate digital proofs.

Already, prints from the DuPont 4Cast are very useful as preliminary proofs. They show the detail and resolution of the image very well, but more color accuracy and consistency are needed before they can be trusted as accurate reflections of the file.

Kodak's XL7700 printer, which uses the kind of dye sublimation process as the 4Cast, was demonstrated in late 1990 and produced prints of remarkable clarity and fidelity.

It's probable that lithographers will always require actual proofs of the negatives (as opposed to proofs of the computer file that was used to create the negatives). Even if you could find a printer who would print from a 4Cast or other digital proof, it doesn't make sense to risk the expense of a press run without knowing precisely what's on the negatives. The number of things that can go wrong between your files and separation negatives (such as a poorly adjusted image-setter, bad development chemistry or procedures, rough handling) far outweighs the cost of making chromalin-type prints for final examination.

QUALITY IS STILL JOB ONE

None of the advantages of graphics computers matter if the images they produce don't measure up to the quality of comparably priced conventional separations.

It's unlikely that any combination of desktop gear will outperform a full-featured Scitex or Crossfield system in the near future. If you're designing catalogs for Sotheby's, using eight-by-ten chromes of familiar Old Masters paintings and printing on a Heidelberg press, you aren't going to turn any heads with output from a desktop system. Not this year, anyway.

Those eight-by-ten chromes and Scitex separations come at a high price, however. If you're doing less demanding work, PostScript separations compare very favorably with run-of-the-mill commercial-grade separations, yet cost less. And, because you control the color, *you* can decide when "good enough" is, in fact, good enough for you.

Newsweek printed one of its covers from a desktop separation in 1990. *Time* has printed photos scanned on the Nikon LS-3500 as double-truck spreads. Even *Playboy* is experimenting with desktop separations.

BUSINESS OPPORTUNITIES

The options opened by high-quality desktop color technology are only now starting to come into focus. The most obvious is to sell clients composed film for projects you're already handling. Others include the following.

Retouching: Scitex houses commonly charge $250-$300 *per hour* for an operator and console. If your labor rate is $75 per hour, selling two hundred hours of retouching at $150 per hour will net your full rate *plus* enough extra profit to pay for a Nikon scan-ner and upgrading an existing Mac II workstation to color capability. Whether or not it makes sense to do your clients' work on the desktop, of course, is more important than the simple economics. Do you want to spend that much of your time on such exacting technical work? If you're a free-flying design-driven studio with little interest in production work, gearing up to make separations may not be your cup of tea.

Montage: Combining color images is a popular illustrative technique, but it's expensive when done by traditional means. There are direct techniques, such as retouching a transparency with dye and a brush, or working on top of a print with an airbrush. Photo-mechanical montages are more common and are made by masking and double-burning a transparency or print. Unless they're done with great skill, photo-mechanical montages often show distinct edges where the images butt. The best way to montage is electronically with a high-end system such as a Quantel Paintbox or a Scitex workstation. However, if you start with high-quality scans, you should be able to assemble montages on a desktop computer that rival the output of a high-end system, but at a far lower cost. This takes both a clear eye and considerable retouching skills. Knowing *what* to do is as important as knowing *how* to do it.

Photo-illustration: Good photo-illustration is always in demand. Combining photos and illustration gives you a bit of both worlds: the "believability" of a photographic image and the rich subject matter of the natural world, plus the dimension of imagination. Bending, stretching, shaping, redrawing, drawing over, coloring, tinting, and dozens of other techniques are made simpler and more foolproof using a graphics computer. One photo-illustrator said that the greatest advantage of the computer is the "undo" feature. It allows you to try out a wide variety of effects and, if they don't work, undo them. Try that with a Cibachrome print and an airbrush!

BLOUNT & WALKER

Shaking the high-end habit with vibrant PostScript color

Put up or shut up. No one has ever said that to us; at least not directly. But after three years of pushing desktop graphics to publishers large and small, we were beginning to think we'd never get the chance to apply PostScript to a complex job with photographic separations. We'd run enough files with screens and spot color created in Illustrator and enough PostScript tests to be reasonably certain of our results. But we'd never gotten the green light on a fully PostScript production.

That changed when Gulf Publishing of Houston agreed to accept composite film rather than mechanicals for a novel product we'd designed for them. Part of our difficulties had been economic: Most of the projects we do are separated and printed in the Orient, where cheap labor and abundant capacity keep prepress prices almost unthinkably low. Typically, a letter-sized page with three photos, separated and stripped, ready for plating, costs $110 in Hong Kong, maybe a little more in Japan, a little less in Singapore. The price includes printed press proofs, roundtrip air express for the materials, and one round of revisions. If you're pushy, you can ask for a few silhouettes and some color correction without incurring extra charges. Even using desktop equipment and a PostScript imagesetter, that's hard to beat.

But Gulf had special needs. While it has traditionally done much of its pre-press and printing in the Orient, this project was unique: a new kind of fish identification book for scuba divers and fishermen. The fish were to be reproduced from photos taken underwater, rather than from color renderings. Also, it would be printed on Kimdura (a waterproof plastic-base paper manufactured by Scott), trimmed to two-and-one-quarter by seven inches and its ten pages riveted in the lower right corner. The size would allow it to be carried in the pocket of a scuba diver's buoyancy vest and fanned out underwater using one hand.

One hundred fish—all brightly colored tropical species—were included, five fish per page. The fish were to be silhouetted, a delicate operation that required cutting around oddly shaped translucent fins, much like outlining hair against an indistinct background.

Gulf responded to our proposal to do the job totally in PostScript for three reasons: price, turnaround time, and control. The silhouettes made the job uneconomical to do by hand. If we made mechanicals with rubylith masks, the labor required would be prohibitive and the results less than perfect, owing to the difficulty of making precise masks for the photostats or black and white scans. If the job had been put on a Scitex, the expense would have been enormous.

Instead, we teamed up with a long-time supplier, Graphic Connexions of Cranbury, New Jersey. We supplied the files and they supplied the scans, film from their Linotronic L-300, and Matchprints.

TAKING THE RAP

Before deciding to offer to take the project to composite film, we had to wrestle with several thorny issues. Gulf wanted to separate and print in the United States in order to better control this new product and to make it available quickly. However, we were placing

---

SNAPSHOT: BLOUNT & WALKER

Blount & Walker Visual Communications, Inc.
136 Buckskin Way, Winter Springs, FL 32708
TEL: (407) 699-7444
FAX: (407) 699-1480

Equipment: (2) Macintosh II-family workstations with 24-bit displays, (1) Mac Plus, (1) LaserWriter Plus, (2) 100 mb hard drives, (1) 45 mb removable cartridge drive, (1) video scanner, (1) flatbed scanner.

Staff: (2) designers, (1) computer production artist.

Typical clients: Corporations and publishers with a need for concept-to-finished-product service for books, brochures, magazines, and other promotional or editorial materials.

ourselves in the position of guaranteeing the suitability of the film to a printer we'd never worked with. Worse yet, the printer was located in Texas, several hundred miles and several time zones away. The window for production of the job was less than four weeks. If something went awry with the separations—if the printer found some fault—we'd have bills from Graphic Connexions, no product, and an angry client.

On the flip side, we had originally priced the job without silhouettes. They'd been added as the design evolved. Gulf said they wanted the mechanicals submitted with color photos in position and to-size so that the pages could be gang-separated. A Scitex house was outside the scope of the budget. We would have to cut rubylith masks or pay a photo lab to make mechanical silhouettes. Either would dramatically increase the cost to Gulf and possibly blow the economics of the whole project. The risks posed by submitting composite film seemed the lesser of the evils.

Doing the job in PostScript also gave us some creative freedom. We'd designed four bars containing color blends (each two or more colors, fading to white) for the cover. These would have taken several hours to airbrush had we separated the job conventionally. Using Illustrator, all four bands were created in less than an hour. And we were able to adjust the colors in the bands to match the four small fish on the cover after all the images had been separated.

MAC SCANS

There wasn't enough room in the budget to accommodate scans from a conventional high-end scanner. All of the photos were 35mm and, convinced by our tests, we went with the Nikon LS-3500.

The photos were taken by a well-known ichthyologist. Some, of rare species, were made under less than ideal conditions. The transparencies ranged from very good to marginal, with most showing at least some of the excessive blue cast usually present in photographs taken underwater. We would not have sent these transparencies to an Oriental separator with a clear conscience and an expectation of excellence. But, because the scanning was being done in the States, we had the luxury of using the best poses of the most desirable fish. If some didn't pan out, it would be simple enough to drop in replacements.

The page files were prepared in Quark 2.12 (3.0 was still in pre-release). Because the pages were so small, we were able to put four pages in each letter-sized file to economize on film. That meant twenty fish per file. Initially, we were afraid the page files would be too big for the L-300 to handle.

SIZE WISE

The LS-3500 has a maximum resolution of 6,000 pixels by 4,000 pixels. As our photos were enlarged less than 300 percent, scanning at full resolution would have been overkill. Instead, the transparencies were scanned at 2,000 by 2,000 pixels, resulting in smaller, more manageable files—about 5 mb each rather than the 25 mb needed for a full-resolution scan. It also cut the scanning time from twenty minutes per photo to less than six. Smaller files are physically easier to handle, open and close faster, reprocess faster (when being resampled or resized), take less time to separate, and run faster on an imagesetter.

Matching the resolution to the project, keeping it at a minimum for the quality required, saves time, money, and your nerves. There are rules of thumb for this: Most separators will tell you to oversample by two to one (that is, for every dot you need on the printed page, record two dots off the original). There's no direct relationship between lpi (lines per inch), the measure of the fineness of a halftone screen and ppi (pixels per inch), which is how a computer sees images. But since we were printing with a 133-line screen and our photos were about four inches wide at maximum enlargement, we felt that 2,000 ppi would give us a comfortable oversampling. Graphic Connexions did a quick test and, after reviewing a color key, we all agreed that 2,000 ppi would work.

CHOP SHOP

After the scans were made on the LS-3500, they were brought into Adobe PhotoShop. While it's not quite Scitex, PhotoShop delivers a full load of capability: undercolor removal and gray component replacement, layer by layer color correction, sharpening and softening filters, contrast correction, selective (spot) corrections, color inserts, masking, outlining, blending, and, of course, color separation. While it may not quite be Scitex, PhotoShop is a *lot* less expensive.

The silhouettes were the trickiest part of the operation. While the "find edges" function of PhotoShop normally works well in outlining an image, the murky backgrounds and translucent body parts of the fish gave it fits. The silhouettes had to be drawn by hand, but this was still far easier than cutting a mask from rubylith laid over a muddy photostat.

The usual expression is, "garbage in, garbage out." Yet, despite the shortcomings of the transparencies, only two out of the hundred had to be rescanned. One of those was a fish that was very nearly transparent; its pale peachy flesh initially came up a dull gray-orange. The other ninety-eight fish looked terrific with only minor, global corrections applied.

More than one designer we've recounted the project to has snorted, "Yeah, but there weren't any flesh tones." That's true. But the range of colors of tropical fish is infinitely wider, and just as subtle, as human flesh. Cardinalfish are a delicate, orchid-petal pink. Royal grammas are iridescent purple and rain-slicker yellow. Midnight parrotfish are cobalt blue, while ordinary parrotfish are brilliant peacock green, and stoplight parrotfish are stop-sign red. And the side of a Spanish hogfish is almost exactly the peaches-and-cream color of an Irish barmaid's cheeks.

Unlike humans, the individuals of many species of fish are not only the same color, but exactly the same *shade*. If the guide was to be credible, the colors had to be accurate. The LS-3500 and PhotoShop nailed them on the first try. The two problem fish and a few others that looked muddy were cleaned up by scaling back the black and blue in the images.

Once the images were silhouetted and balanced, the separations were made in PhotoShop. For each image, the program makes five files: one for each plate—cyan, yellow, magenta, and black—plus a composite file in the TIFF format that can be placed in a Quark or PageMaker document for cropping and positioning. When the file is sent to an imagesetter, the composite image indicates the proper percentage of enlargement and positioning. The page layout program then calls each of the plate files in sequence as it makes the four pieces of film.

Despite our reservations, running the files to the L-300 proved simple. Scaling back the resolution helped and despite having twenty images per page, Graphic Connexions was able to produce one set of film (four pieces) in under twenty minutes per page.

PROOF ENOUGH

The flexibility of the desktop system really proved its mettle when the proofs arrived. The Matchprints were precisely as we had hoped. The colors were true and vibrant, the trapping accurate.

To this point, Gulf had only seen the product in a crude hand-made form. Also, due to the short deadline, they had not seen an accurate color comp of the covers, which had been modified repeatedly—the last time the day *after* the files had been shipped to the service bureau. (A revised cover file was then sent to the service bureau by modem). After surveying their marketing staff and some wholesalers, Gulf asked us to add a photo of one of their other books to the back cover, and change the promotional copy.

Again, the changes were sent to Graphic Connexions by modem.

A new Matchprint was pulled and expressed to Gulf. New and different members of the staff made recommendations about the title treatment on the back cover. Another patch was created and sent by modem.

The next day, new film was in Gulf's hands.

The miracle is that, for us, the correction cycle was handled entirely by telephone. And it happened fast. The cover went through three sets of proofs within six days—despite the fact that our studio is in Florida, Graphic Connexions is in New Jersey, and the publisher is in Texas. If the separations had been done by a conventional pre-press house, each set of corrections would have required new type, a new mechanical, an overnight express package, camera work, and hand-stripping before new proofs could be made. Six days would have been impossible; nine to twelve more likely. Also, because a completely new set of composite film was run for each set of corrections, the cost was the same whether the corrections affected one element or ten. Gulf was able to exercise tight control over the product, fine-tuning it to a much greater degree than would have been possible had the film been made conventionally. And, the printer got the film on time.

We were happy about that, but not nearly as happy as we were when the printer's rep called and said the film "looked good." The final hurdle was cleared when Gulf's production manager made her press check—and it checked out.

COMMUNICATIONS BREAKDOWN

The biggest difficulties with this project were related to humans, not hardware. The publisher's staff was set up to accept mechanical boards and had never worked with supplied film. The printer was new to us. There was no standard procedure understood by us, the printer, and the publisher to rely on to make sure every detail was correct. Gulf was accustomed to receiving mechanical boards and then sending out for random separations. The pieces were then collected in the production department; verified by editorial, marketing, and production; and shipped to the printer.

Because the project ran outside the normal channels, it bypassed the publisher's normal checking procedure. It was checked in laser proofs by an editor and was in final film before any of the marketing or production people saw it. The revisions to the cover might have been eliminated had their full staff had a chance to review an accurate color comp. Although the schedule was tight, we probably should have pulled a 4Cast proof, at least of the cover, before running the film.

The lesson: As a design shop, you're expanding beyond your ordinary role by providing composite film. The person who ordinarily deals with you may not be the person who ordinarily approves film for the printer. Ask the client about their normal approval procedure—who, how, when—and make sure to make arrangements *yourself* to route the materials to them.

ONCE IS NEVER ENOUGH

Would we do it again? You bet. Despite the uncertainties, moving up from providing PostScript-generated mechanicals to four-color film was easier than converting from traditional mechanicals to Macintosh. One reason is that we already knew the machines. But, more important, the technology works more smoothly now, *even at the level of four-color separations*, than black-and-white desktop technology worked in 1987.

Composite film is now an option for nearly every project we bid. We're currently helping to launch a series of regional catalogs. With eight color images per page and a short fuse, these are an ideal use for PostScript color. The client likes the turnaround time and, even pricing our composite film less than the cheapest conventional film house, we're making as much profit on the film as we are on the design. That's the kind of computer performance you have to love.

· · ·

ELECTRONIC IMAGES

Why one retoucher exchanged camera and airbrush for a mouse

It seems that all the hype about digital color swirls around making separations for printing, while other important and potentially lucrative specialties go begging for publicity.

Retouching is surely one of these.

The days of the dye specialists bent over a chrome with a high-power magnifier and a brush with a single hair aren't over quite yet. There's still a strong demand for airbrush artists capable of seamlessly laying frescoes from the Sistine Chapel onto the ceiling of a service station. But some of them have seen the future, and it looks very digital. The revolution in retouching begun by Scitex has filtered down to the desktop.

A native New Yorker, Nick Fain moved his shop, called Electronic Images, to San Francisco. Back East, he couldn't find buyers for the *nouvelle* service he offers: computer-based photo-illustration, retouching, montages, and what-have-you. Without buyers, he had no tear sheets; no tear sheets, no credible way to market the service. But you might say the ground trembled when he arrived in San Francisco—he moved in three days before the September 1989 earthquake. Since then, Fain said, his phone hasn't stopped ringing. Bay Area clients are already sold on the efficiencies of desk-top-based services. And they're willing to take a few risks, maybe even take a beating on a job or two, to push high-end jobs down to the desktop. They know that, once they work the bugs out of the process, they'll begin saving days and dollars.

But what they get, Fain said, has to be first rate.

"I try as hard as possible to come up to the standards I've always applied to my work instead of settling for the usual Macintosh standards," Fain explained. "The Macintosh is actually capable of doing most of the high-end kinds of color manipulation you'd want to do. You have to fudge things a bit, work around some shortcomings. And occasionally you have to clean things up on the back end using a Scitex.

"That's the great thing about working in color on the Mac; you always have the Scitex on the back end to save your butt if something goes wrong. But you really shouldn't count on the Scitex for anything except global changes; if you get into any kind of serious masking, you'll blow the savings you achieved by using a desktop computer."

The Scitex used to be one of Fain's standard tools, but now, he emphasized, it's just a back-up: "Trade pre-press shops need to be looking over their shoulders. Designers using desktop computers are going to be able to give budget clients everything the trade shop can give them, but at desktop prices."

That includes manipulated images. Rather than limiting him, the Macintosh has greatly expanded Fain's repertoire.

"I try to offer images that are a little different. A lot of the effects can be imitated using traditional media, but there are some effects you can only get using a computer," he said.

POSTER CHILD

One recent project that brought all of Fain's experience to bear involved a twenty-four-by-thirty inch poster of a heavily manipulated color image. Desktop designers,

---

SNAPSHOT: ELECTRONIC IMAGES

Electronic Images
221 Sansome Street, San Francisco, CA 94105
TEL: (415) 882-9961
FAX: (415) 882-9977

Equipment: (1) Macintosh II f/x workstation ; 24-bit, 19" Supermac Trinitron monitor; (1) Macintosh IIx with 50 mhz accelerator; Apple high-resolution 13" monitor; (2) Syquest removable cartridge drives; (2) 300 mb hard drives; 150 mb tape backup; 12"x17" graphics tablet; Pantone color viewing box; LaserWriter II; Microtek 300z flatbed color scanner.

Staff: (1) illustrator.

Typical clients: Design studios, advertising agencies, and corporate clients who have a need for four-color montages, four-color retouching, and photo-illustration.

---

accustomed to dealing with letter-sized pages, may blanch at the thought of working at such large sizes, especially in four-color, but Fain said it was no sweat. The original color image file was only 5 mb to boot— about a fifth the size of a standard Scitex scan. Generally the more data in an image file, the better the clarity of the image and more accurate the color. Fain applied a little digital sleight-of-hand known as re-sampling, a technique often used to improve the quality of image files that will be output at large sizes. The result was "terrific," he said.

As a starting point, Fain was given two trans-parencies. One, taken underwater, was of a woman in a flesh-colored bathing suit diving through a swim-ming pool, bubbles streaming off her body. The other transparency was of the sky. The client wanted to show the woman diving through the sky, with sky visible through the bubbles: A tricky bit of masking no matter what tools you use.

Unfortunately, neither transparency was very good: The woman's skin was the typical yellowish-green seen in underwater photos taken without strobes. Rather than rely on a low-end scanner, Fain sent the transparencies to a color house to get a file from a drum scanner. The files came back "looking just as bad as the originals" he said. What followed was, in his words, "a total PhotoShop success story."

The color balance was adjusted. Fain removed the lines of the woman's bathing suit so that she appeared to be nude. Using the "paint on lighter" and "paint on darker" commands in PhotoShop, he was able to pick up the translucent bubbles from the water and layer them over the sky without obscuring it. Also, there wasn't enough sky in the original transparency to fill out the format of the poster, so Fain cloned big sec-tions of it to create a bleed image.

The resulting file was sent to a Scitex house, resampled to increase the amount of data in the file, separated, and output to a Scitex film plotter. Even at his standard rate, $125 an hour, Fain said the job was an "incredible bargain" for the client, who would oth-erwise have been paying $250-$300 per hour for the Scitex house to do the whole job, rather than relying on them only for the separations and film output.

BETTER THAN SCITEX?

Despite his occasional reliance on Scitex for output, Fain doesn't see it as the best tool for his type of work.

"I just finished a project that couldn't be done on a Scitex," Fain claimed. "The job was to take a scientif-ic rendering of a particle accelerator and make an illus-tration from it. The drawing had to have straight lines, Bezier curves, and circles, with a neon glow effect on a black background. The drawing had to be accurate and the colors had to be accurate as well."

Given a skilled operator, the Scitex will beat any desktop graphics computer on color accuracy. But drawing is another story. You can't render Bezier curves on a Scitex because it only understands bit maps rather than the angle-and-proportion vector format used by PostScript to describe shapes.

The client gave Fain a print of the rendering, which he scanned with a Microtek 300z® flatbed color scanner. The scan was pulled up in ColorStudio and used as a color template.

"I created masks for each color in ColorStudio using the shapes annex. That allowed me to draw the lines, curves, and circles very accurately and play with the line weights to get them to match the rendering exactly," he said. "Then I took the masks into PhotoShop. I used the paint on darker command, so that the colors don't overlap each other, yet they fill the black background completely. To give each color a neon glow, I outlined the shapes, blurred the edges of the outlines, and filled them with color. The glow actu-ally looked a little thin, so I blurred the edges and filled them again. The edges feathered perfectly. It's beautiful."

The PhotoShop file was saved as a Scitex CT format image and sent to a Scitex house for final output because Fain was concerned that the intense saturation of the colors might result in moiré patterns if it was output on a Linotronic. Currently, Macintosh separation programs have a tendency to pick up moirés in areas where all four colors are heavily saturated, such as in blacks, browns, and some grays when output through a PostScript imagesetter. Results have been improving rapidly and moirés may no longer be a problem by the time you read this. Scaling back the color for each of the plates usually eliminates moirés.

"I picked up a little too much dot in the black, but we fixed that by altering the contrast when the separations were made on the Scitex," Fain concluded. The result, he said, pleased the client, who got just the right effect at a price that was very right.

RULES OF THE ROAD

Flying by the seat of his pants, Fain has developed some rules that he said have helped keep him out of trouble.

Never promise a job if you're going to be using new software. And try not to take any jobs unless you've already tried to accomplish some part of it.

"I've done a lot of work in PhotoShop in the past year, spent a lot of time on trial and error. As a result, I've gotten to see a lot of the holes in the program," he pointed out. "But I realized as new jobs came in that no matter how much I work with it, I'll never see them all. No one will. So a certain amount of research—time to fiddle around with things to make them work—has to be built into each job. Some of that time might go into dead ends, and clients generally don't want to pay for that. You have to explain right up front that there's a built-in fudge factor. If you finish it quickly without tripping over anything, you might choose to refund that part of the fee. You never really know where the limits of the new processes are going to be. If you don't

know your limits on a particular job, try it before you promise a delivery deadline."

This uncertainty, Fain said, makes pricing difficult. He prices by the hour, but it's sometimes hard to guess exactly how long a new or unfamiliar procedure is going to take.

"If I make a serious blunder and waste a lot of time, I don't charge for that," he said. "That's probably not good from a business sense. People coast on the excitement of graphics computers for a while; I've been coasting for three years. Now I've started building in a little buffer."

The buffer protects Fain if things go wrong and he can refund it if everything goes off smoothly.

"Just buying an expensive computer doesn't give you the right to charge $200 an hour. You have to deliver the product professionally," he said. You can't do that, he noted, if you're constantly squeezed by schedule and budget. "Avoid rush jobs like the plague. No matter how good you are, if you're rushing, you'll forget things."

Even small things, like forgetting to tell your service bureau to turn on crop marks for your file or reminding them to substitute your Quark Data file for theirs while running your job can blow deadlines and precious cash.

"Always build in some emergency time. When you're working with color, you can depend on something going wrong," he cautioned.

One way to minimize accidents is to concentrate on one aspect of desktop work, rather than taking it all. Most people are best at what they do the most.

As did several of the designers we spoke with, Fain recommended making notes as you work. "I keep an incoming checklist, a client checklist, an outgoing checklist, and a service bureau checklist. And I take notes on everything I do," he added. "There's an incredible amount of detail that can crop up later. If you have to backtrack through a PhotoShop file, you better be able to remember what colors you threw in. There are a lot of kludges—work-arounds —that you're going to have to invent to get a job done. You need to have a system for tracking them." If one gives you a particularly ugly result, at least you'll know what to avoid next time.

"Open architecture" is a computer hardware term meaning a computer has been constructed so new modules that expand or improve its basic functions can be added easily. Fain calls his method of building files a kind of "open architecture" for design. Open architecture in a file means building it in a way that makes it easy to dissect and alter later.

"For the illustration of the particle accelerator, I saved each one of my shapes layers—masks—separately. That way I could go back at any time and rework parts of the drawing, or re-render it at any resolution," he explained. You can do the same thing in Illustrator or in Freehand by saving drawing layers separately. If later on you have to alter an object that overlaps another object, you don't have to redraw both.

CALIBRATE! CALIBRATE!

One of Fain's rules is to relentlessly calibrate his equipment with that of his service bureau. While there are various color calibration devices available, Fain's method makes sense.

"I feel okay about PhotoShop's calibration software. It does allow you to have different sets of calibrations for different service bureaus," he said. "I have two different bureaus. If you've been working with a color house for a while, they should be willing to pull a set of test negatives and a Matchprint for you. I have a file with a color chart and a picture of a woman's face. I can see immediately if the skin tones are off. You need to have the proper environment to view the proof in, one with a balanced light source, and you must keep that original file the negatives were made from intact and in an unadulterated form."

You should probably keep the original of the file on a removable device such as a 45 mb cartridge or a floppy and keep it in a safe place.

With the Matchprint in hand and the file loaded in the computer, Fain then tweaks the monitor until it closely matches the print.

There are some unavoidable gaps in the procedure: A true color viewing light should be at 5000° Kelvin, the approximate color temperature of sunlight, while monitors put out light at a considerably lower color temperature. Also, monitors tend to "drift" as they heat up. It's probably a good idea to turn the system on and let the tube reach operating temperature before tuning it.

PARTING SHOTS

"If you're going to do color, get a good education. Learn as much about color, especially electronic color, as you can. Do a lot of experimenting. And when you start working, don't take on critical jobs. If someone says, 'I want this color to be PMS 450 or you're not getting paid,' that's very, very tough. Instead, take jobs where the client wants 'pleasing' color, where they're only expecting something that looks nice. It's less demanding, it's much easier to achieve, and a whole lot less worry for you," Fain advised.

"I wasn't that much of an ace on color reproduction when I started this, and so much of the knowledge hasn't been written down yet. My intuition gets me through a lot of things," he admitted. "I'm lucky. I have experts I can call when things get scary. I know the product managers for PhotoShop and ColorStudio. Designers need more education. They need experts to teach them how color works; how color works in the computer. The people who are doing well with color are people who know the baseline truths about film, who know the physics and the chemistry. If you know color photography and you understand what gamma is, it'll make things go a lot easier."

PHOTONICS GRAPHICS

For Alan Brown, "whatever it takes" takes off from the desktop

Desktop graphics computers have opened a back door for designers to sneak into the domain of the color separator, the type house, even the video studio. But they've also opened the door to artists who weren't trained with a T-square and number two pencil.

Alan Brown is one of them.

A partner in a three-photographer commercial studio, Brown began experimenting with photo-illustration a decade ago and with still video several years ago. The Macintosh was a logical extension of his experiments. A devotee of the Mac, he nonetheless looks at it as just another tool; no more or less important than a view camera or strobe light.

It has, he said, made his life a lot more interesting.

"I began working with what you might call 'mood' images a long time ago," he explained. "I often shoot with very grainy film, or use soft focus. I was compositing color images by having them double-burned onto a transparency or print by the photo lab. Unfortunately, when you work that way, you always end up with cut lines or hard edges. So I'd hire an airbrush artist to smooth them out. Sometimes the airbrush pigments didn't match the image, and they stood out too much when the piece was separated.

SNAPSHOT: PHOTONICS GRAPHICS

Photonics Graphics
815 Main Street, Cincinnati, OH 45202
TEL: (513) 421-5588
FAX: (513) 421-7446

Equipment: (1) Macintosh II f/x with 20 mb RAM and virtual memory software, (1) 100 mb internal hard drive, (1) 600 mb external hard drive, (1) 45 mb Syquest removeable cartridge drive, (1) PLI Sony magneto-optical drive, (1) Howtek flatbed color scanner, RasterOps 24-bit 21" monitor.

Staff: (1) designer.

Typical clients: Design studios, advertising agencies, and corporate clients who want composite color images, special effects, and highly stylized photo-illustrations.

"When the Scitex came along, the clients would say, 'You shoot it and we'll assemble it on a Scitex.' That worked well, but I was less involved; I had to let go of the project before it was complete. Also, I didn't get transparencies for my portfolio. Most Scitex operators are technicians. That's not an insult, it's just that they aren't generally artists. They're computer operators. They're not always as sensitive to the creative aspects of image making as an artist might be."

WELCOME ABOARD!

Like many photographers, Brown is something of a technophile. He bought a Mac 512 in 1986 and learned how to use it: "I was intrigued with the drawing and painting software." In 1988, he recognized that the machines had matured to the point that they could be used for photo-illustration, so he bought a Mac II.

"I like the idea of being a little ahead of the pack," he explained. "Two years ago, a lot of people were shaking their heads, asking what kind of real projects I could use the Mac for and how I was going to get the images out of it. Sometimes I had answers. Sometimes I didn't. Two years later, I feel particularly vindicated. A lot of people are jumping on the bandwagon, and they're very excited about the capabilities. I just say, 'Right.'"

DRAMATIC POSSIBILITIES

Enduring the slings and arrows of skeptical colleagues began paying off in dollars as Brown matched up the work he was doing on the computer with the studio's commercial accounts. One of them, the Cincinnati Opera, came in with a request for a campaign to promote a series of four operas: *Don Carlos, La Traviotta, Cozzi fan Tutte,* and the *ne plus ultra* of romantic operas, *Romeo and Juliet.* They wanted soft, warm images. Brown felt he had their ticket.

"They were looking for images that could be used in newspaper ads, a brochure, bus cards, and billboards. They wanted soft, ethereal, moody—those kinds of adjectives.

"I had just started experimenting with still video and thought it might work for them. We made the shots: two were tabletop still lifes and two were live models."

At the time, Brown had no way of getting the video into a Mac, so he worked with a friend who had an IBM PC-XT with a frame grabber. The frame grabber digitized the still video image.

"The PC would only display sixteen-bit color, so it altered the tonality of the shots. The software for manipulating images was pretty crude, so they got pretty much what the PC was able to grab off the video. We thought it looked pretty good," he recalled.

The client thought it looked pretty good, too, and Brown began thinking that still video and a computer were a pretty impressive combo.

CATALOG OF ERRORS

"Still video was very new at the time, and the resolution wasn't very good," Brown said. "The images had a lot of texture to them, akin to exaggerated grain in a photo. There was no Scitex link with the Mac to clean up a poor separation, and there was no standard for twenty-four bit color. If they were used small, though, the images did hold up."

Because still video shortens and simplifies a studio shoot, Brown jumped at a chance to use it to produce a catalog—a type of project he normally avoids.

"With conventional film you have to light, shoot a Polaroid, relight, shoot another Polaroid, then make a test shot, wait two hours for it to come back from the lab, make the actual shot, and wait for the lab again to make sure you got it," he explained. "With still video, you light, you shoot, you look at it on a player. If you like what you see, you've got it."

Brown estimates that he can work about twice as fast with still video as with conventional materials.

And the costs are lower, too. Image disks cost about eleven dollars and hold twenty-five images. That compares to a dollar a sheet for four-by-five film. There are no Polaroids to make, either, at a dollar apiece. The result was a savings of two-thirds on the cost of materials for the project.

Even production is simpler. Rather than waiting for a service bureau to scan a transparency, a frame grabber can import the video directly to a computer. The files are much smaller, too, averaging a single megabyte rather than the 25 mb files that come from a drum scanner. That makes it easier to store, manipulate, and ultimately output the images.

It also limits their resolution. Like the speed rating of photographic film, the size of a digital image file has a direct effect on how sharp and smooth the result will be. The bigger the file, the more information the output device (whether a film recorder or an imagesetter) has about what the image is supposed to look like, and the better the result.

"Like the opera photos, the catalog photos had an interesting, textural quality," he said. "However, it turned out to be a horrible experience. We weren't dealing with Scitex and had nothing but PhotoMac® to manipulate the images. The images used small looked terrific; the ones used letter size looked horrible. The client signed off on the whole job, all the way across, but six months later, decided they didn't like it and got into a wrangle with the designer over payment.

"At the time, everyone—the designer, the client— thought this was a really neat textural look. Personally, I found it kind of limiting for that type of work."

Would he try it again?

"I would if I had the time to test everything out first and to make sure—by going right through to making film and pulling a Matchprint with test images—that everybody bought it and knew what they were getting," he said. "I've gotten a lot smarter that way. Under those circumstances, I'd embrace it because it's a lot of fun to shoot that way and it's so much quicker. The monetary savings of still video are pretty nominal for most of the work I do—annual reports, brochures, book covers. But when you're shooting a large quantity of photos for one job, they can be significant."

Despite this early setback, Brown remained enthusiastic: "I'm an optimist, but I'm not starry-eyed. When the enthusiasm for the technology dies down a bit, you realize it has to fit into a real budget and a real schedule. You have to make money with it.

"We've done a lot of successful work with the computer; I tend to focus on the less successful projects because I think I learned more from them than from the ones that went well."

DON'T FORCE-FEED THE CLIENTS

One thing Brown definitely learned was not to force-feed technology to clients. "There have been dramatic improvements in the technology in the past two years, but still video is still a very difficult sell," he explained. "People are freaked out by the process. There's no film, no test shots, nothing you can hold in your hand. The whole experience is unsettling; it's unfamiliar to them.

"You're asking clients to stick their necks out further than you're sticking your own neck out. Photographically, I'm confident that if you give me an assignment, I pretty much know what's going to happen. I can shake your hand, smile, look you in the eyes and say, 'No problem.' And I mean it. I don't like reshoots. I pride myself on not having to do them.

"When I began working with the computer, things changed. I would think that getting from point A to point B was easy, because it followed *logically*. In fact, that wasn't the case. Every project took twice as long as I estimated. All sorts of brick walls popped up that I smashed into at a full gallop. In our photographic business, we know how to go over, around, or through obstacles. But these hurt a little. And when clients see

the labor pains in the process, they start to get nervous. And that's a problem. When they starting getting nervous and lose confidence in the approach, it's surprising how their mind-set shifts.

"It's very demoralizing when you hit one of these obstacles. You get this awful sinking feeling when you realize whatever it is isn't going to work."

LIFE GOES ON

How does Brown keep his verve when the inevitable potholes grow into yawning chasms?

"I've never enjoyed myself more thoroughly than when I started working with images on the Mac," he insisted. "It's not that I was getting bored with photography. But there are so many good photographers out there, so many people doing so many talented things, and I'm just one of thousands. I realize that isn't good enough. I'm driven because I enjoy exploring these areas and there is a market for it. Plus, I'm not the sort of person who does what everybody else does.

"I am not a purist, as you can tell. Whatever effect I'm trying to achieve, I'll do whatever it takes to get that effect. The computer has allowed me a greater degree of safety, for one. The undo and revert features are probably the most powerful features in the creative world. You can walk the edge and jump off, and then jump back on again. You can experiment, you can try, you can play with, you can explore, and you can still go back home. It may be hours down the road, but you can get back unscathed, minus some time and patience, maybe, but still basically okay.

"As an advertising photographer I'm used to clients screaming, 'We need it yesterday,' and never allowing enough time to experiment. You get conditioned to go with your best instinct and somehow make it work. The computer is a wonderful device because you can do more in the same amount of time. You can explore and see whether your assumptions are accurate, or just see what happens.

. . .

"The difference between being an amateur photographer and a professional is that we know how to create an environment in which happy accidents can happen. And we know how to recognize and capitalize on those accidents. The computer has extended that and given me more tools to work with."

NON-REPEAT BUSINESS

When the Cincinnati Opera asked for another brochure—this time for *Aida* and *Faust*—Brown did not run to the still video to try to repeat his previous success. The tools have to be used appropriately, and he felt that the storylines of these operas wouldn't be served well by the soft-focus look he'd done before.

"They wanted something more vibrant, but still something that looked illustrated," he recalled. "We shot these on conventional film and scanned them into the Mac. Using PhotoShop, we were able to oversaturate the colors."

This gave the images a look that was clearly not a photograph, but still had an underlying realism that clearly said they weren't renderings, either.

This led to yet a third brochure. This time, Brown photographed his scenes on conventional film, transferred them to Polaroid, and then transferred to a rubdown, which was then applied to watercolor paper. The image was scanned into the Mac and hand-tinted for output to Scitex.

"It was a long way around to the final result, but the client likes it," he chuckled.

EASY DOES IT

Although Photonics has a Howtek flatbed color scanner with a mirror unit for scanning transparencies, Brown sends all of his commercial work to a Scitex house to be digitized on a drum scanner. The quality of the scans from the Howtek—an older 300 dpi unit—isn't up to his standards. He says the Scitex isn't a panacea, either. Whether a scan is good or bad, whether the file works easily on the Mac or doesn't, depends on the scanner operator.

"Recently we did a job for which we were asked to combine two color images," he recalled. "The first Scitex house we used for the scanning couldn't seem to get us a file that would behave on the Macintosh. The second got us a file, but when we sent it back to them for output, they weren't able to translate it. They ended up re-creating our work on their machines. We figured out the problem, but about four months too late."

These and other bumps make desktop scanners attractive, he said, but their cost, effectiveness, and features don't yet meet all his criteria.

Brown shoots a variety of film formats, from 35mm through four-by-five inches. The least expensive high-quality desktop scanners only handle 35mm. Scanners capable of handling larger formats cost too much (about $20,000) to make sense for the type and volume of business Brown does.

"The system we use now, passing scans down from Scitex to our Macintosh, then passing the file back to them for output, works well," he said.

Brown likes the arrangement. When the system hiccups—something doesn't match, calibration is off somewhere, or an operator makes a simple error—Photonics doesn't have to eat the cost of debugging and rerunning.

"The difference between a small operation doing this kind of color work on the desktop and a trade shop with a Scitex," he said, "is that the trade shop has its own film plotter, processor, and computer all in the same plant. If something goes wrong, they don't have to charge themselves extra to rerun the file. If you have to rerun a file to someone else's imagesetter, you're going to pay for it."

By leaving two important phases of the project with the film house, Brown has significantly lowered the statistical probability of hitting a costly snag in his own shop. Brown said he likes those odds—a lot.

· · ·

CHAPTER 4

SERVICE BUREAUS

How studios find profits in their suppliers' difficulties

For most designers, making the decision to buy into desktop computer technology involved some difficult questions: how much to spend, what equipment to buy, on whom to inflict responsibility for keeping the machines running. But at least there was a choice. There are still studios that manage to operate quite well without graphics computers.

The typographers and prep houses that studios deal with haven't had that luxury. The technology that makes it possible for designers to set type from their desktop quite obviously threatens to put typographers on the endangered species list.

For many typographers, the only avenue that doesn't lead to extinction is to become a PostScript service bureau, providing high-resolution hard copy on film or paper from PostScript files. Their basic business has changed from manufacturing—converting manuscript into typeset copy—to service. Some of their most profitable products (keystroking, specifying) have been usurped by their clients, while the capital investment they must make in equipment hasn't dropped appreciably; if anything, their need for equipment has increased. To make up for lost revenues, some service bureaus have geared up to make composite color film directly from clients' electronic files. This, in turn, is squeezing prep houses and even printers, for whom film work often carries a higher profit margin than printing and binding.

By and large, while suppliers compete for shares of a shrinking pie, these changes have enriched designers nimble enough to take advantage of them.

BREAKING OUT OF THE BOX

For at least the past two decades, print production—from concept to finished product—has been neatly divided into four closed-end processes: design, mechanicals, prep, and printing. The structure of the graphic arts industry reflects these divisions. Typographers, photographers, and photo labs feed into design studios, which design and produce mechanicals. A prep house makes film for the printer. The printer manufactures the product. Simple. And effective. But the burgeoning use of graphics computers is disrupting this system.

Working traditionally, at the end of each step there was a product that could be picked up and carried forward by another supplier. The design phase resulted in tissue sketches that could be given to a production house for typesetting and mechanicals. Mechanicals could be given to any prep house and converted into film that met universal industry standards. Any printer could use the film. That's not necessarily true anymore. Studios, typesetters, and prep houses are taking chunks out of each others' turf.

Two fundamental changes have taken place.

First, the roles of the players have changed. Design studios can now create files that can be converted by service bureaus into composite film. Work once done by typographers and prep houses—typesetting and page composition—is being done by designers. The profits associated with those tasks are also going to the design studios.

Second, because graphics computers are so new, there are few universal standards. A conventional mechanical is either complete or it's not. It has type, overlays, and position images in place or it doesn't. Those standards don't apply to electronic files.

The Apple Macintosh is (for now) one standard. PostScript is another. But how electronic files are constructed, which elements are present and which aren't, and what kind of equipment the final output is produced on are all matters of negotiation that have to be cleared up *before* the design process is started, rather than afterwards.

This has created a new relationship—ideally a partnership—between studios and their suppliers; a relationship that some studios and service bureaus have learned to work to their mutual benefit.

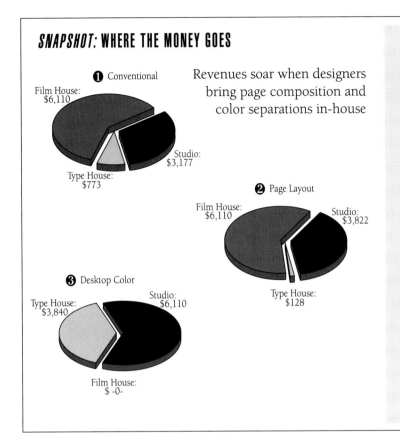

SNAPSHOT: WHERE THE MONEY GOES

❶ Conventional

Film House: $6,110

Studio: $3,177

Type House: $773

Revenues soar when designers bring page composition and color separations in-house

❷ Page Layout

Film House: $6,110

Studio: $3,822

Type House: $128

❸ Desktop Color

Type House: $3,840

Studio: $6,110

Film House: $ -0-

By moving from conventional paste-up to creating composite film on graphics computers, design studios can raise gross revenues, net revenues, and profit margins. In the example shown by the graph at left, the client's total cost to get a sixteen-page catalog from design to composite film is $9,950. The total billings for this project for each of three suppliers — the design studio, service bureau (type/stat house), and film prep house—are shown.

In scenario ❶, the design studio creates conventional mechanical boards. In scenario ❷, the design studio creates mechanical boards from electronic page layouts. And in scenario ❸, the design studio sells the client composite color film made from electronic files.

Switching from manual to electronic mechancials shifts some of the service bureau's revenues to the studio. By creating composite film, both the studio and the service bureau increase their billings and profits at the expense of the film prep house.

YOUR ADVANTAGE

The design studios that have profited most are those that have taken on the most production functions. Where a studio might once have bought type and marked it up 15 percent, setting the type in electronic files is more profitable in three ways. First, the actual type expense from the service bureau will be less if you specify the copy in an electronic page layout than if you have them keystroke it from a manuscript. But you can charge the client the same amount. The difference goes into the "profit" column. Second, the labor expended to put the type into page layout form is more than compensated for by the reduction in labor required to make camera-ready mechanicals. You win again. Third, the money you used to spend on type can be used to pay for the computers you need. You've therefore converted an expense into a capital asset. Your profit-to-billings ratio should be higher, your balance sheet looks better, and the equipment—unlike plain expense items—can be used to increase the amount of credit available from your bank.

To realize these advantages, take on as many production tasks as you can. The further along in the process you go, the more profit you make on each job.

As an example, you're asked to provide a design and camera-ready art for a sixteen-page catalog. The client provides copy in a word processing file and the photographs. The design is of medium complexity—formatted pages with eight four-color photos per page:

❶ Using conventional methods, you might charge as follows:

Design	$ 2,500
Layout/paste-up	600
Type (with 10% markup)	300
Photostats (with 10% markup)	550
Billing	$ 3,950

Your actual costs would be:

Direct expense	$ 773
Net before overhead and labor	3,177
Cost of labor	2,120
Net before overhead	$ 1,057
Profit before overhead	27%

❷ Using a graphics computer to produce camera-ready mechanicals, you might charge the same amount, but your costs would drop:

Billing ....$ 3,950
Direct expense 128
Net before overhead and labor 3,822
Cost of labor 1,600
Net before overhead ....$ 2,222
Profit before overhead 56%

❸ Each page has eight color separations, so the client's cost of creating composite color film, even at very friendly prices, would be at least $375 per page, or $6,000.

The amount of labor needed for you to submit color files ready to be made into composite film is only slightly more than that needed to produce files for camera-ready mechanicals. At 1990 prices, your cost for composite color film (with the service bureau scanning the four-color art) would be $300 per page.

Billing ....$ 9,950
Direct expense 4,800
Net before overhead and labor 5,150
Cost of labor 2,000
Net before overhead ....$ 3,150
Profit before overhead 32%

As you can see, creating composite film is not the most profitable part of this project. And, granted, the computers needed for scenarios two and three cost money to buy and maintain. To take the job to composite film, you'd probably want to have a twenty-four bit color monitor on at least one of your workstations. But look at the bottom line. On this one job, you boosted billings from $3,950 to $9,950. Net increases before overhead rose from $1,057 (conventionally) to $2,222 (using a computer to create camera-ready art)

to $3,150 (submitting composite color film). Submitting composite film gives you almost 300 percent more net revenue than doing conventional mechanicals and 140 percent more net revenue than submitting mechanicals created electronically.

The client's bill to get the project to plate-ready film is the same: $9,950. What's happened is that the computer has worked a kind of subtle Three Card Monte on the players. And designers are the ones who end up with the most cash.

SO WHAT'S IN IT FOR SUPPLIERS?

Why not just buy a scanner and an imagesetter and dispense with the service bureau altogether? No doubt, some studios will do just that. And, no doubt, some conventional typographers and film prep houses will go out of business. However, for the foreseeable future, most studios and corporate clients will not have the means or the desire to produce composite color film or even high-resolution paper output in-house.

Therefore, there are still several vital functions that can be provided by the service bureau:

Carry capital costs of advanced equipment: High-resolution scanners, imagesetters, and color output devices will continue to be expensive items. Service bureaus can spread the cost of that gear over a large number of pages submitted by many clients. So their cost per page to own and operate color equipment will be lower than it would be for all but the largest studios and corporate clients. The time and expertise needed to operate this equipment will gradually decline, but if service bureaus maintain attractive pricing, there will be little incentive for small-volume studios to acquire color gear. According to its manufacturer, as of mid-1990, about 65 percent of the QMS color laser printers sold in the United States went to services bureaus rather than individual users.

Assume risk of obsolescence: Any computer that can produce a PostScript file will continue to be useful for a long time to come. The same can't be said of color scanners and imagesetters. In buying them, service bureaus assume the risk of recouping their investment before clients begin pressuring them to upgrade or begin taking their business elsewhere.

Skills transfer: Graphics computers are complex beasts. Using them for simple tasks is hard enough, but learning to build traps in four-color film for different kinds of presses and printers is more than a little confusing. Because they can spread their knowledge over a large number of clients and projects, service bureaus are in the perfect position to become an institutionalized means of transferring graphic arts technology from the developers to the users.

In practice, this means that the service bureaus maintain a staff of highly skilled production artists. They experiment with new software and hardware as it is released, working out the bugs and figuring out how to apply it to their clients' projects. As clients bring new kinds of projects to them, the service bureaus work out the technology, teaching the clients how to apply it.

This requires that the service bureau stay a couple of steps ahead of their average client in technical proficiency and experience.

However, it also potentially strengthens the bond between the service bureau and the client. When swimming in uncharted waters, most folks will pick a swim buddy they know and trust over one they don't.

In 1990, the average time lapse for new computer technology to penetrate the graphic arts marketplace was about six months for software and a year for hardware. That's the lag between the time a technology is available for sale and the time a large number of users purchase it. Service bureaus tend to be the first purchasers. Until the studios begin buying the gear for themselves, they tend to buy its output from the service bureau. That's been the case with color laser printers; many studios simply send out for color prints instead of buying a color printer. As the price on color printers has dropped, more studios have felt it is cost-effective to buy one of their own. Obviously, the longer a service bureau is the exclusive provider of a new technology, the more return it gets on the time and money expended in developing it. Interestingly, most service bureaus seem quite willing to share their expertise with designers without "holding back" knowledge they could milk for profit a little longer.

Create and vend new services: As new technology appears, service bureaus can offer new products to studios. A current example is high-resolution color comps made from electronic files. Few studios have color printers capable of producing color output good enough for a high-quality composite. Additionally, service bureaus can sell technical expertise. It doesn't make sense for studios to buy the equipment or invest the training time required to produce composite color film if they have only one project they can use it for. A service bureau that already knows how to scan and separate four-color images can do the job for them.

The time required to get up to speed in a three-dimensional drawing program is prohibitive for a one-shot project. At Graphic Connexions, a service bureau in Cranbury, New Jersey, production artists are available to create three-dimensional video graphics from their clients' Illustrator files. Their artists can also create three-dimensional CAD-type renderings from two-dimensional drawings.

A FORK IN THE ROAD

Two kinds of service bureaus are emerging. Practically, any quick printer with a Macintosh and an imagesetter can give you paper output from page layout files. However, to maximize revenues, designers should hook up with a large, well-equipped service bureau, one that is investing in new technology and can offer services—like making composite film or three-dimensional renderings—that you can resell at a profit.

DIGITAL PREPRESS

Teaching designers how to integrate process color in PostScript files

Digital PrePress Inc. (DPI) in San Francisco is one of the new breed of pre-press suppliers now helping studios realize the full potential of their graphics computers.

"Everything we do is in the area of outputting color film from PostScript files," said Sanjay Sakhuja, president of DPI. "We help designers integrate color graphics and color photographs into Macintosh page layout files and output them as film for the printer.

"We feel we have two jobs. The first is to help our clients by telling them what they can do with their equipment, how they can apply the technology to specific jobs. After we've done that, then they come back to us later to actually run the film for a job.

"There's a new role that's been created, the role of a computer production artist. The computer production artist implements the design into an electronic file for final output. In some cases, that's the designer himself. Or it might be a freelancer or a person on our staff. In general, the things our computer production artists do are things that are a lot more complicated than most designers want to get involved in, such as heavy electronic image manipulation."

Sakhuja has a straightforward way of dealing with what should be done by the client and what should be done by his staff: "The things we do in house are experimental, unique situations. If there's a hundred-page catalog to create, we'll figure out how the electronic files should be built—how the traps should be done, what parameters need to be entered into the software—teach the designer how to build the files, then let him implement the pages. If a client needs something that's unique, non-repetitive, we'll do that for them.

"We don't want to be simply an alternate production house, an alternative to a Scitex facility. You can't justify this process just by changing the tools. The effort required to produce four-color film is the same for DPI as it is for a Scitex house. The equipment costs a bit less. But the quality is not quite as good yet. So it doesn't make sense for anyone to use us unless we can offer them a lower price. We do that by having them assemble the files."

Designers who're using graphics computers are already doing nine-tenths of the prep work DPI needs for its process just by making up page layout files with images in place. Therefore, the labor a conventional prep house would expend in shooting boards and mechanically assembling pages is saved, with much of the proceeds going into the designer's pocket.

SERVICE PLEASE

Sakhuja admits that the expertise DPI dispenses so freely was expensive to develop. While he seems bent on giving away the shop, there is a modus to his operandi: Because PostScript color is so new, designers can't use his service at all unless he teaches them how. By the time what he's teaching becomes common knowledge, DPI will have developed new services and acquired more advanced equipment. Also, DPI doesn't have salesmen.

"We are investing money in product, in new services, in equipment, but we don't have any marketing expense. Our philosophy is that we don't have any

---

SNAPSHOT: DIGITAL PREPRESS INC.

Digital PrePress Inc.
1201 Folsom Street, San Francisco, CA 94105
TEL: (415) 882-9961
FAX: (415) 882-9977

Equipment: (12) Macintosh II-family workstations with 24-bit RasterOps displays, (3) NeXT workstations, (3) 9000-series Agfa/Compugraphic imagesetters, (1)Array As-1 large-format scanner, (1)Barneyscan 35mm scanner, Syquest and Bernoulli removable storage, 150 gigabytes of optical storage.

Staff: (15) computer production artists, (3) production managers, (2) technicians.

Typical clients: Design studios, corporate clients, and publishers with a need for four-color composite film at very competitive prices.

salesmen, we only have technical people. We're not ready to sell our service actively to designers who aren't already using a graphics computer at some level," Sakhuja said.

Some of the ways DPI's clients have used its services are novel. A local packaging studio was asked to create composites of ice cream packages to be used in a series of focus groups. The manufacturer wanted the packages to be as close to the real packages as possible, and emphatically did not want comps made by manually pasting up photographic prints. Also, ten copies of each package were needed. In a conventional pre-press shop, the entire package would have had to be separated from mechanicals and press proofs made, then folded to shape.

DPI used a DuPont 4Cast thermal sublimation printer to create proofs directly from the design studio's concept files. In one step, they made ten copies of each package. The design studio saved several days in mechanical prep. The client saved the cost of that mechanical prep. Using the sublimation prints (which require no film) cut another 60 percent from the production bill.

HOW DPI WORKS

As Sakhuja pointed out, DPI works only with studios who are already using graphics computers at some level. Generally, that means Macintosh. What DPI does is help designers move from electronic page make-up to film composition.

DPI is very project oriented; each new job is analyzed on its own merits and a production process designed to make the pathway from Macintosh files to printed product as smooth and straight as possible.

If the project is highly repetitive, DPI's reps will teach the designer how to build the Macintosh files. Generally, DPI scans the client's transparencies on a high-resolution scanner, then gives the designer low-resolution files to place into a page layout. The completed page layout files are returned to DPI where the high-resolution images are automatically substituted for the low-resolution scans and composite film is made. From there, proofs are pulled and any necessary corrections are made to the film before it is shipped to the printer. Sakhuja said DPI also assists designers in dealing with printers, as well.

DOT TO DOT

Getting designers to buy DPI's services was less difficult than convincing printers to accept PostScript film for printing.

"In the beginning, we had a few clients who came back to us saying their printers didn't want to use film from a PostScript bureau," Sakhuja acknowledged.

DPI met the objections head on.

"Most people are a little timid. When the printer complains, they don't know precisely what the printer is talking about and tend to just take his word there's a problem," he continued. "When this happens, we ask for a meeting with the printer and then ask him specifically what his objections are. If we need to make adjustments in our film, we make them. We get down to comparing dot sizes and shapes under a microscope. When the printer sees that our dots are the same as the dots in a conventional separation, the objections magically disappear."

Some printers may have other motives for rejecting PostScript film. Printers with their own prep facilities have been known to price jobs so that they make little profit on the printing (thus showing the client an attractive manufacturing cost). They then mark up their prep prices to compensate. When service bureaus and design firms begin dipping into their till by taking the film work away, some printers get a little testy.

DATA MAX

One significant hurdle DPI has helped its clients get over is in managing large, data-intensive color projects.

A single full-color scan may produce five files of 10 mb each or 50 mb for each image. The scans of color images for a hundred-page catalog can easily fill 10 gigabytes or more of storage.

Copy, page layouts with color breaks in place, and illustrations can take dozens more megabytes. Few designers can justify buying that much storage for one or two projects so DPI makes its on-line optical storage available to designers at a nominal price. Especially for projects with repeating page layouts or color elements, the ability to call up a picture from page thirty-four of last year's edition, resize it, and recrop it without the need to rescan is a big plus.

POSTSCRIPT PERFECTION?

Understandably, Sakhuja champions PostScript as the coming standard for graphics computer languages: "In my mind, there is no choice. There are other languages, such as the proprietary Scitex format, but when you compare PostScript one on one with any other language, it outperforms them all. True, PostScript files are large, but there are ways to address that. The NeXT computer, for example, has built-in data compression chips that can reduce the size of an image file from 4 mb to 150 kb in six seconds."

In mid-1990, Kodak introduced software for the Macintosh that could perform similarly impressive compression of color image files.

The quality of PostScript separations is advancing rapidly as well. PostScript was not originally designed as a color imaging language, but Adobe and the image-setter manufacturers have worked aggressively in the past two years to overcome its initial limitations. Linotronic, for example, has introduced a fourth version of its PostScript interpreter for the L-300—one that images color film at a much faster rate. Agfa/Compugraphic's 9000-series imagesetters, such as those used by DPI, were specifically engineered for color imagesetting. Optronics has released a relatively

low-cost film plotter. These new machines are capable of producing excellent separation film without the banding and density variations that were common in PostScript separations made as recently as a year ago.

Interestingly, Sakhuja also champions the NeXT machine as the future platform of choice for designers.

"The problem just now is that there isn't enough application software for NeXT," he said. "The machine was built with color publishing in mind. As soon as there are versions of Quark XPress, Adobe Illustrator, Aldus PageMaker, and Adobe PhotoShop available for NeXT, it will outperform any desktop machine on the market today."

That performance, Sakhuja said, is spectacular, outshining even the much more expensive DuPont Vaster® and Gerber® dedicated imaging systems.

To give you an idea how fast color publishing capabilities are improving, Sakhuja said new software can penetrate the market within six months and new hardware establishes itself within a year. Given the fact that a high percentage of the new software packages and hardware items—especially in the area of color imaging—significantly advance capabilities rather than duplicate the features of existing products, desktop color imaging is evolving at perhaps twice the speed of the original Macintosh. It was three years between the appearance of the first Mac (1984) and the release of the link between it and a high-resolution imagesetter (1987). The Mac first got the ability to import and manipulate color in 1989, and less than eighteen months later, high-quality separation film is being produced directly from the Mac by service bureaus including DPI.

At this writing, in mid-1990, integrating continuous-tone color into Macintosh files is not as simple as shipping boards and letting the separator worry about the film. However, services like DPI are rapidly closing this "effort" gap, offering studios a new stream of revenue and increased control over their color jobs.

• • •

SprintOut

Moving up to full-scale color

SprintOut is a prime example of a trade typesetting and prep house that has seen the handwriting on the wall, and inferred that its future—if it is to have one—lies in converting electronic files to film rather than in keyboarding text from manuscript.

"Since we have a history as a trade typesetter we know what kind of needs our clients have. Some of our clients began getting into Macs and we wanted to be able to help them all the way through the process, from setting up the project right through film," said Jay Higgins, president of SprintOut.

The path that SprintOut chose is neither a purely PostScript solution nor a gateway to high-end (and high-priced) traditional pre-press systems. As a result, its prices also tend to be somewhere between those charged by straight-PostScript service bureaus and high-end facilities.

The company uses a version of the Cyber-Chrome® film production system that they have modified to their own specifications. The CyberChrome system imports page layout files from IBM or Macintosh and inserts high-resolution color images in them before sending the file to an imagesetter to make final film. In the summer of 1990, the CyberChrome system was supplied with an Eikonix® scanner and used an IBM PC and proprietary software to color correct images, assemble the pages, and make the separations.

The variety of hardware and software that service bureaus have to contend with is fully matched by variations in the level of experience of the people using it.

"This is a frustrating business right now," Higgins admitted. "The level of skill we see in the people operating desktop publishing equipment is all over the map. Someone in management decides that they want to move their production to desktop machines, but they think that all they need to do is put the hardware into the offices and it'll work just like a copying machine. It doesn't. Not all designers are fully up to speed on undercolor removal, trapping techniques, and so on. If you buy the equipment you also need to hire someone to run the equipment and teach the others in the department. And you have to give that person an incentive to teach the others."

As a result, SprintOut focuses heavily on education. They will set up a project for a client, teach them how to operate the hardware and software needed to accomplish it, help troubleshoot, and provide technical support. Higgins's goal, in fact, is to set up a formal training facility for desktop color, perhaps in conjunction with hardware manufacturers and the nearby Rhode Island School of Design.

"Our typesetting business is very high quality; most of the clients are ad agencies. What we're striving for is to bring high quality color to our desktop customers," Higgins said. "We're buying Scitex equipment now to help move that along. What we're coming to is that the responsibility for and a lot of the work of pre-press is being shifted to the end user: the designer. Service bureaus will be in the business of making high-resolution scans and running out film. And we'll be educating customers. The programs are getting more complex. You can't teach yourself anymore by buying a thousand dollar software program and a book."

SNAPSHOT: SprintOut

SprintOut
50 Clifford Street, Providence, RI 02903
TEL: (401) 421-2264
FAX: (401) 421-9460

Equipment: (5) Macintosh II-family workstations with 24-bit displays, (2) IBM-PC AT workstations, (2) Optronics imagesetters, (1) CyberChrome imaging and assembly system.

Staff: (7) computer production artists, (2) technicians.

Typical clients: Design studios and corporate clients with a need for inexpensive, commercial-quality separations.

• • •

QUAD TEXT

High-end imaging—end-to-end integration

From a standing start in the mid-1970s, Quad/Graphics has grown into a behemoth in the publication printing industry. Quad has five printing plants, and these are strategically located so that 75 percent of the U.S. population is within a day and a half drive of one of them. The company's matched M-1000 web presses make multi-plant printing a little easier for magazines such as *Newsweek* that need to be on sale simultaneously in all parts of the country. Quad is a favorite subject of *In Search of Excellence* author Tom Peters, who gives the company high marks for flexibility and innovation. One of its divisions, Quad Text, is a leader in developing new offset printing technology.

Against this background, it's not surprising that Quad has moved aggressively to market desktop production services to its clients.

In September 1986, the company appointed Alan Darling to head up Quad Text, a new division whose mission was to "take pre-press services back to Quad's printing clients."

Four years later, Quad has done just that, offering seamless end-to-end integration of high-quality color to desktop publishers. And in this case, end-to-end really means beginning to end: Quad can provide the transparencies for catalog publishers—their exposures

carefully matched to the capabilities of the company's presses—provide color scans for the publication's designers, accept page layout files from a variety of sources, produce color film on its Scitex equipment, then print and bind just about any quantity you have in mind via offset or gravure. A recent catalog run added up to more than thirty million pieces, but was completed on two of Quad's gravure presses in one month. The designers, meanwhile, need nothing more than familiarity with a page layout program.

"We want to be in a position to accept files from anyone," Darling said. "As design studios and advertising agencies begin to work electronically, we need to be able to accept advertisements electronically and integrate them with our magazine work here.

"Donnelly, for example, has a system they grew themselves called Pulsar. It's very much a subset of the tools you have in XPress and runs on DEC VAXstations. You can't see text and graphics together, so it's not a design tool, but it's a very good production tool. Toys 'Я' Us does its catalogs on Pulsar. We can accept their files here and make film through our system. We can accept files from Archetype® and PageMaker. We haven't taken any files from Ready Set Go®, but I'm sure we could. We're reasonably happy with the Open Pre-press Interface [OPI] and want to work more closely with Aldus to advance it. It's simple now, but it works."

OPI is a set of protocols that were designed to allow full file transportability between page layout and imaging systems.

SERVICE MAXIMUS

Like Donnelly, Quad Text has its own proprietary system, called ADEPT: Automated Design and Production Tools. The system is based on the Scitex Visionary® software, which is a souped-up version of Quark XPress. Quad worked with Quark to developed the links between XPress and Scitex equipment. ADEPT

SNAPSHOT: QUAD TEXT

Quad/Graphics Inc.
W224 N3322 Duplainville Road, Pewaukee, WI 53072
TEL: (414) 246-9200
FAX: (414) 246-7289

Equipment: Macintosh II-family workstations with 24-bit displays, DEC VAX, Scitex interactive workstations, Scitex scanners, Scitex Raystar film plotters.

Staff: (25) computer production artists, (7) production managers.

Typical clients: Figi's, Mary Maxim, and other direct-mail catalog houses, *Playboy* magazine, and other publishers with a need for best-quality separations, fast turnaround, and large press runs.

includes other QUAD proprietary software, such as a production tracking system, and a mixture of DEC and Macintosh hardware. At the client site, Macintosh workstations, a laser printer, and color thermal printer are linked on an Ethernet/AppleTalk® network to a DEC VAXserver. IBM PCs and other keyboard units can be included on the network for text entry.

"We give clients a site license for the Scitex Visionary software, we give them access to all 940 faces in the Bitstream library, we give them production control software, and we give them training and support," Darling explained. "It's more or less turnkey. Some people we wean onto the ADEPT system by putting them on Quark XPress first and letting them do their type, then move them on to color at an appropriate pace."

Like most electronic-layout-to-film services, Quad makes high-resolution scans of the client's art and sends back low-resolution scans to be placed in the layout files. When the layout files are sent to Quad, the high-resolution images replace the low-resolution ones and composite film is made.

"We use the Hyphen RIP [raster image processor], which we have running on a DEC computer," Darling said. "We can rasterize a full page, in color, at full resolution in about ninety seconds. It's very fast and flexible. We can fine-tune the amount of ink coverage and the screen values. We do *Scholastic Magazine*, for example, which is run on very thin paper. We can identify their files by name, and when those files are sent to the RIP, it automatically knows to lower the line screen for their images. There's a lot of sly work going on behind the scenes. The whole intention is that clients can send their files in and they come out the back end as full pieces of film without their having to worry about it."

One area that's currently not fully automated is the trapping of images, Darling pointed out: "I think designers have to be a little aware of traps right now. We're not catching all the traps automatically at the moment. We have to trap some of them on the interactive stations after the files arrive here."

DESKTOP COLOR: READY FOR PRIME TIME?

Small but critical details, such as traps, are one reason why Darling thinks that, for many clients, a turnkey, hybrid PostScript-Scitex solution like ADEPT is the best choice until desktop color comes of age.

"My opinion is that high-quality desktop color won't be ready for a few years. Right now, we're saying that high-resolution color scanning should stay in the color houses. That's not to say that if one of our clients wants to try it, we won't work with them. We will. Because if they don't do it with us, they'll do it with someone else," Darling said. "What's holding back desktop color is not technology, it's skill level. Adobe PhotoShop does a really excellent job of emulating a Scitex Imager®. It doesn't have the quantitative control that you have on the Imager, but it'll do a good job for a lot of people. However, you're now asking designers to adjust color for separation. If you want to take color in-house, you must either have that expertise, or you have to make the same quantum leap that it took to go from mechanicals and cold type to desktop publishing. The color tools need to become more intuitive. That's the limiting factor at this point."

Quad will help clients make that leap, even it means doing a smaller portion of the job.

"We're not holding back on anything as far as sharing knowledge," Darling asserted. "Three years ago, when trade typesetters saw desktop typesetting coming, some of them said, 'Ha, that'll never happen.' They ended up out of business. We don't want that to happen to us. We've looked very hard at our investments here to make sure they're amortized over the correct period so that, if everything does turn sour for film houses and people want to do color themselves on the desktop, we're not left with a sheet anchor around our necks."

• • •

PHOTO LAB INC.

Large-format repro-grade transparencies from color PostScript files

Sure, you say. Separations. Great. That's terrific if you're producing final film for printing. But studios need flexibility of output: prints, transparencies, back-lit panels, mural-sized prints, and more. They need *continuous tone* color images, not separations (which are halftones). For illustrators, in particular, the lack of a suitable way to deliver continuous-tone color art created on a computer has been a major stumbling block. Not many clients are equipped to accept a color Illustrator or Freehand file as final art. The only options for hard-copy output have been low-resolution color laser prints, low-resolution transparencies, or prints from a DuPont 4Cast or Kodak XL7700.

The record will reflect that the dam burst in 1990. Resolution hasn't been a problem in PostScript litho negatives for several years. This year, PostScript finally connected to film recorders with reproduction-grade resolution.

PLI, a Cincinnati color lab, has one of these recorders. With 16,000 lines of resolution horizontally, it can lay down more dots than the emulsion of a four-by-five-inch film can image. The result is continuous-tone images that are as smooth and sharp as one made with a fine studio camera. The almost-but-not-quite

images made by relatively inexpensive 4,000-line film recorders look like something viewed through Vaseline compared to a transparency imaged at 16,000 lines. Size isn't an issue either: PLI has backs that will image 35mm, 70mm, and four-by-five inch film, all at 16,000 lines.

"We're running PostScript directly to the recorder," affirmed Dave Rahe, manager of electronic imaging. "There are some real advantages to that. For one, desktop computers deal with color in terms of red, green, and blue. Their images are constructed of percentages of red, green, and blue. When you go to translate that into cyan, yellow, magenta, and black—for an imagesetter—the colors may change subtly. Since the film recorder works in RGB, there's no translation. The files are being written to the film exactly as they exist in the computer."

One of the major strengths of PostScript as a graphics language is the fact that it's device-independent. The resolution of PostScript output depends on the output device, not on an arbitrary limit set by the developer of a computer or software package. That allows it to take full advantage of ultra-high resolution devices. The same file can be sent to a 300 dpi printer for proofing, a 2,540 dpi imagesetter for separations, and a 16,000-line film recorder with no adjustments or changes required.

THE BIG PICTURE

A high-resolution large-format transparency is the ideal way for illustrators to deliver their work. It's familiar to any client. It makes a great impression. And it reproduces well. For illustrators who work primarily on graphics computers, the saturation and sharpness they're used to seeing on their monitors can be translated—even enhanced—by a high-resolution recorder.

Since film recorders accept both positive and negative film, PLI has kicked off a profitable sideline to its imaging service: Mural prints.

SNAPSHOT: PHOTO LAB INC.

Photo Lab Inc.
1026 Redna Terrace, Cincinnati, OH 45215
TEL: (800) 733-3124
FAX: (513) 771-4403

Equipment: (5) Macintosh II f/x workstations with 24-bit RasterOps display boards, 120 mb internal drives, and 8 mb RAM, (1) 80386 AT-class computer with 8 mb RAM, (4) PL and (2) MassMicro 45 mb removable storage drives, Ethernet network, (1) high-resolution film scanner, (1) 16,000-line film recorder, (1) 8,000-line film recorder.

Staff: (5) production technicians.

Typical clients: Design studios, corporate clients, and publishers with a need for reproduction-quality continuous-tone images from PostScript files.

. . .

"If you're working on a trade exhibit and you have some PostScript graphics, how are you going to enlarge them for a booth?" asks Rahe. It was a natural question, since PLI's custom color lab does a lot of trade show work for photographers. "We began shooting negatives from PostScript files and making mural prints. We've made them in various sizes and, given the enlargement, they're quite good. We recently made a six-by-twenty-foot print from an Illustrator file. We started with a four-by-five negative, so it wasn't tack-sharp. But no blow-up that size is going to be ultra-sharp. When you view it at a normal distance, as you would at a trade show, it looks terrific."

THE PRICE IS RIGHT

Another bit of good news is that it you won't have to hock your Rolex to take advantage of the high-resolution imaging. In late 1990, PLI was charging forty dollars for a four-by-five transparency or negative imaged at 16,000 lines.

"The service is so new, it's hard to say what the real price should be," Rahe admitted. "But that's comparable to what it costs to have a piece of flat art copied onto transparency or negative film."

Too many suppliers look at graphics computers as a way to cut service and increase price. It's refreshing to find one that believes in reasonable pricing.

LOTS OF DOTS

Interestingly, the advent of high-resolution continuous-tone imaging may up the ante for designers using graphics computers in several ways.

The first is in file size. Even a 150-line halftone (which is at the upper end of what's commonly used in commercial color lithography) requires no more than 100 kb of data for each square inch of each color screen (a half-megabyte per square inch is a good guess for CYMK files). That many pixels will give you a two-to-one oversampling (two pixels for every dot)

and yield a negative with as much detail as the printing press can reproduce. Not so for high-resolution continuous-tone recording. If the film could capture all of the detail the recorder can produce (which it can't), you'd need about 10 mb of data *per square inch* to max out the resolution of the film recorder. In practice, Rahe said, a file of 15 mb to 25 mb will give you as sharp an image as the film can hold.

Still, that's quite a jump in file size. Accustomed to the limitations of halftone images (whether for black and white or color) and of low-resolution color printers, many designers have consciously geared their work to files of limited size.

Using a flatbed color scanner, for example, a 300-dpi four-color scan of a letter-sized page will yield a file of roughly 23 mb; cutting the resolution to 150 dpi drops the file size to a much more manageable 6 mb. When output at small sizes—a few square inches—these small files make perfectly acceptable color separations. But, Rahe said, when output to the 16,000-line recorder, the rough edges show.

"You can't expect studio-camera quality from half-sized files," Rahe explained. "You're not giving the recorder enough data to plot a sharp image. By bumping up the size of the file, you have a lot more data to plot, and a much sharper image."

That data does come at a price: High-resolution scanners for importing photographs or flat art are expensive. So are the disk drives needed to store the data. The workstations needed to manipulate these images are 30 to 50 percent more expensive than stations that work comfortably with smaller files.

High-resolution imaging is kind of like nuclear weapons: the mere threat of their existence makes everyone spend money—to have nukes of their own, and to defend against being nuked. High-resolution imaging will likely become one of these costly parity games: the haves—those with access to it—will win more jobs and bill more services than the have-nots.

. . .

CHAPTER 5

COLOR COMPOSITES

From four-color to three-dimensional, computers make comping easier

The widespread use of graphics computers will bring an end to many traditional processes in the graphic arts. One of them will be the "kind-of-like" process. That's where, using printed samples, tissues, and marker renderings, designers attempt to pantomime their intentions and obtain client approval.

It's always been possible to show clients a lifelike comp; the question has been how soon in the process to make it and how much to spend. Because of their powerful illustration and color rendering abilities, desktop graphics computers can be used to create a number of lifelike alternatives in electronic form. These can be output as slides, on videotape, in hard copy, or, in the case of products and packaging, in full three-dimensional form. Almost any lithographic or video effect can be simulated in the computer. Almost, but not all. Metallic inks, spot varnishes, foiling, embossing, debossing, and other post-finishing techniques aren't yet available direct-from-desktop. These can, however, be applied by hand to hard copies of a computer file, or by making negatives for use with an IdentiColor® or similar system.

COST AND EFFECT

Surprisingly, we found many designers felt the comparatively low cost (in time and materials) of computer-generated comps was a bigger advantage than their realism. Even though low-cost thermal color printers, such as the QMS, don't have extreme color accuracy, their ability to quickly print a dozen variations on a theme from a single file at less than a dollar a print pleases both designers and their clients. It's a way to begin dealing with something that closely resembles the final product at an early stage of the design process. And, when clients compare the cost of thermal color prints to the alternative—a smaller number of variations laboriously made by hand at great expense—they tend to feel pretty good about the less-than-perfect quality.

Though most studios we spoke with reserve them until the final approval stage, accurate color comps can be made using a DuPont 4Cast or the new Kodak XL7700 sublimation printer. And it's easy to get a set of separation negatives and a Chromalin-type proof from a color file for less than a hundred dollars; usually on a next-day schedule. There are still some limitations: Few service bureaus keep emulsion in stock for every Pantone® color; but if you're using common colors or can live with CYMK simulations, it's the best way to show the client a "live" image.

Alternatives to making separations are dumping the color file to videotape or a slide, perhaps as a backup to thermal color proofs. The colors can be "tuned" to closely resemble the colors of the final product. Also, with the lighting controls available in programs such as Swivel 3-D® and MacroMind Director, metallic finishes and embossing can be rendered quite realistically. PostScript slides are widely available, usually on an overnight-service basis, for less than ten dollars each. Repro-grade transparencies can be had for forty dollars. If you have the hardware (a video board and VCR), a videotape costs about three bucks.

Despite these limitations, the advantages of using computer-generated comps are undeniable. No one we spoke with even hinted they'd go back to doing marker renderings if they had a choice.

Faster sales: A clear presentation of your ideas is almost certain to make a better impression than a murky one; especially one that requires the client to imagine some part of the project. Large studios, with their staffs and ready access to marker specialists, airbrush artists, and machinery, have always had the ability to show the client what they were getting pretty early in the process. Now, using the computer, smaller studios can make realistic presentations without blowing their materials or labor budgets.

Increased customer satisfaction: No one likes surprises. That's why McDonald's is the biggest restau-

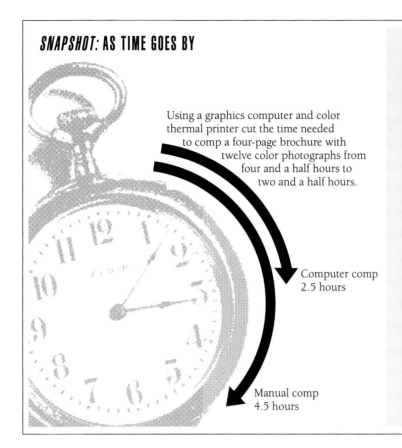

SNAPSHOT: AS TIME GOES BY

Using a graphics computer and color thermal printer cut the time needed to comp a four-page brochure with twelve color photographs from four and a half hours to two and a half hours.

Computer comp
2.5 hours

Manual comp
4.5 hours

Moving up to a full-scale color system may not be cost-effective for some studios. But if your work is primarily color and full comps must be done for each stage of a project, the equipment could pay for itself. At a minimum, adding color capability to one or more of your existing workstations and taking your color files to an output bureau to make color prints might save time and money.

Designers who work with color comps from their computers say that time is the deciding factor. The ability to quickly revise layouts and see them in color on a hard copy makes projects move more quickly. Once clients get accustomed to seeing color comps from the computer, they appreciate the flexibility and economy of color thermal prints.

None of the designers we spoke with have totally given up manual comping. Post-finishing, metallic inks, and some other lithographic techniques cannot yet be adequately simulated using a computer. However, many reserve hand-rendered comps for final presentations.

rant chain in the world. Realistic comps give you the ability to show them what you envision instead of playing visual charades and hoping they're seeing what you're saying.

Shorter final production: *If* you take the time to construct a fairly tight and logically organized composite file, the steps from comp to final film can be as easy as placing the final art and respecifying a few colors. By "tight," we mean using the actual dimensions of the final product rather than approximations; be positive that things line up mathematically, not just visually. By logical, we mean building the files in a way that will make it easy to go back and modify them for final output. Building borders by placing one shape over another, rather than using an outline tool, is not usually logical. Most graphics software uses sophisticated, multi-layer files; objects can exist in front of or behind each other. It's sometimes hard to know precisely how a file is going to print. Fortunately, due to the magic of PostScript, your laser printer will act pretty much like a PostScript imagesetter. If it works on the laser, it will

probably work on an imagesetter. The exceptions to this rule are in using high-resolution images or sending the file through a Scitex instead of a PostScript imagesetter. The data required to print high-resolution graphics at 300 dots per inch (the laser standard) may fit comfortably into your printer's RAM memory. But when sent to an imagesetter and printed at 2,540 dpi, it may overload the RAM. Also, if you intend to send your files from a desktop machine through a Scitex for output (saving them as a Scitex CT file, or using the Visionary link), keep your files as simple as you can. The fewer layers and overlapping images, the less likely you are to have problems when the PostScript description is translated for the Scitex.

COLOR CAUTIONS

Precise comps are a boon for any job; but computers introduce a few twists that, disregarded, can make your life difficult. The first danger is a creative one. It's easy to sit down at your keyboard and whack out a dozen good-looking comps. In fact, it may be too easy.

Designers say you can get caught up in the computer and it capabilities; limiting yourself to what you know how to do quickly on the machine rather than deciding what's best for the product, then figuring out how to adapt it to digital production. One designer said he'd recently been shown a comp for a new magazine. It was painfully obvious the comp had been done quickly on a graphics computer: too many "easy" effects, everything at right angles to everything else, and no attempt to use fonts other than the standard LaserWriter® set.

Don't let the ease of creating comps push you to that stage before you're ready; thumbnails should probably come first for any project. As one New York packaging designer put it: "You can generate a huge number of ideas very fast using a graphics computer, but all of them are going to be in the same realm. The sketch pad is a lot more flexible than a computer; you can jump from idea to idea or style to style without stopping to load fonts or scan in new artwork."

Clients may not be accustomed to looking at nearly finished artwork so early in the process. The details present in a computer comp may distract them, taking their focus off of the overall concept.

They may think that a very rough comp is a final presentation. Conversely, they may think they can make unlimited changes before the negatives are made. Or, they may make inaccurate assumptions about which elements will change and which won't.

One designer recalled a painful experience with a new client: The designer created a package that, because it was very small, required the printer to trim less than a quarter of an inch from the type. The comp clearly showed the trim lines and the live matter to size, and in the final position. The comp was shown to the printer. The client and printer assumed the comp was a rough and that the type would be repositioned. The designer failed to call the tight trim to the printer's attention. When the film arrived at the printer, sud-

denly there was a problem. Two days and several thousand dollars later, the printer had new film with a wider clearance.

It's also quite possible to create effects in the computer that are difficult and/or costly to reproduce using a printing press. The danger is in selling a look that costs an arm and a leg to produce, or which costs you dearly to create the final art. The computer loosens many of the limitations formerly imposed by the ineptness of film houses and the expense of separation and stripping. Presses, however, haven't changed that much. By giving you the control, the computer also imposes on you the responsibility of knowing the limitations of printing, binding, embossing, and any other process you may use.

HOLY HARDWARE, BATMAN!

The near future—1991 and 1992—will offer an explosion of color output options. New technologies that have been in gestation since the late 1980s are coming to market. Combined with the upsurge in the number of designers using color-capable computers, their impact is going to be nothing short of revolutionary.

The tried-and-true color thermal printer will probably continue to be the staple technology. Improvements in color fidelity and resolution have already been demonstrated that put them just one notch below an actual press proof. Prices will continue to drop, and the thought of an under-$5,000 color printer with full PostScript and reasonable color accuracy is far from a fantasy.

The DuPont 4Cast printer produces superb prints. The resolution is superb, though at this time, the saturation of color leaves something to be desired. The prints have a slightly faded look, especially when compared to a chromalin-type proof, which tends to exaggerate color saturation. Kodak introduced its XL7700 dye sublimation printer in 1990. Initial reviews were very enthusiastic. The XL7700 has a nominal resolution of just 200 dpi. But because it is a continuous-tone printer, the output looks sharp and smooth, without the annoying dot patterns that result when colors are simulated by dithering on a thermal printer such as the QMS. The color fidelity of the Kodak printer was superb, and the colors rich. The price was rich, too, with a suggested retail of just under $25,000. While that may keep the XL7700 out of studios in the short term, the first QMS thermal color printer cost over $20,000 when it was introduced in 1988. By 1990, the price had dropped to under $7,000 and they had become commonplace in studios and service bureaus that produce digital color art.

Along with Kodak, the Canon CLC-500® color copier may be an important new technology for studios. Right. A color copier. Unlike older analog color copiers, the CLC-500 is fully digital. And it prints at an ultra-clean 400 dpi with 64 gray levels for each color. Aside from allowing all manner of enlargements, reductions, and color manipulations in its copier mode, the CLC-500 also accepts input *directly* from graphics computers. Through its IPU (Intelligent Processing Unit) interfaces or through an Adobe Emerald® RIP developed for it, the CLC-500 can translate computer files into color prints up to eleven by seventeen inches that are sharper than the Cibachrome prints you were using ten years ago.

Even more interesting is a machine Canon introduced in the fall of 1990 called the Bubble-Jet Copier A1®. Like the CLC-500, it functions in both a copy mode and as a computer printer. Unlike the CLC-500, it makes prints up to twenty-three inches by thirty-three inches. That's an instant poster from your files. And the image can be tiled by the printer, so you can assemble an image as big as you want from twenty-by-thirty inch sections. The A1 also prints with 64 gradations at 400 dpi. When its prints are laminated with a glossy plastic they are virtually indistinguishable from a commercial-quality C-print. Imagine walking into a

presentation with supermarket department signs at actual size, or into a packaged-goods client with a soap package three feet tall. Both the CLC-500 and the A1 accept transparency material, too, so backlit panels can be made quickly and relatively cheaply.

In the past when you worked up a comp, the physical piece itself—a box, a bottle, a booklet—had to be made by hand. That's still true for printed materials, but for packaging and actual products, there's a process called stereo lithography.

Working from a three-dimensional file, such as one created in AutoCad®, stereo lithographic printers build up a three-dimensional form from very thin cross sections. All things considered, the price is reasonable: A package the size of a microwave entree container can be "printed" for less than $2,000. When dealing with packages where the internal volume is critical, carved wooden models are no match for a true, three-dimensional comp. As more package producers add computer-driven tooling devices, it will become possible to design, comp, and create tooling for a package entirely from files created on a desktop computer. This may encourage designers and clients to use more custom packaging, rather than relying on stock containers.

BUSINESS OPPORTUNITIES

Design comps are usually done by the studio commissioned to do the design. However, there do seem to be some opportunities.

By hooking up with a service bureau that has a Bubble-Jet A1 with a computer interface you can offer clients poster-sized visuals for use at trade shows or sales meetings. You can also become a reseller for the bureau, converting other studio's files to color and reselling the printed output with a markup.

If you've become handy with any of the three-dimensional programs, hooking with a stereo lithographer could make you a one-person service bureau for packaged goods and product designers.

• • •

LANDOR ASSOCIATES

If it's good enough for Landor....

A close associate once said of Walter Landor that he had the uncanny knack of making clients believe his studio's best ideas were their own. Landor Associates gained a reputation as a studio that brought out the best in its clients, rather than one that insisted it knew what was best. The delicate balance between give and take in creative presentations was carefully nurtured. Integrating graphics computers into that balance presented some interesting problems. The firm knew that computers were essential if it was to continue to thrive creatively and economically. While it produces mechanical art equivalent to that produced traditionally in every way, computer-generated comps look nothing like the artistic marker renderings traditionally used in the initial stages of a project. They're more final-looking; but at the same time, unless they're printed on a dye sublimation printer or as a Matchprint, the colors aren't quite right.

Landor uses prints from QMS color thermal printers for much of its initial work. These—or sometimes slides from a PostScript film recorder—are used to present the studio's concepts to clients. And that's sometimes been confusing.

"We have run into client resistance due to the inconsistency of the color from the QMS," admitted Glen Setty, group technology manager. "When we've shown QMS prints, some clients felt they were too final. They focused on the details instead of the concept. In a few cases, we've actually gone back and made sketches.

"There's also the esthetic of the presentation. A lot of people like the way renderings are presented; like the way they look and feel. The QMS doesn't really allow us to duplicate that.

"That will probably fade away as clients become more accustomed to looking at color prints. But, because the computer comps look so finished, some clients feel they're being pushed into a design, that they haven't had time to react to it and be involved in its evolution. We have to reassure them that this is just another version of a marker comp, and that the project hasn't been cast in stone."

YOU CAN'T GO HOME AGAIN

Although Landor does use dry transfers to achieve absolute color accuracy for final presentations and for materials to be used in research, computers play a valuable role, too. Not one of the designers we spoke to—at Landor or elsewhere—even hinted they'd stop using graphics computers to produce comps. Most were just anxious for the quality of the output to improve: "It's just too expensive to do comps the traditional way," explained Mark Crumpacker, senior designer. "It becomes a moot point when everything from design to output is being done on the computer anyway. To create a traditional comp of a color file, you have to go into Illustrator or PhotoShop, separate the shapes out into PMS colors, and output them for dry transfers.

"Using the computer, we can generate a huge number of variations very quickly. The most effective way to present those is a thermal print or slide."

Assigned to work on the signage for a Korean amusement park, Crumpacker felt the best way to pre-

---

SNAPSHOT: LANDOR ASSOCIATES

Landor Associates, Inc.
1001 Front Street, San Francisco, CA 94111
TEL: (415) 955-1200
FAX: (415) 391-9563

Equipment: (80) Macintosh II-family workstations with 24-bit displays, 4 mb RAM, 40 mb internal hard disks; Syquest 45 mb removable cartridge drives; (3) QMS color laser printers; (5) LaserWriter IINTX printers; (1) Matrix film recorder.

Staff: (125) designers.

Typical clients: Coca-Cola, McDonald's, and other large national and multi-national accounts. Landor handles identity programs, new product introductions, package designs, signage, and other design projects.

---

sent the job would be in slide form. The colors were to be bright, primary pigments with little subtlety—ideal for a film recorder.

"Besides, the signs were fifty feet tall," he noted. "There was no way to comp them to size. The slides could be projected at a large size to get some idea of the scale of the image.

"Before any project starts I decide how it's going to be presented. That way, I can match the dimensions, format, and resolution of my computer files to the output device. If I'm making slides, I create the files in a two-by-three format, which is the ratio of a 35mm slide. If the comps will come from the QMS color laser, I have to adjust the colors to work around the printer's limitations."

Because the QMS isn't capable of reproducing all colors accurately, Crumpacker has made his own swatch book: a computer file containing hundreds of color squares that he printed on the QMS. That gives Landor's designers a place to start in specifying color for the presentations. Setty observed that computer comping presents unique challenges: "It can get a bit convoluted when a client loves one of the colors in a QMS print and you're not sure how to reproduce it on a press," he chuckled.

ARCH RIVALS

That hasn't stopped Landor from using computer comps for its largest clients.

"McDonald's asked us to do new soft drink cups," Setty said. "They wanted to have the golden arches and logo on them, but with bright colors and a more fun look. We didn't want a hard-edged look, so our designers did marker sketches of the images. We scanned those, used Adobe Streamline® to capture the outlines, then colored them in the computer and presented QMS prints.

"In most cases, we make negatives and Matchprints before sending film to a printer, but since we were printing these flexographically on wax cups, the QMS was pretty close to what we thought the final product would look like. McDonald's approved the QMS prints. From there, all we had to do was put the type in the files, put in stay-aways using stroke-and-fill, then separate the art files out as film. We sent the printer our QMS print and a set of line negatives. The printer made screen tints to match our print."

A TRUCK AND A SMILE

Crumpacker used a slide recorder again for a presentation to Coca-Cola, a longtime Landor client. Coca-Cola asked for a new design for its semi-trailers. By using PhotoShop, Crumpacker was able to place the studio's proposed designs onto photos of actual trucks. When output as 35mm slides, it was impossible to tell you weren't looking at trucks painted in the new colors.

"For any of these processes, you just have to recognize the limitations," he cautioned. "We've never been able to reproduce Coke red on a slide, for example. The one type of project computer output doesn't work for is identity work—letterheads, business cards—you can't get the subtlety of color and detail you need. In those cases, we design in the computer, but we use dry transfers to make the comps. We've not been successful simulating metallics or foil, either."

In those cases, Setty said, they often use a QMS print as a base, adding dry transfers on top of it.

"Get to know the quirks of your equipment," Crumpacker advised. "We found you have to let the QMS rest for a minute between prints. Otherwise, it makes three prints and crashes. And there's something in Apple's laser spooling software that sends the QMS into a permanent waiting state. You have to shut it off and turn it on again to unfreeze it."

Don't forget that clients have quirks too: "Find out what the client *wants* to see. Don't throw color prints at someone who's used to seeing renderings," Setty said. "Try easing them into it, one print at a time."

PROTOTYPE SERVICES

If your computer can image it, Prototype can make a three-dimensional model

Making physical models of packages, products, or buildings is more than a craft; it's an art. Like most arts, it's inexact and it takes time. Now, thanks to stereo lithography, it's possible to render a unique bottle, a complex container, a sophisticated machine part, or an entire product quickly and with digital precision.

Stereo lithography is the most well-developed of several three-dimensional imaging processes that have been introduced. All you need is a file in IGES format (a common three-dimensional format) that completely describes all the surfaces of the object. More than twenty workstation engineering packages will generate IGES files, including AutoCad, Unigraphics®, and Camex®. Some packages available on Macintosh—MacBravo® and Intergraph® among them—will create IGES files as well.

Prototype Services of Chicago accepts IGES files and prints them to its 3D Systems Stereo Lithography Apparatus (SLA) printer. The company also works from blueprints or, in a pinch, rough sketches with dimensions.

"Package designs are pretty simple for us," said Jim Bednar, Prototype's manager. That's understandable. Much of the company's business is in modeling complex machine parts, like the motor mounts for rocket engines. Martin-Marietta is one of PSI's regular customers. "We had a couple of people from American Can [now Primerica] come in to talk to us about mod-

eling a food container. We talked for about fifteen minutes about what we could do for them, how much it would cost.

"They had brought a wooden model with them, and we had a designer in the conference room working at a keyboard the whole time. When we finished our pitch, they asked how long it would take us to render the package; we told them, 'It's already done.'" Bednar chuckled.

Bednar said the company usually charges fifty dollars an hour for design time and one hundred dollars an hour for running the file on the SLA printer.

PRINT SPECS

The SLA is filled with a light-sensitive liquid plastic resin. A laser is aimed at a platform in the center of the liquid. At the beginning of the process, the platform is just below the surface, covered by .002 inch of liquid.

In the computer, the SLA's software converts any three-dimensional image into a series of very thin cross-sections. The laser traces the outline of each cross-section, one at a time, on the light-sensitive resin. As each cross-section is drawn, it hardens the liquid into the shape of the laser trace. A wiper device repeats the trace, scraping excess liquid from the cross-section. Then the platform drops into the resin, and the next section is drawn.

The shape is built up layer by layer, so the SLA is capable of modeling extremely fine detail. Hollow shapes are no problem, Bednar said, though shapes that contain trapped volume are rendered more slowly. This is because the wipers are less efficient in cleaning trapped volumes.

Naturally, the slower a shape is rendered, the more it costs. Prototype billed American Can $1,675 for the microwave container, a simple dish. By comparison, an eight-inch bottle with a four-inch diameter and a very complex shape cost $4,100 to render. Containers that have thick walls also render more

---

SNAPSHOT: PROTOTYPE SERVICES

Prototype Services, Inc.
1660 North Besley Ct., Chicago, IL 60622
TEL: (312) 772-9200
FAX: (312) 772-7117

Equipment: (2) Silicon Graphics workstations, (1) IBM PC-AT, (1) 3D Systems Stereo Lithography Apparatus.

Staff: (2) designers.

Typical clients: Design studios, product designers, and corporate clients with a need for precise solid models of computer-generated designs.

slowly, as do containers built from extremely large data files. As with any printer, when the SLA is given more data points to compute, it works more slowly.

BETTER THAN THE ALTERNATIVES?

SLA is unarguably better than working blind or working from an inaccurate model.

"We were given dimensions for a blister-pack for cotton swabs that was scheduled to go into production in a week," Bednar recalled. "The client was ready to order the tooling, which cost $80,000. A wooden model wasn't practical because they needed to know exactly how many swabs would fit inside. We made three different sizes of models for them in four days for less than $2,000. They confirmed the size and ordered the tooling in time to make their roll-out schedule.

"SLA lets you get a feel for the container—to hold it, turn it over in your hands—and to precisely measure internal volumes. That's important for packaging projects where you're designing a custom container instead of using a stock item."

SLA can provide a critical check step for complex packaging. In another case, PSI was asked to model a foil-cutter for use in producing tamper-proof packaging. The part was very complex, and the designer apparently became confused. In working up an SLA model, PSI discovered that the part wouldn't operate as specified. Using the model, however, it was an easy matter for the designer to see where he went wrong. He marked up the model—just like you'd mark up a printer's proof—and returned it. Using the designer's markings, PSI corrected its three-dimensional database. A new model was made to confirm the revisions and the database was then used to output an accurate set of blueprints.

GOLDEN OPPORTUNITY

There are some designs that are too difficult to model any way except with stereo lithography. PSI created a three-dimensional rendering and an SLA model for a promotional package for McDonald's. Designed to hold a children's Happy Meal, the package was shaped like a watering can, with handle and spout. One side featured a relief of the golden arches logo, while the other carried a relief of Ronald McDonald.

"We had very little to work with; just a rough sketch and the interior dimensions," Bednar recalled. "To digitize the golden arches we took a copy of the logo, traced it onto tissue, then taped the tissue to the computer monitor and selected the points off of it with the mouse. We did the same thing with the sketch of Ronald McDonald."

The watering can comp cost McDonald's $3,100, but they also got some significant bonuses: PSI's Silicon Graphics workstations can transfer images to videotape in real time.

"We provided the can in a specific combination of colors they'd specified," Bednar explained. "But we also gave them a videotape. We took our computer model and animated it, rotating it slowly. Then we videotaped the rotating package and changed the color. That gave them a look at the package in a variety of color combinations."

REPRO GRADE

The SLA resin is a pale white-amber and can be painted any color. The resin is somewhat fragile, so Bednar recommends that the SLA part not be handled too extensively. If multiple parts are needed, for focus groups for example, the SLA model can be used as a master for RTV (Room Temperature Vulcanization) castings. Using a urethane material, a number of RTV copies can be made quickly and inexpensively.

Given its cost, SLA certainly doesn't fit into every project budget. But the ability to precisely mock up packages and refine them electronically could help give clients the confidence to allow designers to attempt unique shapes.

• • •

HORNALL ANDERSON

Mixing and matching techniques

Force-fitting a technology to a problem rarely works. Despite its heavy commitment to the Macintosh as a design station, Hornall Anderson Design Works is still very much a mix-and-match shop. According to technology manager Brian O'Neill, the intent is to use the best tool for the job, no matter what it is.

"Currently about 90 percent of our work is affected by the Macintosh and about a third is done completely by computer," O'Neill affirmed. "We could probably do 80 percent of our work totally on the Mac if we wanted to."

Some of the most important work that doesn't end up totally on the Mac is Hornall Anderson's packaging work. The company's designers have been quick to take advantage of the computer's facility for manipulating type and images, but for final output, sometimes there is no substitute for traditional materials.

"Especially for packaging, we want to be able to show clients something that's as close to a final product as possible at the final approval stage," he explained. "Unlike a dry transfer, you can't print computer graphics directly onto the actual package or label stock that will be used. The stock has such a major impact on how a package looks that we feel it's imperative to show the graphics on the stock before asking for approval.

That said, O'Neill went on to point out that Hornall Anderson pursues every opportunity to use its computers in producing composites. That can mean that the first non-computer comp a client sees is the final one.

"For our packaging projects, we do use our QMS color laser printer to make hard copy of initial concepts," he explained. "And we've been using prints from a DuPont 4Cast dye sublimation printer for color indication."

ONE 4 ALL

The 4Cast, O'Neill said, is a terrific proofer and has proven itself with the studio's clients. It can also save time, money, and effort when used in conjunction with the studio's QMS thermal printer.

"If I want the color as close as possible, I use the 4Cast. It's such a vast improvement in color over the QMS, I haven't gotten really critical about its output," he admitted. "We did a test where we had both a 4Cast and a set of separation negatives made from the same file. Then we made a Chromalin from the negatives and compared them. I wouldn't say the 4Cast was a substitute—I'd always want to see a Chromalin of the negatives before a press run—but it was darn close.

"The big advantage is that you can see your files composited before you spend the money to output them to film.

"It's a realistic color proof direct from Macintosh files. And that's really been a major stumbling block to designers working on desktop machines. I hear independent designers telling horror stories about that. They say they can do color on the desktop, but that too often the film turns out to be incorrect and they have to rerun negatives and eat the cost. By proofing to the 4Cast, if there are any big errors, you can catch them before you make negatives."

SNAPSHOT: HORNALL ANDERSON DESIGN

Hornall Anderson Design Works
108 Western Avenue, Suite 600, Seattle, WA 98104
TEL: (206) 467-5800
FAX: (206) 467-6411

Equipment: (2) Macintosh SEs, (2) Macintosh SE/30, (7) Macintosh II-family workstations with 5 mb RAM, (1) QMS color laser printer, (1) Apple LaserWriter IINTX; Syquest removable storage, Shiva NetModem, Datacopy 730 scanner.

Staff: (15) designers, (14) support and administrative personnel.

Typical clients: Consumer goods and service companies in need of corporate identity programs, packaging, brand and product identity programs, environmental signage, and publications.

. . .

Hornall Anderson recently completed a large project that involved drawing deck plans showing the locations of passenger cabins and public areas on a client's cruise ships. Because each deck, each class of cabin, public areas, private areas, and off-limits areas each had their own color code, the plans were a virtual jigsaw puzzle of screen builds.

To make sure the colors on the deck plans were correct and that they matched the captions, the studio output a series of QMS prints to give the client something to proof. When the files were thought to be correct, 4Cast proofs were done for each one.

"This is a case where we can say to them, 'this area is red, but it won't be quite that red in the printed piece,'" O'Neill explained.

For their part, clients have been very impressed by the quality.

"When you tell them a 4Cast print was made directly from the Macintosh with no film negatives, clients have a kind of 'wowie-zowie' reaction, they're surprised," he said. "And from a functional point of view, it works very well."

COMBINING FORCES

Occasionally, O'Neill said, the studio mixes different kinds of proofs on a single comp.

"Usually, if the QMS is good enough for one part of a project, it's good enough for the whole thing," he pointed out. "But there are times when we mix them. We did a software package recently where we output the front panel on the QMS, then sent out for dry transfers for certain elements that just wouldn't reproduce on a color thermal printer."

PRICE POINTS

There is, of course, a perfectly simple way to get accurate color proofs from a desktop machine: make negatives and Chromalin-type proofs. The downside, of course, is the price. A set of separation negatives will

run you around sixty-five dollars. Depending on the size, a proof can cost thirty to seventy-five dollars.

O'Neill has a novel way of squeezing proofing dollars. He doesn't make page proofs.

"We rarely make full-page proofs before we're ready to go on press," he said. "Instead, we gang the color elements in a Freehand file and run one or two eleven-by-seventeen inch 4Cast prints. The 4Cast prints are costing us forty-five dollars apiece, so if we can get all the color elements down onto one or two sheets, that's not too bad."

Effectively, O'Neill is making scatter proofs of the color elements; and scatter proofs are always more cost-effective than full-page proofs because they cut down on the number of square inches of proofing material that must be used.

GETTING THE BIG PICTURE

For some of Hornall Anderson's work, even the high-end 4Cast isn't quite the right device. That's when they bring in the big guns.

"Our output house has service they call Megachrome," he explained. "It allows us to print color files at a maximum width of forty-two inches by almost any length."

While three-and-a-half feet by whatever is much bigger than any package the studio has been asked to design, the large sizes have come in handy for presentations and environmental signage.

Hornall Anderson has done a fair amount of work for K2, the ski and sportswear manufacturer. One recent project involved the creation of a logotype for a line to be called "Adrenaline."

"The logo contains the image of a man, with a sort of Duffy-group look to it," O'Neill said. "We wanted to show them color studies with a lot of color variations to get some ideas about the color ranges that would be most appropriate."

The presentation was to be made to a large group

of K2 executives. Instead of showing the logos at actual size, the decision was made to show them very large. Working traditionally, the designers would have had to either work their actual-size color studies up into poster-sized presentation comps, or have them photographed and poster-sized enlargements made. Either is time-consuming and relatively expensive.

The original studies were created on a Macintosh, so there was a PostScript file available. The individual logos were brought into a Freehand file and enlarged to poster size, ganged up two-across to fill the forty-two inch width of the printer's paper. The color variations were then applied and the logos printed and laminated for presentation.

"The colors weren't dead accurate, but they were plenty good enough to show color relationships and color families," O'Neill asserted.

Large-scale prints such as this are commonly produced using the Canon Bubble-Jet A1 printer, which was released in the fall of 1990.

The Bubble-Jet uses a unique ink-jet technology to produce mural-sized prints of near-photographic quality either directly from a reflective original (as would a photocopier), from a transparency, or from a computer file. The printer is digital; that is, no matter how the image is input (from an original or a from a computer file) the image is handled by the printer digitally, as a mathematical description. That means the image can be enlarged almost infinitely without a significant loss of quality.

Four color heads (one for each of the process colors) containing liquid ink and small heating elements are employed. The Bubble-Jet's computer pulses the heating elements on and off. As the heaters come on, a bubble is created inside the head. This forces the liquid ink between the heating element and the nozzle of the print head to "bubble" outward, eventually exiting the nozzle and splattering onto the paper. Because the heating elements can be controlled very precisely and

the ink is liquid, it allows the Bubble-Jet to achieve a fineness of resolution that has not yet been seen in color laser printers. The color lasers use ribbons impregnated with a wax-like ink. You might think of the difference between the processes as the difference you might expect between an airbrush and a crayon. The airbrush can lay down a much finer pattern of color and can overlay colors much more smoothly than a crayon can. Canon lists a resolution of 400 dpi for its printer, but visually, it appears much sharper—more like a Cibachrome print than a photocopy.

SIGNS OF THE TIMES

Hornall Anderson has also used the mural-sized prints for its environmental signage division. Part of the studio is devoted to architectural and retail work, and signage is a big part of their work.

Getting reasonable comps or even proofs for signage is costly and time-consuming. Now presentation copies and rough proofs can be made quickly and at their actual size.

"We recently did some work for a hospital cancer center," O'Neill recalled. "They wanted some temporary signs until we could get the actual signs ready, so we decided to use the Megachrome process.

"We did some very sophisticated maps in Freehand, then printed them to size on the Megachrome and had them laminated. I'm not sure how resistant the prints are to bleaching from sunlight, but they were perfect for this application. Our only other choice would have been to make negatives and pull silkscreen prints. For a temporary installation, that's very costly."

Like the other studios we spoke with, Hornall Anderson hasn't found any one perfect solution for all of its composite and proofing problems. It has found, however, that the range of options open to them using desktop computers has made the studio faster and more cost-efficient.

INSIDE *Arts*

EARLY MUSIC:
A PASSION FOR THE PAST

MEREDITH MONK AND JACQUES D'AMBOISE

PERFORMANCE TEXT BY DONALD DAVIS

ON THE COVER:
REPERTORY DANCE THEATER

As the color imaging capabilities of desktop graphics computers have improved, the results designers are able to achieve are slowly merging with the "mainstream" of color imaging. The magazine cover above was created by Wickham Associates of Washington, D.C. Although there are several ways they could have arrived at this result—by airbrushing or hand-tinting a photo—they chose to create the image using desktop computers. The original black-and-white photo was

scanned on an Agfa PIX workstation and the scan transferred to a Macintosh for alteration. Adobe PhotoShop was used to tint the photo and to paint shapes and highlights into it. Separations were made in PhotoShop and then imported into Quark XPress, where the image was combined with the type. When completed, the file was output to negatives using an Agfa/CompuGraphic 9600 imagesetter. The gold magazine masthead was run in metallic ink as a fifth color.

It's possible to make commercial-quality color separations from continuous-tone originals—such as photographs—using relatively inexpensive desktop tools. To make these separations, a 35mm transparency was scanned using the Nikon LS-3500 scanner at a resolution of 1280 x 1024. This is less than a quarter of the scanner's maximum resolution (6000 x 4000). This produced a file of 4 mb. The scan was then imported into Adobe PhotoShop, resampled to 16 mb, separated, and output on a PostScript imagesetter. The large separation (left) represents an enlargement of 815 percent from a 35mm original; the separation above is about 210 percent of original size. At less than $10,000, the LS-3500 is not intended to replace the vastly more expensive drum scanners used by many trade pre-press houses; however, for many color jobs, the quality of its scans is totally acceptable. For more information on the Nikon LS-3500 see Chapter Three: Imaging & Pre-press, page 30. Photo © 1991 John Harcourt.

Obtaining reproduction-quality hard copy of images created on desk-top graphics computers was difficult until the release in 1990 of several high-quality output devices. This familiar image created in Aldus Freehand was rendered on a four-by-five inch film recorder at 16,000-line resolution by Photo Lab Inc. The more common 35mm PostScript film recorders image at 4,000-line resolution. The higher resolution and larger film size make it possible to create repro-grade transparencies of illustrations and computer-manipulated images. The image at left was enlarged to 400 percent while the smaller image above was made from the same transparency at 105 percent. Both were separated conventionally. For more information about the high-resolution recorder, refer to Chapter Four: Service Bureaus, page 52. The illustration is by Scott Campbell. © 1988 Aldus Corporation.

7

8

9

10

Graphic Connexions, a studio and service bureau located in Cranbury, New Jersey, has used its desktop computers to grow from traditional two-dimensional print graphics into high-end interactive and multimedia presentations. These images were created on a mixture of IBM-compatible and Macintosh graphics computers, then separated in Adobe PhotoShop and output as composite film on a Linotronic L-300.

1-6: These frames are from an IBM-based interactive information center for colleges (dubbed CLICK—Computer-Linked Interactive Campus Kiosk). CLICK was conceived primarily as an advertising vehicle to help sponsors connect with the hard-to-reach college market. The kiosk has two video monitors: The top monitor displays video messages, advertising, and other information. What appears on the upper monitor is controlled by the lower monitor, which is a touch-screen connected to a desktop computer. The menu screens include the main menu (1), and variety of sub-menus (3-6) offering maps, information on restaurants, sports, and more. Full-motion video and still photographs stored on a laser disk display behind the menus, accompanied by a high-quality digital soundtrack. When a button is selected, text pops up on the touch-screen. Icons on the sides and bottoms of the screen are buttons that users can touch to view the topic

of their choice, return to the main menu, or dial a modem to connect the kiosk to an on-line service, such as Prodigy®. The kiosk also contains a multi-column alpha-numeric printer that prints coupons, travel information, small advertisements, and other data at the user's direction. CLICK was developed by director/producer Derek White and designer/illustrator Jay Williams for MarketSource Corporation and IBM.

7-10: These are the opening frames from an animated sequence created to demonstrate the multi-media capabilities of the Macintosh to Rohm & Haas Corporation. The four-minute animation developed for Apple Computer Inc., was created using Swivel 3-D Professional, MacroMind 3-D®, Macromind Director, and Adobe PhotoShop. The original presentation was made directly from a Macintosh, which was used to drive a Sony RGB video projector, and shown on a fifty-foot screen. The animation was later output to videotape using a Truvision NuVistaboard.

Flatbed color scanners are capable of producing results that are quite good. Naturally, these relatively low-cost devices have some limitations. As long as you keep these in mind, you'll find that the scanners are excellent tools. The separation above was made from an eight-by-ten inch color print using a conventional drum scanner. The scan was separated and plotted conventionally using a dedicated proprietary film composition system. The original photograph was made from an internegative taken from a four-by-five inch test transparency shot under studio conditions. The separation on the opposite page was made from the same color print, but was scanned at 300 dpi on a Microtek 300z scanner. The photo was separated in Adobe

PhotoShop, imported into Quark XPress, and output as composite film on a Linotronic L-300 imagesetter at 1270 dpi with a 133 lpi screen by Graphic Connexions of Cranbury, NJ.

Although scanners such as the Microtek are commonly used to create composites, they're not often used to create final film. Experiments suggest that as long as you don't enlarge the images significantly (compared to the original art) and select a high enough scanning resolution, they're capable of producing good results. Most scanners allow you to select a variety of resolutions. There is always a trade-off between resolution and file size. The higher the resolution, the bigger the file size. Bigger files are harder to work with. They slow

your computer significantly and they require more storage space. Many separators recommend that you capture two pixels from the original for every halftone dot you will need in the final film. If you're planning to use an image at the same size as the original or smaller and will use a line screen of 150 lpi or less, a 300 dpi scan is adequate. At that resolution, a four-by-five inch original would create a file of 4 mb; a five-by-seven inch original would take up about 10 mb. An eight-by-eight image (such as the one above) requires 16 mb. If you intend to reduce the image significantly (by half or more), consider reducing the resolution to reduce the file size. Unfortunately, there are few hard-and-fast rules. You'll have to experiment with res-

olution and file size to find a combination that works for each specific project. While using conventional separations is easier, there are significant advantages to this low-end approach. You are giving up flexibility and some quality. However, the ability to turn around color projects more quickly and at a lower cost may mean enough to justify these shortcomings for some jobs. Before committing yourself to a totally PostScript solution for a job involving continuous-tone color, be certain that you have the necessary hardware, software, and expertise; that you have a service bureau with the capability to bail you out if things go awry; and that the client has a clear understanding of what the final materials will look like.

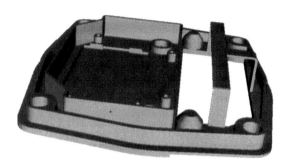

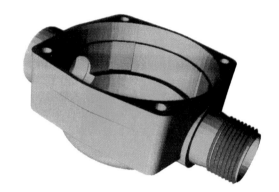

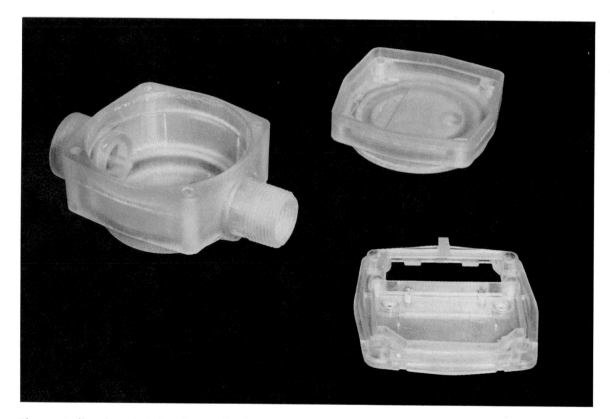

The computer file used to make the three-dimensional renderings (top) was also used to make a plastic model of the parts shown. Using a "printer" called a Stereo Lithography Apparatus (SLA), Prototype Services of Chicago "printed" the files in three dimensions, making an actual working model of the valve. The SLA segments the three-dimensional object into a series of cross-sections, each a fraction of a millimeter thick. Each cross-section is then "drawn" onto the surface of a light-sensitive liquid plastic polymer by a laser. Where the laser beam touches the liquid, it turns into a solid, building the object layer by layer. The SLA can make objects with complex curves on both exterior and interior surfaces. This has enabled Prototype Services to make models for a variety of packaging, such as custom-shape bottles and other containers. This allows designers to experiment, testing a variety of package shapes without having to carve a wooden or foam model. The SLA models are exact duplicates of the computer files so the containers can be checked to make sure they hold the correct volume of product. The SLA model can also be used as a physical "proof" of an object to ensure that its pieces fit together as specified. SLA models are naturally translucent, as are the parts for the model above, but they can be painted any color and graphics can be applied to their surface as well. For more information on the SLA, see Chapter Five: Color Composites, page 60.

THE SMARTEST DISTANCE BETWEEN TWO POINTS
USATLAS
RICHARD SAUL WURMAN'S 1990 ROAD ATLAS

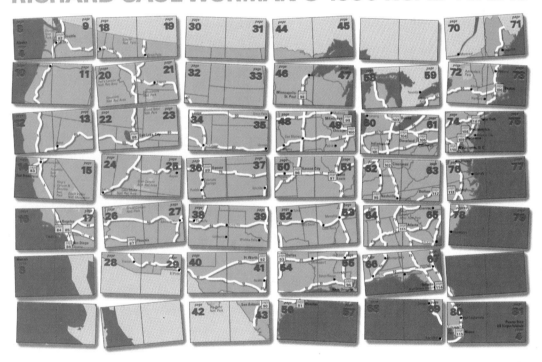

ACCESS®PRESS

Technology alone is rarely the answer to a client's needs. To create a unique and more useful form of atlas, designer Richard Saul Wurman decided to break up the United States into equal-sized grids. This allowed him to portray the entire land area of the country at the same scale. Existing atlases segment the country by state, resulting in a series of maps of widely varying scale. This makes it hard for users to estimate distances. The maps for this atlas were created using Adobe Illustrator and Aldus Freehand. The advantages of using graphics computers were important to the project. The publisher, Prentice Hall, set a very short deadline for the book—six months from start to finish. This meant that the maps had to be drawn before the overall design of the book was complete. In addition to shortening the time needed to produce the drawings, graphics computers allowed the renderings to be modified and updated as the design for the atlas evolved. When completed, the files were imaged and color separations made by Digital PrePress of San Francisco on an Agfa imagesetter. Conventional Matchprints were then made of each page to check for stylistic integrity (such as the coloration of features, typestyles—font and color—for town names, and so on). The atlas was printed conventionally using five colors. For more information on how the atlas was created, see Chapter Two: Page Layout, page 15. Atlas and cover © 1990 Access® Press Ltd. and H.M. Gousha/Prentice Hall.

1

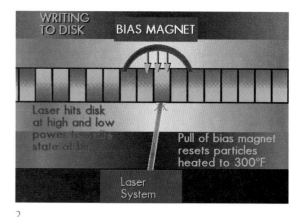

2

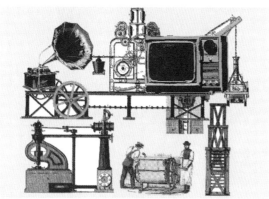

3

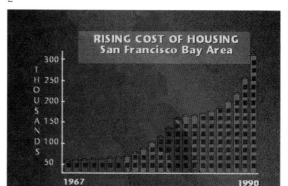

4

A number of studios have used graphics computers as a "springboard" to help launch them into new businesses. Printz Multimedia, which created the graphics on this spread, is one. Located in San Francisco, the studio began using desktop computers for basic layout and typesetting services. As the tools for desktop machines became more sophisticated, the studio moved into the production of animated graphics, business presentations, and television commercials. Eventually, Printz bought its own sound studio and equipped it with desktop-based digital recording equipment.

1. Bally Tour de Fitness: This is a frame from a presentation given by the marketing director of Bally's health clubs at the company's 1990 fall convention. The presentation was designed by Bass Francis Productions of San Francisco and the graphics done by Printz. The presentation was recorded on video and shown on a video projector.

2. Magneto-Optical Interactive: This frame is one screen from an interactive trade show exhibit created for Mass Optical Storage Technologies. Using the interactive program, visitors to Mass Optical's exhibit booth could quickly demonstrate how the company's sophisticated magneto-optical disk drives store data.

3. Bitman: This is one frame from an animated sequence created for video designer Michael Buettner. The piece was intended to humorously portray the propensity of complex systems to break down.

4. Western Development: This chart is from a seven-minute video for Western Development Group. The presentation was used to inform potential investors about the San Francisco real estate market.

5. MacUser: Printz produced an interactive exhibit with a unique one-button interface to showcase the winners of MacUser Magazine's annual Eddy Awards for product excellence. The categories listed on this screen light up alternately; when the category the viewer wishes to explore is lit up, clicking the mouse once will take him to that category. To attract viewers, Printz digitized images of a rapper and matted them into the presentation. The rapper danced with the Eddy and even faced into the camera, "knocking" on the screen from the inside. The piece was created for the MacUser Magazine/Ziff-Davis Publishing Company exhibit at the 1990 MacWorld/San Francisco.

5

Overleaf: Another new option for designers who need quality hard copies of their color graphics files is the line of Canon ink-jet printing devices. The same basic technology is used in both the CLC-500 series of color copiers and in the large-format Bubble-Jet A1 copier. While the CLC-500 is limited to eleven-by-seventeen inch paper, the Bubble-Jet will print images up to twenty-three by thirty-three inches. Color files from Macintosh and IBM-compatible computers can be printed directly to the copiers and to the Bubble-Jet through a special interface also available from Canon. PostScript is supported through Freedom of the Press, a software PostScript interpreter. Inside the printer, four ink heads—one each for cyan, yellow, magenta, and black—spray liquid ink onto the paper through 256 nozzles to create the image. The printers are fully digital—as opposed to the early color copiers that were analog, much like color printing paper— and the ink heads are controlled precisely, printing at a resolution of 400 dots-per-inch with sixty-four gradations for each color. The result is amazingly lifelike color. The image on the next spread was separated conventionally from a Bubble-Jet print. Except for some loss of detail in the deep shadow areas, the print is virtually indistinguishable from a photograph when viewed with the naked eye. The detail in the faces is exacting, even reproducing the texture of the skin and the fine hairs in the clowns' wigs. The small imperfection on the clown's nose was caused by a nick on the surface of the print. The ink will flake off if it's abraded, so a plastic lamination or other protective cover is in order. Especially when covered with clear plastic lamination, the prints are bright, vivid, and sharp; perfect for trade show exhibits, environmental signage, possibly even repro art. The printers also print on large-format transparent film, so back-lit transparencies can be created as well. In its copier mode, the Bubble-Jet automatically segments and tiles images. As the copier enlarges to 1200 percent, murals up to twenty-two feet by thirty-three feet can be created from a single original, with the copier calculating how many tiles are needed and where to break up the image. The machine also sports an optional transparency scanner and 35mm projector for making prints from photos. The scanner reads both positives and negatives in any format up to eight-by-ten inches. The machines aren't cheap: They retail for a bit over $100,000 and lease for $3,600 per month. However, service bureaus and copy centers have already begun installing them. For more information, see Chapter Five: Color Composites, page 64.

This unique new nature guide would not have been produced if desktop tools weren't available. Featuring one hundred silhouettes of tropical fish, the publisher needed the entire job finished in eight weeks. To save time, Blount & Walker Visual Communications integrated the entire process—editorial, design, layout, and separation—into one step. The budget was too small for the silhouetting to be done on a high-end workstation and the deadline was too short for the color to be handled in the Far East. The fish were scanned from 35mm transparencies using a Nikon LS-3500 scanner, silhouetted in PhotoShop, imported into page files created in Quark XPress, and output as composite film by Graphic Connexions, a service bureau. The close-up at left was conventionally separated from a 35mm slide of the printed piece, enlarged here to about twice its actual size. For more information, see Chapter Three: Imaging & Pre-Press, page 30.

CHAPTER 6

CREATING TYPE

Discontent with current offerings spurs "desktop foundries"

For designers most sensitive to typographic quality, the desktop graphics computer is a paradox: The technology is capable of producing excellent type, but it isn't commonly used to do so. Developers have passed over the basics—such as releasing digital fonts with the thousands of kerning pairs needed to produce truly elegant type—in favor of more glamorous applications such as desktop separations, animation, and video.

For designers working in color and animation, the advancements have been a godsend, but it has left some weakness at the very foundation of desktop-derived communications: the written word. Expediency and experimentation have become rules one and two. But in the words of 1960s-style activists, the point of desktop graphics computers has been to give "power to the people," and take it away from institutions, such as developers. Powerful drawing and font-creation software, such as Fontographer® by Altsys, has appeared. By and large, finely tuned desktop typography has not.

In part, designers said, this is because fonts tuned specifically for the desktop are scarce. In plain English, most fonts are not built to produce elegant results easily and haven't been adapted to the way desktop typographers use them. Some designers have taken this as an open invitation to recast type in an indigenous digital form that promises to raise the quality and expand the capabilities of desktop typography. They are actively designing and releasing new general-purpose PostScript typefaces.

They're also raising the stakes for other studios by spreading the word that custom fonts are not only available, but can provide a solid cornerstone for a corporate identity program.

HEAVY METAL

Until quite recently, type was produced almost exclusively by foundries. By definition, a foundry is a place where metal is cast using molds. And for centuries, that has been the way type was produced. Over the past three decades, the foundries were forced to convert to digital, computer-based operations as typographers abandoned hot-set metal for phototype and, later, digital typesetters.

Despite the enormity of this change, the legacy of metal type is still with us. Character spacing, sizing, and leading conventions dictated by the physical process of casting and setting metal type are still in widespread use, even though tastes and technology have changed. Rules of usage coined when type was picked from a drawer letter by letter are still embedded in the digitized fonts released by many foundries.

Typographers say the dilemma is in being careful not to throw out the baby with the bath water: Some of those conventions help the eye see words better and make type pleasing to the senses. The essential question is: How do we free ourselves from the past without losing the wisdom of past masters?

Desktop tools have allowed designers to begin trying to answer that question, and a wild variety of new desktop-only fonts has cropped up.

EASY AS A-B-C?

Why doesn't everyone jump in and create their own fonts, then? At the risk of making a bad pun, there's more to a typeface than meets the eye. Few of the fonts released for desktop use address the fundamental questions of what a digital font should be while, in the quest to be different, others miss the mark esthetically.

Why do fonts such as Baskerville, Caslon, and Garamond please the eyes of generation after generation while others "wear out" in less than a decade?

"Some of these classic faces have been with us since Guttenberg and many of the letterforms were invented long before Guttenberg," observed Joe Treacy, a type designer whose faces have been published by Linotype. "Their forms go back to the way letters are drawn using quill pens or brushes. How the pen is held dictates where the stresses fall in a letter, but the intelligence about where that ought to be, about how serifs should be formed, and so on is the product of centuries of trial and error.

"You have to be able to look at a letter and understand how it was formed with a pen and brush; how to make stresses fall at the correct angle to be perceived by the eye. In calligraphy, the angle of the pen has an enormous impact on how successful the rhythm of a letter is and how that rhythm plays out as you build lines and paragraphs. If you don't have any feeling for these things, all you're looking at is an outline. A letter is more than an outline; it's defined by the negative spaces in it and around it as well. Those spaces dictate how well it's going to combine with other letters."

So, ironically, in the age of the machine, it is still the expression of the human hand that holds the key to the ultimate qualities a typeface needs in order to endure—readability and personality.

George McLean, a designer who for many years worked at Landor Associates and whose brushwork is immortalized in many logos including Del Monte and Seven-Up, was equally emphatic about this. Good faces, he said, show a "good hand." They have obvious and pleasing personalities. Faces created using computers alone, he predicted, are too "plastic" to endure.

TYPE WITH AN ATTITUDE

As with politicians, it is the personality factor that largely governs a typeface's popularity and utility. The object, McLean and Treacy said, is to ensure that the type "fits" the message you want to convey. As with a suit, the ultimate "fit" is one that's custom designed for the task at hand. But the use of custom logotypes and especially full alphabets—never even close to being epidemic—remains a neglected stepchild despite the availability of PostScript and Fontographer.

"There's still a cut-and-paste mentality out there, even among large, well-staffed studios," Treacy com-

mented. "You do see some custom logos, but they're interspersed with a whole lot of Helvetica."

Given the skill required to create a truly elegant new face, that may not be all bad. How many designers have the time to learn the intricacies of type at the calligraphic level?

THE DIGITAL DIFFERENCE

Trade typographers have long done their own tuning on digital fonts. Taking the basic font data supplied by a foundry, they've created their own kerning pair tables and formats that cause the type to act in a way they believe is correct. No two typographers see all of these issues eye-to-eye. The result? Type with personality, with human intelligence applied.

Unfortunately, many of the digitized versions of classic faces being released for use on desktop computers lack the controls and extensions necessary to make them behave in an elegant way. Few desktop fonts are supplied with true small caps, resulting in obvious weight discrepancies when they're set that way. They are commonly released with several hundred kerning pairs. For just one font (one size, one style, one weight of one typeface), the number of possible kerning pairs is 1,950 (or 2,600 if you want words written with the neo-usage "interCap" to look right). Multiply that by the number of fonts in a typical package (roman, bold, italic, and bold italic) and throw in the fact that a computer can print the type at virtually any size, and you see that the foundries are only scratching the surface of proper fit.

Additionally, tastes in typography have changed radically in this century alone. Compare text from a book printed in the nineteenth century to a contemporary magazine ad and you'll see differences immediately. The trend is to larger type, set with less inter-character spacing and with some degree of condensation.

The digitized versions of traditional fonts don't fully account for these changes, nor do they fully com-

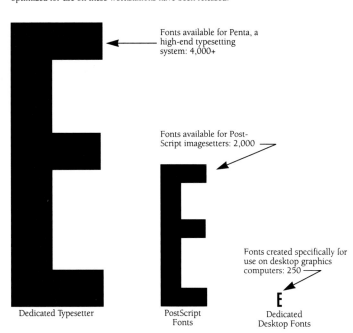

SNAPSHOT: DEDICATED DESKTOP FONTS STILL LACKING

Despite the enormous number of desktop graphics computers, few fonts optimized for use on these workstations have been released.

Fonts available for Penta, a high-end typesetting system: 4,000+

Fonts available for Post-Script imagesetters: 2,000

Fonts created specifically for use on desktop graphics computers: 250

Dedicated Typesetter

PostScript Fonts

Dedicated Desktop Fonts

Not all fonts are created equal. The physical limitations of metal casting had an enormous effect on the design of faces considered to be classics: Times, Palatino, Goudy, Caslon. Despite the removal of that limitation by digital technology, foundries have been slow to update the characteristics of their fonts.

Desktop graphics computers have their own limitations. Often, faces used on them have to stand up to low-resolution output on laser printers and to extreme manipulations such as condensation or expansion, skewing, and rotation. In addition, they should be easy to read on a 72 dpi monitor, even in small sizes.

An adventurous few have challenged the traditional wisdom of font design and released faces optimized for use in desktop applications. But the number of optimized desktop fonts is dwarfed by the number of faces that were simply translated from conventional digital typesetting systems and especially by the number of fonts available for high-end typesetting systems.

pensate for how the fonts will, in fact, be used. Many traditional body faces, for example, were optimized for use at nine or ten points. Yet body copy of eleven or even twelve points is very common. Leading tends to be looser, today, too. To make fonts truly digital, then, means doing more than digitizing existing faces.

"There's nothing wrong with challenging the way typefaces have been historically designed and manufactured, especially if contemporary usage dictates something that ought to be fixed," Treacy said. "If the first thing people do when they begin to set digital type is to change the default size and re-set their tracking to minus one, something is wrong with the way the fonts are designed. I know a lot of art directors who do exactly that."

"Take two classic faces, Baskerville and Palatino," points out Peter Fraterdeus of Alphabets Design Group. "Neither of them were designed with the idea that they would be rendered by a computer using Bezier curves. There may be characteristics of those faces that are hard to render with a small number of

points—which is desirable for a PostScript face. That's one thing that could make a new typeface, designed to be digital from the ground up, more desirable, more appropriate to the technology.

"I don't have anything against the digital version of Baskerville; it's such a cultural icon that it should be used in digital design. That kind of puts me on the fence, but I believe that we need new digital faces *and* that the classics should be made available in as effective a form as possible.

"The faces we currently have weren't designed to 'stand up' to the kind of condensing, twisting, turning, and other manipulations they get put through on a graphics computer. Also, there are only a few true three-dimensional faces. Now that we have software for rendering three-dimensional images, there's a need for three-dimensional type as well."

Fraterdeus proposed the creation of "smart" fonts that could modify themselves according to how they were being used—automatically cutting back on the weight of serifs when condensed, for example, or adding weight to thin strokes and serifs when reversed out of a color.

BUSINESS OPPORTUNITIES

If digital-ready fonts aren't forthcoming from the major foundries, does that leave a vacant niche for computer-conscious type designers? Yes and no. With the thousands of faces already available, making a business of creating digital fonts is difficult. Though the tools needed—a basic, monochromatic Macintosh system—are simple and relatively inexpensive, marketing and delivering the faces is expensive and difficult.

Unless the face is sold through a major foundry—as was Joe Treacy's Bryn Mawr family—distribution is a problem as well. The technical side of creating font files and duplicating disks is easy enough, but marketing—getting them exposed to designers and selling them—is not.

Some of the first designers to sell digital fonts—such as Casaday & Greene—have done it by placing ads in computer magazines. For the small practitioner whose main business is not marketing a full line of faces, that may not be terribly efficient.

"The Font Shop is bringing out a collection of new digital fonts on compact disc," Fraterdeus said. Perhaps other distributors who collect and market faces from a variety of sources will emerge .

Joe Treacy, in fact, has begun licensing rough drawings from other designers and creating PostScript fonts from the drawings. He sells his faces by direct mail and word of mouth.

Unlike general-purpose fonts, custom alphabets are generally sold to a single client or created for a special project. Later, they may pass into general usage, as has the Textron face—a hand-drawn alphabet originally created for a design book.

Even in custom type, the effort-to-reward ratio may be a bit steep. "We generally charge fifty dollars per character for an original alphabet," Treacy said.

That works out to around $2,000 for a full font (the twenty-six letters plus numbers and punctuation) in one case, or $4,000 for upper and lower case in one style and weight. The hours are long, and client direction—even when working with a good art director—can be spotty. There aren't an awful lot of people who really understand letterforms.

Clients have to be sold on the idea of a custom alphabet, and not many of them are highly attuned to the mysteries of type, either.

"I feel that I owe my clients something original, something that is unique and grows out of their marketing strategy," Treacy explained. However, he said, he finds that only the largest corporations are willing to put the necessary time and money into developing a custom corporate typeface: "In plain fact, consumers' lives don't revolve around print ads and collateral materials." That makes custom type a hard sell.

Many of the services offered by digital designers can be proven to be more cost-effective than traditional methods; it's easy to demonstrate significant cost savings. Saving on a necessity, like color separations or color imaging, is a strong lure for almost any client. Custom typefaces are still considered a luxury—albeit one made very much more affordable by the graphics computer.

Treacy does digitize existing corporate faces and logos, placing them in PostScript fonts, and he's sometimes asked to "extend" a custom logo by creating an alphabet to match it. But, for now, Treacy said he believes the big bucks are being mined elsewhere—in pre-press and video.

"Type is not something you do for the money," Fraterdeus agreed. "The faces that have made big money are the ones promoted by ITC and the other large foundries over a long period of time. They have the marketing muscle to promote a new face. Doing a totally new face, as opposed to adapting an existing face, is a long-term proposition."

• • •

TREACYFACES

Modernizing an ancient art

I f there is such a thing as a desktop foundry, Treacyfaces is it. Based in Ardmore, Pennsylvania on Philadelphia's Main Line, the company has found wide acceptance for its line of digital fonts.

Joe Treacy, who operates Treacyfaces with his partner and wife Carol, designed his first font, Bryn Mawr, in 1980. It was released by Linotype for use on dedicated typesetting systems in 1984 (which, of course, was B.M.—Before Macintosh). Treacy acquired the digital data for Bryn Mawr from Linotype and re-released it for the Macintosh in 1989.

Treacy, a former art director for several Philadelphia-area agencies, was drawn to typography because he felt it was so central to the success of print graphics.

"Over the years, I saw what worked and what didn't, and I began to file away notes," he said. "I got the idea that I'd like to design a face that did things other faces didn't do, or didn't do well."

Treacy began designing faces in 1976, but it wasn't until 1980 that Linotype saw his drawings for the Bryn Mawr face and invited him to work with its designers to put it into production.

Treacy had shown Bryn Mawr only in a bold roman, but Linotype wanted six additional weights—which sent him back to the drawing board for another year. After reviewing the new drawings, Linotype decided what they really wanted was eight weights, not six, but felt the face was far enough along to begin production. While Treacy worked up the two additional weights, Linotype's designers began digitizing his drawings using a URW Ikarus® computer. Treacy then worked with the Linotype designers, learning the basics of typeface production along the way.

"In 1984, the only way Linotype had of proofing the face while it was under development was a flatbed device that cut the letters out of rubylith, or printing it to a Xerox printer that made enormous 500-point bit maps," Treacy said. "When the Macintosh came along in 1985, I felt that I could develop type on it without an Ikarus. And when the LaserWriter was released in 1987, that gave me a terrific way to proof."

When Treacy began using type on his Mac, however, he noticed that the faces were being supplied "bare bones"—minus complete kerning pair tables, true fraction fonts, and other niceties. As desktop publishing evolved, he realized that the type that was being supplied didn't completely fit the needs of graphics computer users.

"Desktop publishing is being applied in situations with very tight deadlines, and type is being set in-house, rather than by an outside supplier who better make every galley look good," he explained. "People who previously bought type from vendors are setting type in-house and deciding that they can live with some flaws in order to get the job out on time. If the typeface is supplied with spacing flaws, they may not have the time to go in and fix them.

"These flaws are particularly noticeable when type that's just a digital transcription of a traditional metal face is adjusted to fit the modern esthetic.

"When you start minus tracking the type, you begin to see all kinds of imperfections. Not only is the inter-character spacing off, but the characters just don't fit together well. If people aren't going to take the time

---

SNAPSHOT: TREACYFACES INC.

Treacyfaces Inc.
111 Sibley Avenue, Ardmore, PA 19003
TEL: (215) 896-0860
FAX: (215) 896-0773

Equipment: (2) Macintosh II-family workstations with Radius two-page grayscale displays and 40 mb hard disks, (1) Everex 40 mb tape back-up, (1) Chinon 200 dpi scanner, (1) LaserWriter NTX.

Staff: (2) designers.

Typical clients: Design studios and corporate clients with a need for original typeface designs or digital design and production services.

to fix these things at the job level, then you get what we have today—a lot of DTP-set jobs in which the type looks mediocre."

Treacy said he thinks advertising and especially color television have changed the way we look at type. The preference is for larger body sizes and a much tighter fit than was ordinary just thirty or forty years ago. While trade typographers have kept up with these trends by making adjustments to their digital fonts, the font foundries haven't; out-of-the-box digital fonts don't act the way designers want them too, Treacy said.

"I think the two-inch film font industry has had an enormous effect on how people think fonts should perform. Some art directors and production people believe that, if they begin setting type on a graphics computer, it's going to automatically behave as if it were being set on a Typositor®.

"That's not the case. I don't think a lot of people realize that if you set body copy fonts at forty-eight points on an Alphatype, Linotype, or CompuGraphic device you'd see a lot of inconsistencies crop up. That led me to believe that if we could design digital type that just plain fits together more consistently and works well in both text and display sizes, we could carve out a new niche for ourselves."

FAMILY AFFAIR

Since Bryn Mawr was released, Treacy has marketed a steady trickle of new digital-ready fonts. Forever, a sans serif, was released in 1988, and Habitat appeared in 1989. Instead of rapidly unleashing a flood of new designs, Treacy has concentrated on making the fonts more useful: Forever is now available in Extralight, Demi, Thin, Medium, Regular, and Extrabold weights in both roman and italic styles. Most fonts come with thousands of kerning pairs, rather than hundreds. Illustrator-compatible outline files are included, as are true fractions. Fraction and symbol fonts containing extended character sets are available for all three faces,

and a condensed version of Habitat was released in 1990. Treacy even designed a special font to simplify the creation of crossword puzzles. Just by typing the answers in any word processor, the letters appear inside of boxes that link together to form the crossword. By hiding the text and adding numbers, the crossword is complete.

IF UNIQUE IS WHAT YOU SEEK....

In addition to these general release fonts, Treacyfaces creates faces for individual clients.

With thousands of fonts—including Treacy's own—on the market, why bother?

"As a graphic designer, one of the things I feel I owe to my client is the satisfaction of having a design approach that grows out of the advertising strategy and is completely different from anything the competition is likely to do," he said. "Readers' lives don't revolve around advertising and collateral material. You're asking them to spend time with this promotional material. With the kind of information overload people experience today, their attention being pulled in so many different directions, you have to try to achieve some uniqueness that will set your client's ads apart. One way of achieving that uniqueness is through a custom typeface.

"That face should embody the personality of the marketing strategy. The marketing effort of a company should have a distinctive personality. Most of the time a consumer spends with a print ad is going to be spent reading—reading about the company, deciding whether they like the company, if its products are better than those of its competitors, if the pricing seems to be right. Obtaining a custom typeface is only half the equation. The other half is to be sure it's put to use properly, to use it in a way that *conveys the personality of the company*.

"Once the typeface has been put in PostScript form—say by a studio that's created the face with

Fontographer—it's important they give themselves some breathing room. They shouldn't finish it one day and start using it the next. Take time to work with, and look at, the face.

"It's easy to get too close to the face to be objective about whether it works. You have to give yourself the opportunity to stand back. Type design is a long, drawn-out process. The shapes affect each other in so many ways, you can't assume you're going to get through a whole alphabet on your first draft.

"If you look at Hermann Zapf's book or the writings of any well-known type designer, you see that they've done a lot of intermediate work between the initial concept and the final renderings. Even small changes in character shape can have an enormous impact on the feel of the face. Probably the most celebrated example is the differences between Paul Renner's original drawings for Futura and the final version. They're poles apart. Even though the tools are now available to do the digitizing very quickly, designers need to give themselves time to design the shapes."

THE PEN IS MIGHTIER THAN THE MOUSE

Digitizing—putting the letterforms into the computer and saving them as a PostScript font—is the last step in the process, and, thanks to Fontographer, one of the easiest.

Treacy said he starts with a pencil. "Generally, my best designs start with spontaneous pencil or marker drawings that are then scanned and altered in Fontographer," he noted.

The electronic trace should be as tight as you can get it, he advised, but once it's in the machine, forget about it. Begin dealing with the type as it appears on the screen.

Treacy's next step is to flesh out the control characters, those letters that exhibit the shapes on which he's going to base the shapes of the rest of the alphabet (such as the "o" in Antique Olive, for example).

When that's done, he begins fitting the characters together and proofing them on a laser printer or other PostScript imagesetter.

The face needs to be checked in a variety of different point sizes to find any anomalies. "I look at the letters in a very large size to make sure the drawings are executed cleanly enough and with sufficient quality," he said, "and in a small size to judge whether they're drawn with esthetic balance. Even if the face is very quirky—a script letter—it needs to have balance. It needs to have good shape; the curves should be free of flat spots.

"I've found that using as few control points as possible is an advantage," he said.

Control points are the places where line segments (whether straight or Bezier curves) are anchored or joined. Moving a control point changes the length, angle, or curvature of the line segment joined to it.

"The fewer control points there are, the faster the type will process on a PostScript imagesetter. Also, every place you have a control point is a potential flat spot," he explained. "In fact, if you look at faces that were digitized prior to 1988 when it became possible to do outline tracing automatically, many of them have flat spots. I think that's a direct result of having too many control points."

SELLING BENEFITS

The slow demand for custom faces, Treacy said, is a matter of education.

"If you look at corporate identity work you see a few custom logos interspersed with a lot of Helvetica," he pointed out. "Other elements of corporate identity show a cut-and-paste mentality: 'Your logo here.' If you can educate clients about having a custom face that will make them unique in the marketplace, it will benefit both you and the clients in the long term. But you have to be willing to put in that time, to hold their hand a little, and to play the role of educator."

• • •

ALPHABETS DESIGN

Pressing the outer limits of PostScript typography

Though it may sound a bit like a cereal, Alphabets is actually something of a technological chop-shop: where things get taken apart, rearranged, and welded together in ways that may not have been intended, but make perfect sense.

Peter Fraterdeus, the studio's guiding light, is a typographer and calligrapher turned computer fanatic. His attitude, like that of Joe Treacy, is that he reveres the classic faces, but also has a raging desire to push the concept of what fonts are and should do to the outer limits of existing technology.

"We're working to develop faces that we hope will make a mark," Fraterdeus said. Alphabets has already released a family called Prospera. "The next face I plan to release will be one that is very plastic, that can be subjected to extreme manipulation without destroying its design.

"I have the first few characters of a face that will stand up to all kinds of degrading practices: condensation, expansion, various inter-character spacing. How substantial the serifs are in a serif face is a key question; but as you start squeezing a face, the serifs begin to disappear.

"PostScript letters are, in fact, short, self-contained computer programs. It seems possible to make these programs aware of what's being done to them in the way of manipulation and then have them modify themselves appropriately. It follows the current concept of 'hinting' for PostScript fonts, but is much more substantial. How quickly we can get to that point is unknown, but it does seem inevitable that 'smart' alphabets will be created.

"I believe in creating tools, not predefined ideas. A 'skeleton' structure could be created for a typeface —the underlying shape of letters for many fonts is similar—and perhaps an extension could be written for page layout programs. A dialog box containing slider controls could be used to vary the contrast between thick and thin strokes, angles of the strokes and serifs, weight of serifs, condensation, spacing, and so on. That would allow designers to design typefaces 'on the fly.' It would probably also lead to incredible 'type abuse,' but it would encourage people to experiment very freely with letterforms.

"I think the tools should be there, even if they're abused for a while. Perhaps if people experiment a lot and it doesn't work, they'll go back to the classics. The classic alphabets have persisted a lot longer than the styles we like to refer today."

THE POWER OF THREE

Fraterdeus is also exploring how to project PostScript fonts into three dimensions.

"I can take a Fontographer-based outline and, using a SuperCard® program I wrote, translate it into a Swivel 3-D command set, and create it as a three-dimensional model in Swivel," he explained. "This is important for things like video graphics, hypermedia, and so on. My personal interest at the moment is in designing faces that are not intended for final printed output, but for presentation on a computer monitor or on videotape."

These new media and viewing environments can be very challenging to the skills and persistence of the type designer.

SNAPSHOT: ALPHABETS DESIGN GROUP

Alphabets Design Group
804 Dempster Street, Evanston, IL 60204
TEL: (708) 328-2733
FAX: (708) 328-1922

Equipment: (3) Macintosh II-family workstations with 8 mb RAM, (1) Macintosh SE/30 file server, Apple CD-ROM, Syquest 45 mb removable storage drives, LaserWriter IINTX.

Staff: (2) designers.

Typical clients: Design studios and corporate clients with a need for custom PostScript logotypes or typefaces, or technological consultants.

· · ·

"A lot of new questions come up," Fraterdeus pointed out. "If you have a three-dimensional character, depending on its design, you either see it in perspective or you don't. But if you have a whole line of characters, do you view them as if they were in a straight line—lined up along a straight vector—or do they follow a slightly curved vector so that you get the impression you're the same distance from each letter?

"If the letters are rotated, how does the lighting behave on the surface of the letters? What about the animation of type and letters? Quite a lot of that has been done in high-end video work such as you see in network television graphics. The visual effects are quite good, but I'm not sure the typography itself has been very good in terms of the letterspacing and the lack of effort being put into custom letterforms. I think that will start to change.

"It's not trivial to import a typeface and use it as a three-dimensional object. It's easy enough to import a typeface and use it as a pasted-on texture to a three-dimensional object, but true three-dimensional type gives you substantial control of placement, location, and animation. It's also a matter of having a different choice, because right now the number of faces that have been converted to true three-dimensional form is small. The Swivel package includes a pseudo-Helvetica and a pseudo-Times. That's it."

GOING FOR THE GREEN

A wise publisher once said, "There are better things to do than that for which the world is not yet ready." It was an effective credo; he cashed out at age fifty with three-quarters of a billion dollars in the bank.

Fraterdeus, too, has found that just because you can do new things with new technologies, they aren't necessarily profitable. Instead of concentrating on general-release faces, he focuses on custom type.

"I refine rough sketches made by other designers," he said. "I work on the thick and thin balance, the spacing, and so on. By the time we get through, they're usually a substantially different face from what we start with. We can deliver the finished alphabets as both Freehand files and as PostScript fonts with custom logos in them, if needed."

LETTER PERFECT

Fraterdeus's basic approach to type design is remarkably similar to that of Joe Treacy, but there are some significant differences.

He agreed that it's best to start with rough drawings as opposed to working directly on the screen: "You have the freedom of a pencil; the freedom that comes from the hand. There are the ergonomics of the way the hand and the arm work that help define the arc of the curves, for example."

However, Fraterdeus doesn't use an autotrace to input his roughs, feeling that it's more efficient to put them in by hand. Unless the scan is very clean, he said, it takes almost as long to edit the incorrect control points out of a scan as it does to draw it manually.

"I use Freehand for the actual design work and Fontographer for final output. Until recently, you couldn't cut and paste between them, but now you can," he said. "It's actually something I suggested to Altsys. In Freehand, you have the blend tool and other tools that are very useful. If you want to do multiple weights of a face, you can easily scale them in Freehand as a first step."

Technique aside, Fraterdeus is emphatic about the importance of the designer's eye in typeface design: "You have to have your goals clearly in mind. Is it going to be a display face or a body face? Look at the letters closely and think of it as the sum of its negative spaces. A letter is *not* a line; it's defined by the space around it. If you look at it in a purely analytical sense, then there are two negative spaces—one on either side of the stem—and also a negative space inside the letter. It's really only defined by a line at its edges."

MULTIMEDIA

How computers help some to move beyond the printed page

The most revolutionary impact of computers on the graphic arts will not come from their ability to help artists do more work in less time. It will not come from the restructuring of the relationship between and numbers of design studios, typographers, prep houses, and printers. It will not come from lowering per-unit costs of printed materials.

All of these things are important. All will have an enormous effect on the structure and even the size of the graphic arts industry. *But looming even larger is the gateway computers provide for artists to move beyond two-dimensional graphics and expand into non-print media.* Media other than print—especially multimedia, interactive video and "hypermedia"—will likely account for a large share of the growth in communications spending in the next decade. Some studios are already using graphics computers to pull profits from these new and largely uncharted waters.

Hypermedia is the name used to cover any interactive, self-directed electronic media (which also includes interactive video). It allows the user to move through an electronic communication at his own pace (as opposed to a videotape, which simply plays from beginning to end). Multimedia is a catch-all that includes slides, videotape, and presentations made directly from computers.

WHY JOHNNY DOESN'T READ ANYMORE

Non-print media will supplant some printed communications because *for some purposes* they are more effective than print. In many cases, they attract more *attention* than print, and this alone can make them more effective, especially in advertising or marketing.

For those of us who cut our teeth on magazines, books, and brochures, the challenge facing us as communicators is that Johnny not only doesn't know how to read anymore, he doesn't *want* to read. As opposed to fine arts, the graphic arts are largely about effective communication: of a concept, a point of view, or specific information, such as what colors are available in next season's selection of sportswear. How well a communication works—what effect it has on the recipient—is in part governed by how much attention it can attract and hold.

In general, human beings pay the most attention to messages that involve more of their senses. The "hierarchy" of attributes, from lowest involvement to highest, is in this order:

Form
Color
Sound
Motion

A communication that has form but little color (a newsletter printed in black and white) has a hard time competing for attention with a motion picture or a television program. A whole season's worth of reruns of "Married With Children" aren't necessarily "better" or "more interesting" than a dog-eared copy of Mark Twain's *The Innocents Abroad*. Content—how well it is conceived and executed and its relevance to the person receiving the communication—is critical as well. But first you have to get the viewer's attention.

The fact is, the number of people willing to comb through literary magazines in search of terse, witty text is small and declining. The number of people who spend their time playing "Super Mario Brothers" is large and growing. You're free to draw your own conclusions, but there does seem to be a relationship between level of interest and whether a piece of communication dances and sings.

HYPER ACTIVITIES

Is this change in attitudes the first peal of the death knell for graphic artists? It doesn't have to be. *Because it can transform two-dimensional drawings into three-dimensional ones, animate them, and combine them with sounds, graphics computers may offer artists trained in two-dimensional communication a segue to the future.*

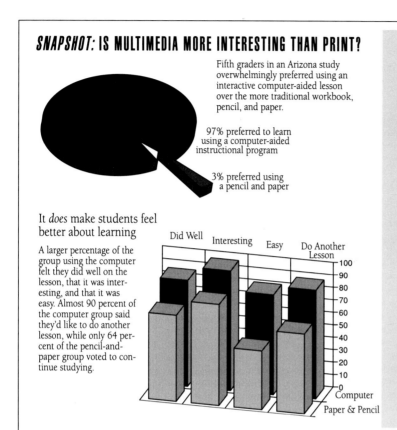

SNAPSHOT: IS MULTIMEDIA MORE INTERESTING THAN PRINT?

Fifth graders in an Arizona study overwhelmingly preferred using an interactive computer-aided lesson over the more traditional workbook, pencil, and paper.

97% preferred to learn using a computer-aided instructional program

3% preferred using a pencil and paper

It *does* make students feel better about learning

A larger percentage of the group using the computer felt they did well on the lesson, that it was interesting, and that it was easy. Almost 90 percent of the computer group said they'd like to do another lesson, while only 64 percent of the pencil-and-paper group voted to continue studying.

Multimedia is hardly new, but until recently, its use was limited to group presentations. It seemed unlikely that individuals would use multimedia as a reference or work tool.

Since the mid-1980s, three important changes have occurred. First, desktop computers have saturated businesses of all sizes and many people now have them at home. Every computer can potentially be used to view multimedia. Second, easy-to-use multimedia programming tools appeared. And third, informational multimedia has been embraced by the television generation—the baby boomers—and even more so by their children. In a study of fifth graders conducted in 1987 at Arizona State University, the children overwhelmingly preferred performing a practice lesson using an interactive computer program. Less than 3 percent preferred paper and pencil to the computer. They also felt more positive about the studying: Nine out of ten students who used the computer said they'd rather do another lesson on the computer than do nothing at all.

Changes of this magnitude move with the alacrity of a glacier, which is to say slowly: You don't wake up one morning and find a glacier in your backyard. Print is not going to go away. The publishing industry is not going to go away. Businesses will continue to rely on the written word for a large percentage of their internal and external communications. But much of the expansion of communications (both volume and dollar value) in the coming decade will be in media other than print. And there are going to be some casualties.

As the publishers of *Life* and *Look* discovered, when color television came in, they went out. Many of their readers found the tube more interesting than photographic essays. Because of this built-in interest, advertisers found television a more effective way to sell products: Form, color, sound, and motion combined to entrance audiences.

After three decades of color television, we've raised a generation (two, in fact) for whom the novelty factor of television is no longer enough. It not only has to talk, it has to talk directly to them; it must reflect their attitudes and point of view to merit their attention. As television struggles to become more specific, some print media have shown remarkable resilience by exploiting their ability to tightly and economically target select groups. Special-interest magazines and direct-mail catalogs are two that come to mind.

In the world of business communications, video has been less than totally effective for sales messages. How many people have the time or the patience to sit through an extended video sales pitch? Two decades ago, the sixty-second television commercial was the benchmark. Today, there are far more thirty-second commercials than sixty-second ones. Some advertisers have gone under thirty seconds, pressing the television networks to accept fifteen-second spots. Research shows that remote controls get a vigorous workout as viewers scan channels during commercial breaks in network programming.

What viewers are doing is tuning through or away from information they don't want to find something they do want. What they want is information delivered on demand, not at the time and the pace dictated by the advertiser or the television network. That's one of the great things about printed communications. You can browse a bookshelf for what you want, open it to any page, and get "information on demand."

As a medium for the delivery of information, the computer has an advantage over broadcast television because it can be controlled by the viewer—it's interactive. And because it can show motion and sound, it has an enormous advantage over print. The "hypermedia" computer tools that came of age in the late 1980s offer a practical way to combine the best features of print and video.

HYPERMEDIA, OR JUST PLAIN HYPE?

Granted, the skills needed to author a hypermedia program are harder to master than simply transferring layout skills from tissue paper to a computer monitor. It involves learning how to structure long communications. And then there are the tools: all hypermedia creation programs require a modicum of what most of us would call programming. But the rewards are there for those who make the effort. Hypermedia isn't the easiest thing to sell to clients, but for trade show exhibits, retail displays, corporate training, and business presentations it has a panache that print graphics simply can't convey. Animated color images accompanied by sound are going to attract more attention than most printed pieces. That's a function of how humans perceive the world. Considering production effort and costs, however, video is probably the best medium for simple animation. What makes hypermedia unique is the fact that the viewer can choose what he wants to see and when he sees it. It's *interactive*. It gives the viewer complete random access to subjects as large as the history of the earth or as detailed as the anatomy of a ladybug.

"Random access is profoundly important, you can make the experience an infinite. You become an active reader: watching becomes subjective and experiential,

not passive," said Bob Stein, quoted in issue 4.2 of *Verbum* magazine. Stein should know. His Voyager Company published a commercially successful and critically acclaimed hypermedia guide to Beethoven's Fifth Symphony. The piece was authored by Robert Winter, a well-known musicologist and professor at UCLA.

The importance of an interactive medium can't be overemphasized. Interactivity has become not only the main strength, but also the main reason for the growing acceptance of hypermedia. In 1990, the school textbook authority for the state of Texas approved a hypermedia program called *Windows On Science* for use in the state's secondary schools. Used with a laserdisk player, the program allows teachers and students to explore natural history subjects interactively. Tests in a number of Texas schools generally confirmed the results of the 1987 Arizona State University study cited in the graph on page 91. Along with California, Texas is the most influential state in the United States when it comes to educational materials. The approval of either of those states can make or break a publisher's products. The adoption of *Windows On Science*, while hardly the first use of hypermedia for education, may turn out to be the most important in terms of spurring general use of hypermedia.

BUSINESS INTERESTS

Education aside, hypermedia's first commercial applications have been to enhance business communications. Like television in the 1930s, not everyone has a computer system capable of replaying hypermedia. Also, people aren't yet accustomed to sitting in front of their computers for the purpose of entertaining and informing themselves. Unless it's to play "Super Mario Brothers," it's somewhat unusual to stroll into the den and flip on the computer instead of the television. However, we *are* accustomed to using computers in our work. And that's where hypermedia has put down its first and strongest roots. People will sit in front of computers to get information about job-related issues.

Catalogs, especially ones that sell products with a large number of options or interchangeable pieces, are prime candidates for hypermedia. So are public information pieces about consumer-products companies and their offerings.

For example, each year since 1988 the Buick division of General Motors has produced hypermedia disks containing its "new model year announcements" in addition to the more traditional new model color brochures. While the floppy disks used by Buick have too little storage capacity to contain color images or live video, they do feature a snappy rendition of Buick's theme song, some two-dimensional animation, and an engaging game for auto history buffs. Oh yes, they also contain illustrations, photos, and technical specifications for all current Buick models. There's even a price-sheet-cum-calculator that lets you figure your monthly car payments on each of the new Buick models. You type in the number of months of the loan, the amount you want to put down, and the current interest rate. The price sheet then displays your monthly bill, cleverly answering the "Can I afford it?" question that stops many potential buyers from even going to a showroom.

Steelcase, the office equipment manufacturer, turned to hypermedia to produce a catalog for its Context system of office furnishings. The catalog, first released in 1988, does more than merely list the system components and their prices, it also has a design module. Using a Macintosh and a mouse, interior designers set up the dimensions of the space they are furnishing, then drag elements of the Context system (partitions, desks, chairs) into it. The system doesn't allow the designers to specify Context items in a way they won't fit together, giving an error message if they try to join two pieces of furniture that can't be joined. At any point, the design can be printed. The catalog automatically generates a list of Context items used in the design, giving the number and model designation of each element and its price.

In this case, the hypermedia is communicating in a way that neither print nor video can. It not only informs designers about Context furnishings, it actually helps specify and order them. If you were furnishing an office, what would you rather do: spend hours with a mountain of bulky print catalogs, flipping back and forth to find elements you could afford that fit together properly, or pointing and clicking with a mouse on a computer screen?

These aren't isolated instances. McGraw-Hill has published Datapro Consultant, a multimedia reference tool for the Macintosh. Designer Clement Mok developed an interactive guide to the TED2 design conference held in 1990. DynEd International has published a hypermedia tutorial that teaches English language and business customs to Japanese businessmen.

BUSINESS OPPORTUNITIES

Hypermedia is much more than this year's buzzword. Though its potential has been recognized since the mid-1960s, when researchers began looking into the possibility of marrying computers to television. It took almost thirty years for the technology that would make this practical to emerge. It's still evolving. But, whereas in 1975, many of the necessary tools were still in the lab, in 1990 the tools exist and are widely available.

Hypermedia is being used now to advertise and promote businesses, to inform, persuade, and educate. The question is how widely it will be used and how quickly its use will spread. Since 1988, Apple Computer has included its hypermedia program, HyperCard®, with every new Macintosh. Undoubtedly, less than 10 percent of those programs are being used. But that still leaves a lot of seeds—seeds that are sprouting as communicators, including designers, learn how and when to use this new tool.

SANTA FE INTERACTIVE

Adding value to their clients' information products

The "trick" to hypermedia, contends Mark Carpenter, is in combining familiar graphics computer tools with knowledge and making them work together for the user. Carpenter, president of Santa Fe Interactive, should know whereof he speaks. Prior to founding Santa Fe Interactive (SFI), he helped create one of the first high-profile commercial interactive catalogs, a hypermedia presentation that was used to launch a new line of office furnishings for Steelcase. Since then, he's worked on interactive projects for McGraw-Hill, Dow Chemical, and other industrial heavyweights.

"Our products fall into two categories: multimedia references and multimedia performance support tools," Carpenter said. "The references are geared to companies that have a large number of products or very complex products that have to be explained to employees or to customers. Starting with the Steelcase project, we found that multimedia is a good way to simplify the flow of information. Often, such as with Steelcase, the volume of material that's needed to communicate the necessary information about the product is overwhelming. By putting the information into a computer, it's all in one place and it's easy to access."

Storing and retrieving information is the obvious part. The other less obvious task is to add value to the information by offering tools that let users manipulate it in ways that are useful to *them*.

That requires linking a product database to a multimedia front end, one that allows users to interact with the database without having to learn how to use a database. SFI then links the database to other software tools that help generate written proposals and specify and write orders for products.

OUT OF CONTEXT

When Steelcase began the run-up to the launch of its Context system of office furnishings, it was looking for a way to impress buyers with the fact that Context was a radically different office design solution, not just another pretty set of panels. At the same time, Apple Computer was looking for Fortune 100 companies to use as a showcase for their emerging multimedia products. A cold call made by Apple on Steelcase resulted in a bite. Steelcase felt that hypermedia might be a good way to introduce Context. In the spring of 1988, Apple put Steelcase in touch with Creative Interactive Media in Santa Fe, where Carpenter worked before founding SFI.

"We made a short concept piece using HyperCard and VideoWorks®," Carpenter said. "We used Steelcase products so the content would be familiar, but the real purpose was to show them how powerful the technology was."

Steelcase was duly impressed. From March through June of 1989, six people worked to create a Macintosh-based information presentation about Context. The piece debuted in June at the furniture industry's NEOCON trade show. It stole the show and, according to some, put the office furnishings business into future shock.

The presentation was divided into three parts, or modules. The first was an introduction to the Context system, its philosophy and design rationale. The second was an animated three-dimensional overview of

---

SNAPSHOT: SANTA FE INTERACTIVE

Santa Fe Interactive, Inc.
1807 Second Street, Santa Fe, NM 87501
TEL: (505) 982-3738

Equipment: (12) Macintosh II-family workstations with RasterOps 24-bit displays; ColorSpace 2 card; various pieces of hardware under evaluation for manufacturers.
Staff: (12) computer production artists.
Typical clients: Dow Chemical, Steelcase, McGraw-Hill and other large corporations with a need for high-performance sales and training multimedia materials.

the system complete with color, motion, and sound. The third was a detailed reference that included design guidelines and specific information about styles, fabrics, and so on.

The entire piece was interactive so that viewers could navigate through it at their own pace. Multiple levels of detail were available, too. Clicking the labels in a drawing of a chair, for example, brought up extended information on materials and colors.

An extension of the presentation is planned that will allow designers to construct furniture groupings on screen. The groupings will be shown in plan view and isometric view, can be printed out for study, and the program will generate a bill of materials based on the drawings with prices.

Steelcase already supports Intergraph architectural design stations with databases and symbol libraries for its office furniture systems. Dedicated Intergraph workstations are expensive, however. The design system planned for Context will be based on the Macintosh, making it available to many more designers. Also, its tools will be more specific. Where existing databases represent desks with a single all-purpose rectangle, the Context system will place the actual style and model of desk selected in the drawing.

In the spring of 1990, SFI updated the basic Context presentation, and the design tools were scheduled for release in 1991.

SFI HELPS DOW DO GREAT THINGS

Catalogs, even interactive catalogs, are close enough to existing media to be grasped quickly. SFI's expertise in "performance support tools" is a little more esoteric.

A performance support tool is something that helps a worker do his job better. The tool can be as simple as a printed train schedule for train conductors. Obviously, there's no real advantage to computerizing tools that simple. But when the information and specialized knowledge required for a task are complex,

the computer becomes an invaluable medium.

"The key is to reduce the amount of information presented so as not to overwhelm the user," Carpenter said. "The system has to know what specific information the user needs at any given moment and then provide it."

In the case of Dow Chemical, SFI's assignment was to build a software program that would help managers make crucial decisions.

"It was part of an overall curriculum on quality that was developed at Dow," Carpenter explained. "The main problem they had was that people were jumping to conclusions about new products, new processes, and new markets without enough data. When you consider the amount of money needed to launch a new product, it can be costly to jump to conclusions. Dow's instructional designers had developed quite a bit of information on how to investigate before making a decision: where to get information about a problem, how to figure out if you have a valid answer. They had outlined a process that had a lot of checks in it and offered a lot of guidance.

"Problem-solving is a difficult process to manage. This software was designed to provide another level of support. The goal was to standardize the way in which problems were investigated and solutions proposed."

Using content supplied by Dow, SFI designed a Macintosh application built on Silicon Beach's SuperCard hypermedia software. Depending on the type of problem being studied—new product, new market, internal process—the program leads users through a series of action steps (akin to a flow chart) to formulate the problem clearly and accurately and to propose and test solutions.

Along the way, users can tap modules to help them with brainstorming, outlining, question-and-response tests, and with presentation of their findings.

The ability to document the logical steps taken in formulating and investigating the problem are just as important as finding a solution. Especially when groups work together on problems, it's crucial to keep track of the issues raised, data collected, and options explored as solutions percolate upward through successive layers of management.

Problem-solving, discussion, and presentation are not exactly new. Why bother to write a computer application to "control" them? Why not just publish a workbook containing the instructors' suggestions and the company's guidelines?

"Presenting conclusions to management is an important step in Dow's decision-making process. When people work with the normal tools—flip charts, notecards, and pieces of paper—it's incredibly hard to put together a presentation for other managers," Carpenter said. "Our program consolidates the information as it's generated and gathered, and it has built-in presentation tools to help users communicate the information to others clearly and effectively.

"During the investigation process, users attend a series of group meetings. The group brainstorms, examines data, and so on, then goes away for two weeks before it meets again. The program keeps track of where the group is in the decision-making process, the status of the investigation, the information they have, and the decisions they've made. All of the documents are easy to retrieve and present to others.

"Dow is working to implement a standard format for problem-solving presentations. It works out that there's one slide for each step in the formal process. The slide explains the results of that step and why the team went on to the next step."

The program carries with it a full record of what decisions were made and why they were made as the proposal moves upward through management.

From within the application, users can create rudimentary presentations, a variety of printed documents, and even slide shows that can be played back on a Macintosh for a group of people.

Where more power is needed—to create 35mm slides, for example—SuperCard's XCMND external commands are used to tie the application to third-party software such as Aldus Persuasion®. Software that provides support for financial data, statistical analysis, and other specific tasks can be accessed through XCMNDs or by cutting and pasting between those applications and SFI's program.

"Just having all of the information on the Macintosh where it can be shared between applications is a huge advantage," Carpenter said. "It makes the whole process easier. Where there are specific tasks called for by Dow's process—making charts based on statistics or group voting for example—we're writing applications in SuperCard to do that without leaving the program."

VALUE ADDED

SFI is using its expertise in visual communications to add value to the information developed and supplied by the client.

"One of the most important things we do is help clients with the design of the information flow," Carpenter pointed out. "We get the content in a variety of forms. It comes to us as memos, spreadsheets, or even databases. In no case have we been given information in a form that a computer can use readily. And in some cases, the information we're given is not really appropriate to the purpose of the project. In the design phase, we have to create an effective structure for the content and then find the holes in the logic of how the information flows.

"Those holes are more apparent when the information is in electronic form than they might be in print. We can see what information should come next and see the possibilities for accessing related information. That is an editorial function, but it's different from the kind of editorial functions that are required for print media.

"A lot of it has to do with structuring the data for retrieval through the computer. It's quite a challenge to take a client's database and use it with a multimedia front end. Databases aren't usually designed to communicate to a large number of people. They're basically set up for the management information services people to go in and extract data. Linking them to an object-oriented front end isn't easy, but it makes the information readily available to more people."

BACKGROUND CHECK

It's obvious SFI gets into its software a lot deeper than the average designer. But that doesn't mean you need a degree in computer science to delve into hypermedia. Most members of the SFI staff have backgrounds in graphics or education. Carpenter, for example, worked as an exhibit designer, creating computerized displays. Two of the art directors came to SFI from broadcasting, bringing with them experience using high-end paintbox systems.

Carpenter and others at SFI worked at Wilson Learning, a videodisc production company that produces interactive training materials for corporate clients. Most of that work was done on IBM-PC compatibles, but when the Macintosh II was released and HyperCard appeared, Carpenter and the others at SFI were quick converts.

"We can turn things around in four months that would have taken us two years to produce in a DOS environment," he said. "We were doing things in InfoWindow® on the PC, but when Mac tools came out that could replicate some of what InfoWindow could do, it became an attractive low-end option. The ease of building an application in the first generation of HyperCard was attractive, though it took a while to convince corporations that a presentation based on small black-and-white cards could have value. As the tools have become more sophisticated, we're now doing full color on the Mac."

SFI is solely Macintosh. Carpenter said the cost of a full-blown interactive system developed on a Mac is usually less than the cost of one developed on high-end equipment. The biggest difference, he said, is capability: "Before the Macintosh we were limited in what we could offer the client. How good our program looked was restricted by the technical limitations of the graphics card or video card. Also, we were limited to a simple branching structure for the content. With the Mac, we can manipulate files on a global basis."

SALES PITCH

Selling design is hard enough. Selling informational design, Carpenter said, is even harder. It's easy to sell shoes; everybody knows what they do and everybody needs them. That's not the case with hypermedia.

"It often takes a while to educate our clients about what they're buying. They get the general concept, but few of them have had enough experience with hypermedia to know what the economic benefits are," Carpenter said. "Training is kind of soft; it's not hard dollars and cents. The measurements are hard to define: Are people still using it a year later? Are they enthusiastic about it? The general economic slowdown affects how many people businesses hire and how many they need to train."

It can also affect their desire to get into new businesses or enlarge existing operations, two points at which training—and perhaps hypermedia training tools—is often called for.

"How quickly a client grasps our product depends on what business they're in," Carpenter observed. "If they're in a business that depends on communications, they usually get it pretty quickly. If they deal in hard goods and have a corner on the market, it takes a little longer to explain the benefits."

Despite these difficulties, Carpenter is enthusiastic about hypermedia: "It will become a major business; it's just a question of how soon."

• • •

PRINTZ MULTIMEDIA

For this studio, the future really is now

When people say "multimedia," they tend to mean one medium—one that mixes photographic images and sounds. Computers, however, are true multimedia machines. Work created on a graphics computer can be output as mechanicals or negatives for a printer, as transparencies or slides, or as video. This flexibility offers designers who are facile with a computer the opportunity to expand their services across a whole range of what are now specialized fields.

Until they get very, very large, design businesses tend to be boutiques, specializing in one or two narrow aspects of visual communication. That's the usual approach. It's not the Printz approach. If you're a Californian, you might say Printz is the Ralph's of design shops. If you're an Easterner, you might say it was the Safeway, Grand Union, or Kroger's. Either way, it's a veritable supermarket of services. As partner Charles Wyke-Smith put it: "We offer clients one-stop shopping for their graphics, from business cards to three-dimensional video animation. We'll print their logo on a letterhead or fly it across a video screen."

By diversifying its offerings, Printz is able to con-

centrate more of a client's media budget in its shop. The resulting volume and ability to handle diverse tasks also helps Printz build stronger overall relationships with its clients.

THE LONG AND WINDING ROAD

Like most computer art studios, Wyke-Smith and his partners, Michael Nolen and Ken Ruatalo, didn't wake up one morning and say, "Let's get computerized and start a new business."

Prior to co-founding Printz, Wyke-Smith was using a Macintosh 512 to do title slides and storyboards for slide presentations. In 1986, he and Nolen began doing theater programs and other print jobs on the Macintosh. Eventually, they bought four Mac Plus workstations and a LaserWriter. They hired another artist and they were in business.

In late 1987, they bought a Mac II. Soon after, Jack Norton Productions of San Francisco asked them to help stage a convention for U.S. West, one of the "Baby Bell" companies created by the breakup of AT&T.

"They really wanted to do live video projection from a computer, so we bought a Computer Friends video board for the Mac and worked up the graphics. We ran it in the slide show mode of Cricket Presents," Wyke-Smith recalled. "That same year we did video projection for a Kawasaki convention in Reno, and that was the beginning of multimedia for us."

As the Printz reputation grew, so did its capabilities. By late 1990, the company was split into two divisions. One handles print work. The other, Printz Multimedia, handles everything else. Printz acquired an eight-track audio recording studio with a thirty-two channel MIDI. A MIDI (Musical Instrument Digital Interface) is a link between a computer and a musical synthesizer. Scores created on the computer can be played back through the synthesizer. Each channel can be programmed to sound like a different instrument,

---

SNAPSHOT: PRINTZ MULTIMEDIA

Printz Multimedia
340 Townsend St., San Francisco, CA 94107
TEL: (415) 543-5673
FAX: (415) 543-5994

Equipment: (5) Macintosh II-family workstations with 24-bit color displays, 8 mb. RAM, 40 mb internal hard disk, external Syquest 45 mb removable drives; (1) SE/30 file server with 300 mb main disk; (2) 160 mb auxiliary disks; streaming tape backup; 8-track audio recording studio; 32-channel MIDI; Digidesign analog-to-digital converter; NTSC video board; NTSC monitors; Laserwriter IINT.

Staff: (3) partners, (7) computer production artists, (3) administrative associates.

Typical clients: Broadcasters, advertising agencies such as Hal Riney Partners, and large corporations with a need for animated graphics and sophisticated print media production.

so a thirty-two channel MIDI is your basic symphony-in-a-box.

"We're also using a Digidesign® analog-to-digital board to record voice-overs directly onto disk using the Macintosh," Wyke-Smith pointed out. "We can cut-and-paste audio the way you cut-and-paste text in a word processor. If someone doesn't like the way they said a particular word, we can re-record and replace just that word. Or we can completely rearrange the order of a sentence. We use it a lot to remove pauses or the click of a tongue. You can see these things in the waveforms and select them with the mouse."

A Macintosh workstation with four monitors is used primarily for creating animations in MacroMind Director.

"Director allows you to have ten windows open at once. Animation occurs in one of those windows, and the others are for color palettes, a paint program, and so on. We have three of the monitors set up as a single continuous desktop, so you can move the mouse right across all three of them. That way, you can keep all of the windows open and visible. While you're painting an object in one monitor, you can be animating it in another," Wyke-Smith explained. "The fourth monitor is an NTSC [television] monitor to preview video. We have video output, but we're just installing frame-by-frame recording."

SELECTED TARGETS

That kind of hardware arsenal has given Printz the muscle to work for some very large corporations, and the ability to price jobs right for smaller ones.

In early 1989, the company created a unique piece for Levi Strauss & Co. As part of its marketing effort, Levi's invited the public to its headquarters to view the company's line of summer clothing and complete a computerized marketing survey. Everyone who completed the survey received a free Levi's watch.

"People were lined up for twenty minutes to go through this process," Wyke-Smith recalled. "We put together a four-minute piece that was played back on nineteen-inch monitors in the waiting area. It's purpose was to prepare people to take the survey. The piece was a mixture of two- and three-dimensional animation that was made in Director using Swivel 3-D elements. We created a three-dimensional model of the display booth that flew into the screen. The animation then highlighted the various areas of the booth and told what went on there. Basically, it showed them how to use the survey computers so they were prepped and ready to go when they got to the front of the line. Levi's was very pleased."

That same year, Printz did an extensive animation for Hal Riney Partners, the San Francisco advertising agency that created the memorable Bartles & Jaymes wine cooler campaign.

"Channel 4 in San Francisco was doing a piece on cosmetic surgery, and the animation was part of a promo for that piece," Wyke-Smith said. "We used a frame grabber to digitize a model's face, then scanned in about twenty photos of various facial features from other models. We used an airbrush to cut the features out and give them a soft edge. The face appeared on a faked-up computer screen that was supposed to represent a cosmetic surgeon's computer. A woman's voice was recorded asking, 'Should my eyes be wider, like Cher's? New eyebrows? No, my neighbor just got those.' And so on. The basic face stayed the same, but the nose, eyes, and mouth kept changing as she asked questions. It was a very witty script. The changes started out moving slowly, then sped up as the spot progressed."

Printz also created animation for a video for Lucky Stores, a large West Coast supermarket chain. The video was an in-house piece designed to introduce the installation of the company's E-mail system. In it, a manager overwhelmed by paperwork is rescued by the company's new E-mail system.

"We built a box in Swivel 3-D, and this dissolves in on his desk. A winged envelope comes out of the box, flies around the room and goes into his computer, which then lights up and displays the E-mail interface," Wyke-Smith said. The box and envelope were matted into the live video of the manager's office. Using Director, the artists were able to match up the flight of the envelope with the manager's eye positions so that it really looks as if he's following the envelope with his eyes, Wyke-Smith said

MEDICAL PRACTICE

Printz has even delved into medical animations, in one case, to demonstrate how an operation on a patient's hand caused numbness. The animation was used in a malpractice suit against the surgeon, who had cut one of the patient's nerves. The animation showed, step by step, how the surgery was supposed to go and where it went wrong. Peeling back layers of skin and muscle on screen may not be for the squeamish, but at least you can remind yourself that it's only a cartoon.

Another video animation was done for an insurance company to help its adjusters better understand how to evaluate knee injuries.

"When a doctor sends his report on a client's knee injury to the insurance company, the adjuster needs to know how to read between the lines to determine if the claim is legitimate," Wyke-Smith said. "The company set up a script that featured an inexperienced adjuster encountering his first knee injury report. He doesn't know what to do, but his computer has this persona called Angel, and she comes to his rescue. We built a very futuristic-looking interface so that it appears you're looking way back into the computer through a tunnel.

"We built wire frame images of the bones in Swivel 3-D. Then we created a bone texture in PhotoShop and texture-mapped it onto the wire frames. They really do look quite like bones. When the adjuster calls the various bones by their common names, the computer corrects him, 'No, that's not your shin bone, it's your tibia.'

"Slowly, we built up the entire knee area with all the bones labeled, then added the ligaments, cartilages, and muscles. We built up the whole leg layer by layer and showed it in cross section. The animation then showed how injuries occur in accidents, what parts are damaged, where liquids gather in some injuries, how cartilages get scratched when you fall on your knees, and so on."

APPLE WORKS

Printz has combined work from its two divisions for Apple Computer.

"They recently surveyed their employees worldwide and are producing a video about the results of the survey," Wyke-Smith said. "The envelope the survey was mailed in had a map of the world on it. For the title sequence of the video, we brought in the envelope, made it spin, and created a globe out of it. The globe changed to an apple, and the apple changed to the Apple logo. We did other graphics, such as animated charts and so on that appear in other sections of the video."

PRICE POINT

Like other multimedia producers, Wyke-Smith said pricing these services is a little tricky; it varies so much from project to project that it's hard to generalize about the numbers.

"For animated graphics that a speaker would show on a screen—bar charts that grow, a pie chart that cuts into slices—we charge between $1,000 and $2,500 per minute, depending on the complexity," he estimated. "It works out to about $75 an hour. The cosmetic surgery project for Riney consisted of ninety separate video frames created on the Mac. There was a lot of scanning, repainting, and so on. It took us about three days, thirty-three hours or so, and we billed about $3,000. For trade-show graphics, things that might be shown on a computer at an exhibit stand, we charge $1,000 a minute. For those we scan a lot of images in 24-bit color, resize them, and repaint them."

RECYCLED ART

"We're discovering that the form we output in makes very little difference. One of our clients is a distribution firm, and we do all their print work. Since we have all of the corporate identity graphics stored on hard disk, it's easy enough for us to quickly do 35mm slides or video titles for their corporate presentations," Wyke-Smith said.

Not only does saving prepared art help Printz by giving the studio a vast library of "clip art," it's also a great convenience for customers.

"A lot of companies, even ones with corporate communications departments, don't want to touch creative," Wyke-Smith said. "They farm it out. We try to build up relationships with those people." Being able to create graphics in a broad range of media helps.

American President Lines makes maximum use of the Printz "media combine." APL is an ocean shipping company that buys both print and video graphics. Printz does the complex, ever-changing sailing schedules for APL. And based on them, it does promotional work, even video titles. APL gives the work to Printz even though it has its own video production department because of the speed with which Printz can turn around high-quality graphics.

The key, Wyke-Smith said, is that Printz archives every piece of every job it's ever done.

"That's the key, archiving everything. We have a massive library of client work. We can assemble a new presentation or promotion from existing components," he explained. "Everything is cross-referenced in a FileMaker II® database. You can walk up to any Mac and type in 'U.S. map' and it will list every U.S. map in the inventory. Type in a client's name and it will give you every job we've ever done for them. The database also lists the number of the disk the file you're looking for is on. If you need to pull something from an existing file, you can find it and access it very quickly."

Wyke-Smith admitted the storage is expensive: "A typical video job takes up 30 mb, so every one of those we do costs us a Syquest cartridge, about $80. That cost is passed on to the clients, however. We have a box for that on the job card. When we're taking an order, filling out the card, we ask the client if they want us to archive their job. We've never had one say no. We charge $7 per megabyte for the first ten megabytes. The more megabytes in the job, the less they pay per megabyte. They quickly see the value of it. If they pay $3,000-$4,000 for a video, they're very understanding about paying $100 or so to keep the job on file.

"Archiving is the best way to retain clients. If we've done a proposal for Presidential lines, we have the basic format, the shell, already printed. They modem us the body copy for the various sections and we can print it up on the laser and have it ready for them very quickly—overnight in some cases. We have camera-ready art, effectively, of everything we've ever done for them. In cases of bids, we can sometimes go in and just change the name in the 'bid for' box.

"What's selling our multimedia services to clients is control, not cost," Wyke-Smith said. "It does work out to be less money for them, but the real value is in other areas. They can guide the process and get what they want. Clients don't always know what they want, but they know what they don't want. If we can show them something, they can tell us which way to go. We can rough up three different animations out of the same elements for someone very quickly, then have them choose the look they like best, change the typeface or the color palette, and go on to a finished product without wasting a lot of time."

HARVARD ED/TECH GROUP

Would you trust a lawyer who was trained by a computer?

Did you ever long to be Perry Mason, leaping from behind the defendant's table and shouting: "Objection! I object to this continuing harassment of my client, your honor"? In the fantasy, of course, the judge agrees and instructs opposing counsel to behave or face contempt of court. The Harvard Law School Educational Technologies Group has made something like that possible, though without the histrionics. No, it's not a video game. It's a way to train law students to be more effective in the courtroom.

Ed/Tech's products are one of the most high-profile and well-established educational uses for interactive computer technology. And, because of their length of experience with the medium and the rigorous standards of performance they must meet, the members of the Ed/Tech Group are uniquely qualified to talk about the promises and limitations of interactive video training programs.

"Interactive works when you can involve the person who's viewing it. It has to be a situation that requires a response from them," said Scott Glanzman, acting director of Ed/Tech. "In a driver's education course, you may listen to a lecture about traffic signals, the rules of the road, defensive driving, how a clutch works, and so on, but you really don't understand how it all works until you get behind the wheel of a car and experience it for yourself.

"With lawyers, one of the things that's very hard to teach is trial advocacy. Using the interactive programs, the students can learn to think on their feet."

The programs give students the experience of a real trial without risking anyone's life or liberty. Without these interactive sessions, the first time an attorney had to manage a trial on his own would be in a real courtroom with a real client.

The programs are contained on twelve-inch videodisks. A lab containing IBM PCs networked to a Digital Equipment VAX minicomputer is available to the students. They simply find an open workstation, slip a disk into the videodisk player, and—presto— they're Perry Mason.

Programs produced to date run the gamut of trial situations: personal injury cases, criminal trials, direct examination of witnesses, cross-examination, and so on. The students play the part of one of the counsels. First, the student selects which lesson he wants to view, say, "objections" for example. The trial, which has been filmed with live actors, begins to unfold on a video monitor next to the workstation.

The scripts are written by senior law students and professors at Harvard Law. In the objection lesson, they have written in sequences where opposing counsel presents questionable evidence and where it would be appropriate for the student to object. Objections are entered via the keyboard. At that point, the trial stops and the video cuts to a close-up of the judge, who asks the student for the basis of his objection. The student types in the reason he objected. Using keyword searches, the computer checks a database to find if that objection is warranted at that point in the trial and whether the student's reasoning is correct. If it doesn't

---

SNAPSHOT: EDUCATIONAL TECHNOLOGIES

Educational Technologies Group
Harvard Law School
Holmes Hall, 18 Everett Street, Cambridge, MA 02138
TEL: (617) 495-1000

Equipment: (8) IBM-compatible PCs, both 286- and 386-based models networked to a DEC VAX minicomputer; (2) Macintosh II computers with 2 mb RAM, 24-bit color displays, and Data Translation ColorCapture frame grabber boards; (1) Macintosh SE; Sony 8mm videocassette recorder for making rough cuts; (12) Pioneer laser disk players.

Staff: (5) producers, (2) adminstrators, student interns and faculty advisors.

Typical clients: The work done by the Ed/Tech Group is prepared for Harvard Law School. Some of its products have been sold to private law firms for use in fulfilling continuing legal education requirements.

recognize anything in the student's answer, it asks multiple-choice questions to determine the basis of the objection. If the student's reasoning is faulty, the system provides hints to nudge him toward the correct answer. Once the student understands the points under dispute, the judge sustains or overrules the objection and the video of the trial continues.

THE BLUE SOLUTION

Hypermedia enthusiasts are, justifiably, high on such Macintosh software as HyperCard and SuperCard for controlling their presentations. At the time Ed/Tech got involved in hypermedia, 1982, the Macintosh was still a mere glimmer in Apple's eye. Though some hypermedia authoring software was available, Ed/Tech's John DeGolyer wrote his own. DeGolyer's software is the package used to create and control Ed/Tech's programs.

Partly for this reason, Ed/Tech's work is geared to IBM compatibles, even though the Macintosh has "a real smooth still video interface."

Also, Glanzman explained, "the IBM is what's out there." The programs are used at more than eighty law schools throughout the United States. Unfortunately, he said, that limits Ed/Tech to a lowest-common-denominator technology and limits the flexibility of the authors in scripting and the technical quality of the final product.

"We have to be as compatible as we can, and the IBM is a cheap way to deliver the information," he pointed out. All viewers need is a basic 80286 machine with a VGA monitor, a standard television monitor, and a videodisk player. The players cost about $500.

Despite this reliance on IBMs, much of the design work is done on the Macintosh stations. The trial situation is transferred directly from videotape to videodisk. The supplementary still images—close-ups of the actors, of pieces of evidence, drawings—are created using a video camera and a Data Translation ColorCapture® frame grabber. Using Data Translation's

proprietary software, the images are cleaned up, sized, and cropped. Then they're transferred back to videotape to put them in analog form before being stored on the videodisk. The moving video is then merged with the still video, and DeGolyer's authoring program is used to tie the images into the lesson script.

FAILURE TO COMMUNICATE?

The chief limitation facing Ed/Tech, Glanzman said, is securing the time of Harvard Law professors to script new programs and help maintain existing ones. It's the content, not the flash of hypermedia, that makes its products valuable. To get that content, Ed/Tech needs someone who's an expert in the law. It doesn't hurt if they're a good communicator, too. The Ed/Tech producers act as communications designers, molding the presentations to the hypermedia format to get the message across effectively.

Maintenance is a problem as well. Like parts catalogs and marketing campaigns—two areas where hypermedia is used in the private sector—the law changes. Existing programs have to be updated to reflect new rules of evidence and new statutes.

"Write-once media, such as videodisks, make maintenance difficult," Glanzman noted. "Some of our early programs were done on videotape, rather than videodisk. In some cases, they're better than later programs because we were able to revise them more easily. Once you put a sequence on videodisk, that's it. With tape, you can go back and revise if a segment isn't working."

Though CD-ROMs can be rewritten, they're not the ideal medium because the time required to access data on CD drives is too long to play full-motion video. Fast hard drives will support video, but would be too expensive to distribute.

"Animation is one way to solve that, for now," Glanzman agreed. "But the final solution is to find a cheap way to put full-video on a PC."

CHAPTER 8

VIDEO/ANIMATION

Video has changed the landscape and the language of design

Right now you may be asking what a section on video is doing in a book for designers. Designers do print. Video houses do video.

That's almost accurate. But it's also changing. And it's only part of the story. The importance of video as a medium for cultural communication is well-documented. It's also growing—rapidly—as a medium for artistic and especially *business* communication. Without a knack for identifying projects where video is the most effective way to communicate and the skills to create effective video, designers may be dealing themselves out of a large and growing segment of the communications market.

For dozens of studios, the graphics computer has become a "bridge" between the two-dimensional world of the art table and the fluid, three-dimensional world of video. Getting from one side to the other takes money for equipment, it takes time, and it probably takes a certain temperament. For at least some, it's also proved profitable.

VIDEO REALITY

You're already operating in a visual environment at least partly defined by video. Long before there was MTV, video had a powerful hold on us. MTV didn't create the marriage of television and graphics, but it did consummate it. Using quick cuts and a collage-like look, MTV kicked broadcast television into visual overdrive, raising the visual ante for mainstream programming. MTV's frenetic visual style spread to more mainstream programming and helped "market"—or at least prepare consumers to accept—the rebellion against formalism in graphics that marked the 1980s.

MTV also proved that a visual reality—in this case video—can be more important than physical reality. MTV showed that visual reality can not only affect physical reality, it can create it. Making visuals that change some external reality is what design, at its best, is all about.

Video's facility to manipulate reality hasn't been lost on businesses with products to sell.

"IS IT LIVE, OR IS IT MEMOREX?"

One of the most potent forces pushing businesses to use video communications is that "it works." Video communicates. A study done at the Wharton School of Business in 1987 found that a well-produced video increased viewers' retention of advertising messages by 50 percent over print ads. The video also shortened the time consumers took to make a purchase decision by almost a third.

One of the reasons video works is because video is accepted as reality. What's seen on the screen is perceived as "real," whether it is or not, whether it makes sense or not. If you've ever observed bettors at a racetrack craning their heads back, rivetting their eyes to TV monitors while the horses thunder by a few yards away, you know what we mean.

The very first color television broadcast provided a clear demonstration. The program was to begin with a shot of a bowl of fruit; their colors, instantly recognizable to the audience, would prove that color television worked. The crew labored long and hard to get the lighting and color just right, then took a dinner break, returning a half-hour before the live program was set to air. When they checked their carefully tuned monitors, panic struck. The bananas were purple, the apples were orange, and the oranges were green. Several heart-stopping moments raced by with technicians furiously twirling their controls, until someone thought to check the set: A prankster on the crew had painted the fruit during the dinner break! The technicians took what was on their monitors at face value without checking the reality—the fruit on the set.

More recently, customers in a convenience store called police to apprehend an armed man who was attempting to rob the store. When the officers arrived, there was no robber. What happened? The customers

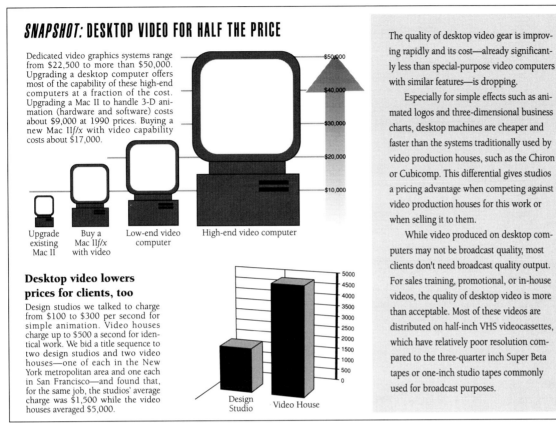

SNAPSHOT: DESKTOP VIDEO FOR HALF THE PRICE

Dedicated video graphics systems range from $22,500 to more than $50,000. Upgrading a desktop computer offers most of the capability of these high-end computers at a fraction of the cost. Upgrading a Mac II to handle 3-D animation (hardware and software) costs about $9,000 at 1990 prices. Buying a new Mac IIf/x with video capability costs about $17,000.

Upgrade existing Mac II

Buy a Mac IIf/x with video

Low-end video computer

High-end video computer

Desktop video lowers prices for clients, too

Design studios we talked to charge from $100 to $300 per second for simple animation. Video houses charge up to $500 a second for identical work. We bid a title sequence to two design studios and two video houses—one of each in the New York metropolitan area and one each in San Francisco—and found that, for the same job, the studios' average charge was $1,500 while the video houses averaged $5,000.

Design Studio   Video House

The quality of desktop video gear is improving rapidly and its cost—already significantly less than special-purpose video computers with similar features—is dropping.

Especially for simple effects such as animated logos and three-dimensional business charts, desktop machines are cheaper and faster than the systems traditionally used by video production houses, such as the Chiron or Cubicomp. This differential gives studios a pricing advantage when competing against video production houses for this work or when selling it to them.

While video produced on desktop computers may not be broadcast quality, most clients don't need broadcast quality output. For sales training, promotional, or in-house videos, the quality of desktop video is more than acceptable. Most of these videos are distributed on half-inch VHS videocassettes, which have relatively poor resolution compared to the three-quarter inch Super Beta tapes or one-inch studio tapes commonly used for broadcast purposes.

---

swore they saw the man on the store's security monitor. In fact, what they were watching was not a security monitor, it was a soap opera in which an actor was stalking the corridors of a hospital with a gun.

If it appears on a TV screen, it's automatically credible. People believe video more readily than any other medium; they may believe it more readily than the evidence collected by their own eyes and ears.

Since most business communications are created to persuade others, that's a pretty powerful argument for understanding and using video. The fact that business communications make up the bulk of the products sold by designers only adds to the importance of becoming video-literate.

Need more proof? One of the most widely covered "news" events of 1985 was the question of "Who shot J.R.?", the villainous character played by Larry Hagman on the prime-time soap opera "Dallas."

It's common for soap opera stars, especially evil female types, to be accosted on the street. Strangers walk up to these actresses and say, "I hate you!" The

person they hate, of course, exists only inside the tube. The viewers are clearly confusing the real person with the actor's fictional persona.

Video's ability to confuse fiction with reality has become a pervasive part of our culture.

It isn't surprising that television can make singers into stars overnight. Elvis Presley became a sensation after the infamous neck-up telecast on the "Ed Sullivan Show" portrayed him as a rebel. (At that time, white people generally didn't move their hips when they sang.) The Beatles were popularized by television ("Sullivan" again) and, for most of their careers, existed as disembodied media icons rather than live performers. Their last live performance was at Candlestick Park in San Francisco in 1969. That was long before *Abbey Road*, before the *White Album*, before *Sergeant Pepper*. Still, Elvis and the Beatles were real musicians.

The Monkees have the distinction of being the first widely popular prefabricated video band. They were actors who could sing. Their weekly situation comedy transformed them into a legitimate band.

They had a string of hit records and performed live.

The difference between Elvis, the Beatles, and The Monkees is that, in the first two cases, the musicians had created a cultural currency—an act—before being popularized by television. The Monkees showed that television could get people to accept non-musicians as musicians. By saying there was a "Monkee mania" sweeping the nation's teenagers, television made it so. The show succeeded in not only altering reality, but in creating it.

MTV has had a great deal more success in fabricating "stars." And its techniques are spreading rapidly, becoming an accepted part of our communications culture. The idea that dramatic (i.e. "reality-based") images can be enhanced with illustrative music and graphics helped spawn "Miami Vice" and the more recent "Cop Rock."

Perhaps we need a name to distinguish simulated personalities from real persons. How about SIMs? That's what Broderbund Software calls the simulated humans in its SimCity® game. Remember Max Headroom, the synthetic character of a few seasons back? Max "lived" inside the computer at a television network. He could only be "found" by calling him up on a monitor. Max was a SIM. That is to say, he wasn't flesh and blood, but he was a very real member of the cast. The other cast members interacted with him as if he were fully real, if not quite corporeal.

Here's a prediction: the Monkees of the 1990s will be totally digital. Someone will use a MIDI computer and music synthesizer to create a "sound," an act, a musical genre. But instead of using human actors to make videos for MTV, they'll use computer-generated images to create their SIMs. The SIMs will be *perfect*. And they'll be wildly popular. They will reflect an attitude and a visual image that synchs to the popular mood with digital perfection. Eventually they'll go on the road and do performances. The SIMs may even appear "live in concert" via holographic projection.

If this sounds far-fetched, think back to the year 1985. Where was the Macintosh in 1985? It was a lovable but woefully underpowered appliance. There was no LaserWriter and no interface to high-resolution imagesetters. It was not a serious tool for graphics professionals. Five years later, we're making quality color separations on it.

The technology to create the SIMs described above exists today. It's being used today. And it is, occasionally, being used for business communications. Commercial design is largely devoted to creating or manipulating perceptions about a product, a person, a political notion. Video is a powerfully persuasive tool.

Designers are in an excellent position to harness the power of video for business communications. Some have already begun to do so. The graphics computer can provide the means to substitute silicon chips and a bit of experimentation for the years of yelling "fade to black" that video journeymen must endure.

BUSINESS OPPORTUNITIES

No one we interviewed was able to "bootstrap" a video-capable workstation by signing a video project that would pay for it before buying the hardware. However, several said they were able to quickly recover the costs once the initial investment was made.

One ready market for video graphics may be local video houses. Because dedicated animation systems are so expensive, many small production companies buy graphics services from larger and better-equipped video houses. In urban markets, the kind of electronic paintbox effects achievable with a desktop computer cost $225 to $350 per hour. You can price your labor at $75 to $100 an hour and still charge the small video houses less than they're currently paying for animation and titles. If labor costs you $35 an hour, seven title sequences should pay for upgrading a Mac II into a respectable color video workstation, complete with scanner and software.

• • •

GRAPHIC CONNEXIONS

Using video graphics services to bolster the bottom line

One effect of the proliferation of graphics computers has been to blur the line between studio and supplier. While printers and typographers have long offered basic art services, the graphics computer has given some suppliers the means and the motivation to go beyond the basics of cut-and-paste. A typical service bureau with a Linotronic L-300, a couple of Macs, and a color thermal printer has well over $150,000 invested in equipment alone. There's also the cost of finding and training computer-capable staff. You have to run a lot of PageMaker files at six dollars a page to make a profit. Many, like Graphic Connexions, have bolstered their design services to pump up the bottom line.

Designs for print are still the largest percentage of their work, but Graphic Connexions has also found a lucrative niche in video production. While their gear is expensive by the standards of most design studios, it's inexpensive compared to the cost of the high-end animation systems commonly used by broadcasters. Combined with their ability to quickly master new software, it's given them an edge and opened the door for sales to video production houses, broadcasters, and corporate communications departments.

SNAPSHOT: GRAPHIC CONNEXIONS

Graphic Connexions, Inc.
10 Abeel Road, Cranbury, NJ 08512
TEL: (609) 655-8970
FAX: (609) 655-0612

Equipment: (12) Macintosh II-family workstations with two-page monochrome monitors or Sony 1302 color monitors, (1) Macintosh SE/30 server with 300 mb hard disk, (1) Macintosh IIci with 8 mb RAM and NuVista video board, (1) VID I/O expansion module, (1) analog-to-digital converter, (2) videocassette recorders, (1) Farallon MacRecorder, (1) Linotronic L-300 imagesetter, (1)Microtek 300z color scanner, Syquest 45 mb removable-cartridge drives.

Staff: (15) computer production artists, (1) production manager, (2) marketing/administrative.

Typical clients: Video production houses, corporate video departments, design studios.

"We get a lot of basic requests from people who want two-dimensional animations of their logos for video title sequences, or technical illustrations to cut into live video," says designer Jay Williams.

While that may be "basic" for Williams, the equipment and expertise required *do* take time to master.

GEAR BOX

Graphic Connexions is a high-volume service bureau, so it has more than a dozen Macs on site. The video work done primarily on one station: a Macintosh IIci with 8 mb of RAM, 300 mb hard disk, Pioneer 4200 laser disk player, Sony CD player, Microtek 300z color scanner, Sony 1302 multisynch monitor, Mitsubishi nineteen-inch monitor, NuVista video board, a Farallon sound recorder, and an analog-to-digital converter. Animation is recorded onto a Toshiba VHS videocassette recorder for previewing effects. When a piece is finished, the Mac is transported to a local video production house and the output recorded on three-quarter inch videotape. The software toolkit is just as extensive, but the names are more familiar: Adobe Illustrator, Streamline, PhotoShop, SuperCard, Swivel 3D, MacroMind Director, and PixelPaint Professional®.

For Williams—as for many of the animation and video artists we interviewed—MacroMind is the cornerstone program for video work. The program has built-in visual effects, such as fade to black, fade to white, wipe, dissolve, cross fade, and more. Users can animate computer-generated graphics by drawing them frame by frame or by using the program's powerful "Go Between" (tweening) command.

Given a starting point and an ending point (a geometric shape and a logotype, for example), the program draws the frames that would fall between those two points in an animated sequence. It also has a programming language, Lingo®, through which users can control a number of computer actions, from launching an animation sequence to shutting down the computer.

MacroMind even has an auxiliary program that allows MacroMind presentations created on a Macintosh to be viewed on IBM compatibles.

"Lingo is fairly simple. It's similar to HyperCard in that it uses English-oriented commands," Williams said. "I took a two-day class from a MacroMind instructor. It helped. But most of what I know I learned from reading—lots of reading—and playing with the program for forty or fifty hours. It took about six weeks after that to get comfortable with the program, but you're always looking things up, referring to notes. MacroMind has a technical support line that helps quite a bit. The interactive programming mode takes the most time to learn."

FAST FORWARD

One of the first projects Graphic Connexions tackled was a video title sequence for the New Jersey Network, the state's public television network.

"They gave us a logo and asked us to animate it, with a finished length of six seconds," Williams recalled. "We scanned the logos in black and white, used Streamline to produce an editable PostScript outline, then bumped it over to Illustrator to clean it up. From there, we took it into PhotoShop and began coloring it and adding effects as needed. We saved the images at 250 percent of actual size in Illustrator, then saved them at 40 percent in PhotoShop. That's our anti-aliasing routine."

Computer-generated video images sometimes have annoying "fuzz" around the edges. "Anti-aliasing" is a term used to describe any technique that gives images solid, flicker-free edges. Blowing the images up in Illustrator and shrinking them in PhotoShop is the equivalent of altering an oversized photostat with a pen, then shrinking it so the pen work doesn't show.

"MacroMind creates animation frame by frame. For each second of full-motion video, you need thirty frames. So, for this title sequence, we had to build 180

frames," Williams said. "Their logo was a circle intertwined, so we built two sequences. In the first, the circles come apart. In the second, they join back together. The two sequences were linked together and output to videotape."

To show the circles coming apart, Williams built two frames. The first showed the logo together. The second showed the logo apart. Using the MacroMind "Go Between" command, Williams automatically built the intermediate frames showing the logo gradually coming apart. A dialog box allows the user to specify how many frames will be in the sequence. Specifying 300 frames will yield ten seconds of animation, while thirty frames will yield one second.

The whole process took about four hours, Williams said, though more complex animations can take longer. Still, Macintosh animations take far less time than do pieces created on high-end video production computers. That means they cost less overall.

"We're doing a fair amount of work for video production houses. Especially for corporate videos, they're looking for a low-cost way to create titles and simple animation," Williams said.

One of these "simple" pieces involved animating a chemical reaction. The visual effect the producer asked for was easy to create. Two chemicals flow into a container, then the liquid flashes several colors to indicate a reaction is taking place. A single frame showing the vessel and the chemicals was built in MacroMind. Then the program was instructed to "cycle" through a sequence of colors. The resulting effect—colors flashing behind the liquid in the container—was videotaped straight from the Macintosh.

QUICK REVERSE

The computer's facility with video lets you go the other way, too—from video to still images. In one case, Williams said, he grabbed a series of images from a videotape and put them onto 35mm slides for an advertising agency. The agency was making a storyboard presentation on slides and wanted to incorporate some frames from an earlier video. The Macintosh proved the ideal way to "shuffle" the pieces from tape to slides.

"We grabbed the video frames by digitizing them from a quarter-inch VHS tape, so we really wondered how good the slides would look," Williams said. "We did it in 32-bit color and the slides came back very, very nice."

THE PRICE IS RIGHT

Pricing video work or animation is no different from pricing other design services: How much capital do you need to buy the equipment? What's the cost of the gear? How long will it be useful? How many minutes of product will you be able to sell during that time? How much is your time worth? And, of course, what will the market bear?

Contrasted with other design services, what the market will bear may be more than you're accustomed to billing.

Graphic Connexions charges $100 per second for simple animations such as three-dimensional logos flying across a screen. The New Jersey Network piece, which took four hours to complete, billed out at about $600. Even considering the high cost of the video workstation, that's a better buck than Graphic Connexions earns on typesetting. Other designers interviewed charge up to $150 per second for simple animated graphics.

In a few cases, Williams said, they've been able to earn an even higher hourly rate by using MacroMind's automatic features. In the case of the chemical reaction, all that was required was redrawing a technical illustration supplied by the client, then hitting an effects button (in this case, making the drawing flash a sequence of colors), and capturing the result on tape. The whole process took less than an hour, yet the video producer was very happy to pay "only" $500 for the finished piece.

UPPING THE ANTE

Using the lessons learned in producing animation and video, Graphic Connexions is moving into interactive advertising. Interactive advertising—where consumers can choose what information they want and when to view it—has a powerful appeal to marketers. Trials of interactive advertising services done in the 1970s and 1980s weren't spectacularly successful. So far, no one has found the right combination of content and technology. Still, interactive media has become a very real part of mainstream marketing: many supermarkets now have interactive displays that help shoppers locate specific products and featured specials in the store.

The parent company of Graphic Connexions, MarketSource, is heavily involved in direct marketing, targeting small groups of consumers including college students. Williams, Derek White—president of Graphic Connexions—and designer Greg O'Lone created the concept for a free-standing kiosk that would contain a Mac, large-screen television monitor, laser disk player, and touch-screen computer monitor. Information and advertising recorded on the laser disk could be accessed by the students using an interactive program running on the touch-screen monitor. They would be able to view information about spring break destinations, recruitment advertising from companies seeking college graduates, even consumer advertising.

The question is, of course, will college students stop in front of a video screen—even an interactive screen—to view advertising? They've been known to do stranger things. Initial support for the college kiosks from national advertisers was "positive," Williams said. "They like the concept and they're excited about having their videos played on campuses. Now all we have to do is get the students excited about watching them."

JURIS GRAPHIS

Legal videos make strange bedfellows

There are a lot of things about Juris Graphis that would feel familiar to most designers. Bob Scott, president of Juris, is a veteran of both in-house retail advertising departments and traditional graphics businesses. He owned a print graphics studio before starting Juris and still does books, promotional literature, and advertising for a variety of clients. Most of the staff have backgrounds that are solid and expected: airbrush illustration and print design.

What would be unfamiliar is that the bulk of the clients served by Juris aren't advertising agencies or corporate marketing departments: They're lawyers. As a profession, law is about as far from art as you can get. The distaste Americans profess for lawyers is rivaled only by the speed with which we resort to their services. According to the National Center for State Courts, Americans filed approximately 17 million lawsuits in federal and state courts in 1989. Many of these will never be tried. They'll be dropped or settled before coming in front of a judge and jury. In some, especially cases involving injuries or deaths, the evidence can be overwhelming, complex, and hard to understand.

That's where Juris comes in. Through graphics, Juris makes the complex simple and the puzzling clear, reducing hundreds of pages of documents to one-page diagrams or a few seconds of animated video. Given the vast sums at stake, this is a case where a picture—if it's clear and convincing—can be worth hundreds of thousands of dollars. The value of a well-executed, convincing legal exhibit to an attorney or client can be almost unlimited.

MOVING BACKGROUND

Before Juris, Bob Scott had a conventional graphic design practice: brochures, product literature, advertising. He's also a sculptor and mixed-media artist. One of Scott's friends, an attorney, came to him in 1985 with a very difficult case. He thought Scott's ability to visualize the abstract might help him find a way to explain the case to a jury.

The case involved an electrician who had been wiring a new office building. There were two complete electrical circuits in the building: one connected to the local utility's power lines, the other powered by an on-site generator. A switch in the circuit was designed to automatically go to the back-up power should the utility company's lines fail. The switch, however, was not working right. It kept switching back and forth between the outside power and emergency power. The attorney's client, the electrician, was attempting to fix it. For some reason, the switch turned on both circuits while the electrician was holding one wire from each, sending 220 volts through his body. Remarkably, he wasn't killed, though he was seriously injured.

Scott built a four-by-six foot graphic diagram using colored lights to represent the two circuits. A control panel turned the lights on and off to illustrate the malfunction of the switch and show what happened when both circuits went on.

The diagram was presented in court and the jury took very little time to award the electrician more than a million dollars in damages to be paid by the manufacturer of the switch.

SNAPSHOT: JURIS GRAPHIS, INC.

Juris Graphis, Inc.
255 S. Orange Avenue, Orlando, FL 32815
TEL: (407) 882-9961
FAX: (407) 882-7200

Equipment: (1) Macintosh IIx workstation with 2 mb RAM and 100 mb hard disk, (2) Amiga 2500 workstations with 50 mhz accelerators and 24-bit color monitors, (1) video camera, (1) LaserWriter IINT, (1) quarter-inch VHS videocassette recorder.

Staff: (3) computer production artists, (1) medical illustrator, (1) administrative.

Typical clients: Attorneys involved in personal-injury lawsuits and insurance companies investigating or litigating claims.

• • •

That one incident turned Scott into a cross between Perry Mason and a painter. Rapidly, it became a career.

"Right after the jury came in, the opposing attorney came up to me and asked if I could build an exhibit for him, for another case he was involved in," Scott recalled. "Word got around, and before long, the bulk of my work was coming from attorneys."

Although legal exhibits is a burgeoning field, Scott said there are only a half-dozen firms on the East Coast that specialize in it. "We probably offer the most full-service approach of any of them," he said.

That service now includes computer graphics and video animation.

"The thing that's been hitting everyone's hot button for the past six months is computer animation," he said. "It sings, it dances. It has a direct relationship to the way people gain information today, which is through television. People can see a complex situation and understand it intuitively. And it has become more acceptable to judges. If it's properly prepared, it can be admitted into evidence."

LOOKING FOR AN HONEST PICTURE

Getting judges to admit animations into evidence has taken some time, Scott said. The potential for abuse is very, very high. While the common folk wisdom is that "pictures don't lie," in fact, artists are trained to make them do just that. Perspective itself is an illusion, not to mention *trompe l'oeil*. With the facilities of a computer, an artist can take even greater liberties with reality, and judges have been wary of presentations that prevaricate, or distort the facts.

"The most common use of animations is in automobile accidents. There's a lot of opportunity to fudge an animation to favor your client," Scott said. Time can be compressed or expanded, the position of vehicles can be moved slightly, and physical features—hills or curves—can be emphasized or minimized.

To get its animations admitted, Juris employs an expert witness. "We have someone who specializes in re-creating accidents and testifying about them," Scott explained. "We work with him on the animation." The expert tells Juris the sequence of events and their timing. These are built into the animation. When it's finished, the expert reviews the animation to be sure it conforms to the results of his investigation.

"He looks at a rough cut, then tells us how to make it conform to his report. He might tells us to add a half-second between the time the car hits a wall and it bounces back into the road or whatever," Scott said. "In effect, he's directing us."

In court, the expert witness is called to the stand first. He states that he investigated the accident and made a report. The attorney can then play the animation for the judge or jury and the expert can vouch that it's an accurate representation of what happened, in his opinion. Unless his testimony is thrown out, the animation should then be admissible.

Usually, Scott said, the procedure is to start by consulting with the attorney and the reconstructor to draw out the facts that need to be illustrated. These are written on a large, erasable-surface wall in the Juris studio. When all of the facts and the relationships between them are clearly outlined, Juris builds a three-dimensional model of the accident scene. The scene is videotaped, digitized, and dumped into the computer.

Usually, a preliminary rough of the animation is done in HyperCard on the Macintosh to get a feeling for how the piece should be structured.

"Then, depending on what's needed for the case, we'll either develop a two-dimensional animation using the digitized video of the accident scene as background, or we'll do a three-dimensional animation if one of the vehicles rolled over," Scott explained. The final animations are done on a Mac II or Amiga, with the final video work all done on an Amiga before being transferred to videotape.

MARKETING BY THE NUMBERS

"When we started this, I had no idea what the market was, what kind of a universe there was in terms of companies producing demonstrative evidence," Scott said. "I had to find out who was doing this and what they were doing. I met people from some of the other companies, but none of them were approaching the business quite the way I wanted to, making Juris a one-stop shopping center for visual evidence.

"I did find out the number of potential clients is enormous. There are something like 700,000 attorneys practicing in the U.S.," Scott noted.

Selling the product was one concern. Making the product was another matter. Scott had to learn what is admissible in evidentiary hearings (such as trials). He had to learn to interpret expert accident reports. And he had to learn how to translate reports, testimony, and physical evidence into visuals.

Building a life-scale replica of a heater (which Juris has done) or making a two-second animation of an accident is actually the easiest part of the job, Scott contended. Except in very simple cases, the bulk of the time spent on a project goes into consulting with the attorneys, reading evidence, agreeing on what parts of it should be presented visually, and deciding how to interpret the evidence visually to make the greatest impact on the judge or jury.

GETTING DIGITAL

Those lessons were merely time-consuming, Scott said. "Emotionally, it was easier for me to make the transition to doing art for lawyers than it was to accept the computer as a tool," he admitted. "At the time, 1985, the Macintosh 512 was the only computer available for artists. We began to see that some of the things we were doing on mechanical boards might be handled better on the screen. The output options were pretty limited at that point, but it was still useful.

"I was also starting to incorporate photocopies and such into my paintings at that time, so I guess that helped me get over the hump. As I worked with the computer and got to know it, I realized it was actually very friendly and easy to use. That realization coincided with our decision to pursue trial graphics as a major part of our business."

Scott appears to have made the transition from technophobe to technophile flawlessly.

"Most of our presentations are done on videotape now," he said. "The majority of courtrooms are equipped with a VCR and a monitor to play back taped depositions. That's fine for most cases. We can see a market, however, for presentations made right off the computer in some complicated cases. If you have a passenger airplane crash, for example, you might have multiple attorneys and multiple accident experts, not to mention millions of dollars in claims.

"In that case, we might build a basic animation that we could then vary to present each expert's view of what happened. The computer would allow us to create and replay multiple scenarios, each different, very quickly."

From the humble Mac 512, Juris has moved steadily up the technological ladder. Its current system is based on Amiga 2500 CPUs with 50 mhz accelerator cards.

"We went back and forth from Amiga to Mac before making a decision," Scott said. "The Amiga does have a smoother video interface than the Mac, but cost was a big consideration. The Amigas cost less."

The accelerators, which are also available for Macs, boost the speed of the CPU, a critical need for anyone doing real-time animation.

"We've also looked at UNIX systems," Scott said, referring to the operating system that some predict will eventually supplant both the current Macintosh operating system and IBM's Windows environment. "Our feeling is that the data is becoming more interchangeable. We should be able to port images created on one machine to another machine fairly easily."

In fact, the Macintosh version of PhotoShop, for example, already supports the import of files created on the Amiga.

The next step, Scott said, is to move up to multiple-view three-dimensional animations.

"We're working to develop a system that will allow us to input all of the various information about an accident into the computer mathematically," Scott said. "That way, we can have multiple views. We can put the camera in one car, then, without redrawing the entire sequence, have the computer show us what the accident looked like from the point of view of the other driver."

It's a question of adapting, rather than creating, software. Multiple-camera views are already available on some high-end CAD systems.

Juris has also gotten some interest from Groupe Bull, the international parent of Zenith Data Systems.

"We've talked to them about doing basic software packages for attorneys that would allow them to construct their own animations," Scott says.

Using a library of pre-drawn elements—four-lane intersections, two-lane intersections, trucks, cars—the attorneys could set up the basic scenario for the case they're working on. They could then send their work to Juris for animation and output to videotape.

Just as Graphic Connexions, a service bureau, is becoming a design studio, Juris, a studio, may soon become a service bureau.

WHAT'S IT WORTH?

Scott admitted it was hard to peg the "market" value of the work Juris does. What's it worth to an accident victim to have an animation that convinces the jury they deserve compensation? What's it worth to the victim's family? Beyond that, what's fair?

Juris bills about $5,000 for a typical project. For that, the attorney and client receive counsel from Scott and his staff, a fifteen-second videotaped animation of the accident, and perhaps a three-dimensional model of the accident scene. In total, Juris may spend sixty hours on the project: forty hours in consulting and research, and twenty hours in executing the products.

What it's really worth was graphically illustrated by a telephone call Scott took while we were talking. Insurance companies often delay making fair settlements in injury cases because the awards are high. The longer they drag out the process, the less money the injured party will accept. And, the longer they delay making the payment, the longer the money can sit in their bank earning interest. Even if a case is scheduled for a jury trial shortly after occurring, it can take three to six years before the insurance company runs out of legal excuses to avoid starting the trial. Meanwhile, the victims of the accident are left with mounting medical expenses—or the death of a family's breadwinner—and no compensation.

Juris had just delivered an animation depicting a serious accident involving two semi-trailers and a car. The car ran a stop sign. One of the trucks swerved to avoid the car and hit the other truck, which hit the car. Two people were killed. The attorneys Scott worked with represented one of the truck drivers. As he put down the phone, Scott said, "That was the attorney. They had a meeting with the insurance company this morning. The insurance company was reluctant to settle the claim, but when our clients whipped out the animation and played it, the insurance company's attorney folded and offered a settlement on the spot."

The animation wasn't the only factor; Juris had the facts on its side as well. In the law, having the facts isn't enough; you've got to be able to present them convincingly. With their sound, motion, and clarity, the videos produced by Juris are very convincing evidence indeed.

CHAPTER 9

CLIENT SERVICES

Using the computer to squeeze out a little extra effort

Designers never tire of telling "impossible client" stories. We're sure you have a few of your own. It sometimes seems customers will go to almost any extreme to make your life miserable. It's not true, of course. It just feels that way. As the pace of business has quickened over the past two decades, clients' expectations have soared. How do you respond to a question like, "If Federal Express can pick up a package in Burbank at five p.m. and deliver it in Bangor, Maine, by ten the next morning, why can't you whip up a half a dozen logos by next Friday?" The answers, "Because you don't have to be inspired to fly a 747," and "Because we only have four employees, not four thousand," are good. They're accurate and true. But they are impolitic. No matter how feeble their grasp of your business, they *are* always the customer. They deserve your respect and understanding. And—maybe—they have a point.

Should design studios rethink their view of service? Good design takes time. No one is arguing that. But it also takes time to sort out which of the thirty-seven folks named "S. Patrick" who live on Dunleavey Road in County Cork, Ireland, is the addressee for an overnight package. Is it Sean, Seamus, or Sarah? Businesses expect instant delivery of all kinds of services. Design is no exception. Federal Express can do it. Why can't we? While some tasks can be shortened by applying more manpower, design isn't necessarily one of them. Making each delivery person more productive has been the engine that drives Federal Express. Making each designer more productive is one way of boosting service without comprising quality.

For many clients, it's a given that you've raised productivity and shortened turnaround times by using graphics computers. The questions they're asking now are: How much further can you go? How many new services can you deliver? How fast is fast? How inexpensive is inexpensive? The studios that come up with effective answers stand to gain business.

In the large urban markets, the benefits of graphics computers are taken for granted. Clients expect to pay less for more work and to get it faster than they did last year. They realize that, in order for you to do that, they may have to accept new ways of doing things. As clients have opened their minds to new methods, studios have begun to respond.

THE POWER OF TWO

Before you start squeezing design time, take a hard look at your design and production process. Are there tasks the computer could facilitate, make smoother and less time consuming? For example, have you tried picking up the telephone? Remember the Unisys Corporation ad campaign that used the tagline, "The power of 2"? That was a double entendré alluding to the cliché that two heads (Unisys and the customer) are better than one and to the fact that computers use only two digits: ones and zeros. For studios, there is a kernel of wisdom in the Unisys tagline: The power of two machines is better than one machine alone. When you connect your computer to the telephone line through a modem, you literally open your studio to a world of new opportunities.

The modem can reduce the time needed for some mundane tasks, such as delivering files to a typesetter or comps to a client. This can shorten your overall production cycle without reducing the amount of time you spend on the design itself. It can also free you to work with suppliers—illustrators, production people, service bureaus—outside of your immediate area with few of the time penalties that normally entails.

DIAL C FOR CLIENTS

We began telecommunicating copy from a CPM-based computer to our typesetter in 1980. So telecommunicating copy and correspondence to clients seemed like a logical next step. Or it did to us, anyway. Our clients had other ideas. A decade ago, we found only one

SNAPSHOT: FAST MODEMS SPEED FILES

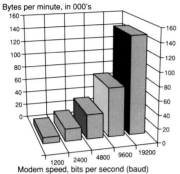

Bytes per minute, in 000's

Modem speed, bits per second (baud)

High-speed modems make the transmission of large graphics files practical. A 1,200-baud modem can only transmit 9 kb per minute, but a 19,200 baud modem can send up to 144 kb in the same time.

Using a simple compression utility, a 5 mb file containing a high-resolution color image can be shrunk to 1.25 mb. While a 2,400-baud modem would take more than an hour to send the file, a 19,200-baud modem could cut the transmission to under eight minutes.

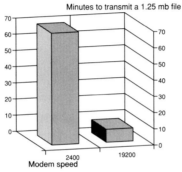

Minutes to transmit a 1.25 mb file

Modem speed

Getting there first with the most has helped create success for businesses in many industries. As graphics play a more integral part in the delivery of services and products, pressure has increased to reduce the amount of time needed to complete and deliver graphics projects.

While graphics computers help designers work faster, especially by reducing duplication of steps in the design process and speeding production, working faster isn't the only answer.

Telecommunications offers a way to speed delivery without compressing internal processes. Some design firms have begun using direct computer-to-computer transmission to send files to clients for approvals and handle last-minute corrections. The time needed to transmit a large graphics file has been a problem. But prices are dropping on high-speed modems and compression utilities, such as StuffIt® and Kodak's ColorSqueeze® can reduce file sizes by up to 75 percent.

client ready to take our copy over a modem. Because we were on the East Coast and the client was on the West Coast, we had only a five-hour window each day to work together. Their project—a new packaging system for nutritional supplements—was on a tight deadline. Complicating that was the fact that the product literature we were producing had to be cleared by the U.S. Food and Drug Administration.

The solution? We set up a bulletin board. At the end of their workday, their computer called our computer with corrections, additions, deletions, and clarifications to that day's work. By noon the following day, we'd have the revisions finished and back to their computer in time for their nine a.m. staff meeting. Their legal department worked on the revised copy during the day, cleared it with FDA, then wrote us a memo recapping their progress.

The brochures bounced back and forth between our office and theirs until the FDA felt they were acceptable. Thanks to the magic of long-distance phone service and the three-hour time difference, the client got overnight turnaround on the copy and made

an important trade show deadline. Today, it's easy enough to send copy via facsimile, but the fax machines of 1980 were maundering, cantankerous beasts that took three to five minutes to transmit one page and needed an attendant to run them.

Design firms commonly use facsimiles to get copy and design revisions to and from their clients. But an adventurous few have begun using their computers instead. The benefits are faster transmission time and the ability to send and receive color graphics. The biggest hurdle is getting your clients to use their computer modems. In 1980 we found few clients who knew how to use their modems or were willing to try. It was much easier for them to ask us to drop a package in Federal Express.

Today, many companies have internal electronic mail systems in place. Those who have offices in scattered locations often have their own wide-area bulletin boards. Using a modem, you can connect directly with the client's internal E-mail system. In the U.S., many businesses subscribe to MCI Mail, a telecommunications service run by MCI Communications.

The popular utility Glue®, from Solutions, Inc. will allow your clients to open view your graphics files on their own monitors, even if they don't have the program you originally used to create the files. They don't need the layout program, the illustration program, or any fonts. All they need is a copy of Glue. (Glue is offered as part of the telecommunications package Microphone®.) Using it, you can send graphics (even entire page-layout files) to an E-mail system or MCI.

COMMON CALLS

To be sure, it's unlikely that clients in Desplaines are going to drop a studio because they don't telecommunicate. But that time may be coming.

Telecommunicating page files to service bureaus is a common practice. On a recent project, we sent files to be converted to color film to our service bureau in New Jersey. Their price was too good to pass up, and by using the modem, we avoided delays in receiving the film.

Other studios are even more adventurous. Primo Angeli Inc. of San Francisco uses telecommunications to support its drive to increase its business around the Pacific Rim. In 1990, it began telecommunicating prototype designs to an Australian client. Peterson & Blyth of New York occasionally sends prototypes and revisions to Procter & Gamble in Cincinnati. Ronn Campisi of Boston routinely modems prototypes to clients in New York and elsewhere. Illustrator Dale Glasgow of Virginia modems complex color Freehand illustrations to clients across the United States. Ad agency BBDO/Atlanta has hooked up several clients, including Delta Airlines, to its internal E-mail system (*see page 19*). This allows the clients to interact with all of BBDO's departments without suffering the frustrations of voice-mail delays and telephone tag. It also lets BBDO serve its national accounts better: the Southeastern account team for Sizzler restaurants is in Atlanta while the national account team and creative group are in Los Angeles. *Time* magazine gets the prize for the most unique telecommunications use: Its photographers no longer air-express film from the world's hot spots back to New York for processing. Instead, they process their own Ektachrome on the spot, digitize the images using a Nikon LS-3500 scanner, and then modem the files back to New York.

GRABBING A FAST BYTE

Moving color images destined for reproduction is still unusual, partly because of the time required to transmit high-resolution color. That same hurdle—transmission rates—has also made it inconvenient to send color images to clients.

Even at 19,200 bits per second (the fastest transmission rate available over standard telephone lines), a single uncompressed 24-bit color image would take half an hour to send. *Time* does it by compressing the 5 mb files produced by the scanner to less than 1 mb, which will transmit in five to eight minutes. File compression software and high-speed data lines—which allow you to send computer files in their original digital form, without being converted to an analog signal as they would be if you were using a standard telephone line—that make it cost-effective to move large color files around are readily available.

A dedicated T-1 data line, for example, moves data at 1.5 megabits per second. An uncompressed 5 mb color file could be sent over a T-1 line in twenty-six seconds instead of thirty-five minutes. A T-3 data line operates at 44 megabits per second, and will move a 5 mb file in less than one second. These lines are already in service in many areas and can be leased from your local telephone company or from national carriers such as AT&T or MCI.

Suppliers, such as mega-printer Quad Graphics in Wisconsin, are already gearing up to accept publication files over high-speed telephone links. According to Alan Darling, manager of the company's Quad Text

• • •

division, Quad is readying itself to be the final production site for magazines. Darling envisions ad agencies sending ads to Quad in electronic files that would then be merged into page files created by a publication's art staff. The completed magazine pages would be separated electronically and plotted to film or directly to plates for printing. Since Quad prints *Time*, *Playboy*, and a number of other mass-circulation periodicals, it's in a position to have a profound effect on the entire publishing industry. The machines and methods are in place; publishers are already telecommunicating page files. In this case, the rest of the world is waiting for those of us in the design community to catch up.

PEER PRESSURE

It goes without saying that if a faster, cheaper way of producing something is available, it will be used. The advent of graphics computers—which produce mechanicals faster and cheaper—forced some trade typesetters out of business. Many designers have been forced to add computers to their studios. Studios that adopted computers early have an advantage over those that are just converting.

Studios that are now taking their first steps in interacting with clients through telecommunications will have a strong and salable competitive advantage in the very near future—one to two years. In 1992, clients who now expect you to show them laser proofs of their revisions overnight will expect you to modem them those revisions within the hour. And they'll expect film output in hours, instead of days or weeks. Without a solid grounding in telecommunications, it could be hard to keep up.

The news isn't all bad, however. You can literally have a sketch revised in Spokane and the copy recast in Chicago and back to your production people for layout in a matter of hours, not days. The faster you turn around the work, the sooner you can bill for the work. The adage about preferring a quick nickel to a slow dime is just as true for a design boutique as it is for a dress boutique. Time is your inventory; the faster you can use it and bill it, the better your cash flow.

BUSINESS OPPORTUNITIES

It's hard to imagine what a design business built around telecommunications might be like; that is, it's hard to imagine it today. As pressure from clients to speed up, shorten, slim down, and tighten belts continues, it seems likely that telecommunications will become as important to designers as it is to other businesses. In 1985, who would have predicted that delicatessens would install fax machines to take written lunch orders from nearby offices? It didn't seem to make sense to use a fax machine when the office workers could order in person or over the telephone. But it happened—because it's faster and easier. And faster and easier equals cheaper.

Studios are now testing telecommunication processes that may ultimately prove to be faster, cheaper, easier, or all three.

We've always thought of design as a rather contemplative sport, requiring lots of noodling and doodling to come out right. That's still true for some fraction of a studio's business. But the part of the business that has to do with interacting with clients shouldn't be done slowly: For most clients, faster is better. Production work doesn't require a great deal of dawdling, either. Faster is definitely better in production. By linking their computers to clients' E-mail systems, designers waste less time in the process of responding to a request or waiting for a response. It seems likely that telephonically networking studio computers to clients' E-mail systems will become common very soon. Studios and their clients already have the hardware and software. All they need is a reason to break their old habits. As it has in many other facets of our business, it seems likely that economics—hard, cold cash—will provide that reason.

RONN CAMPISI DESIGN

Always looking for a little edge

After ten years at the Boston *Globe*, including a stint as director of design, Ronn Campisi was more than qualified to set up as an independent publication designer. And, it being 1987, he had something few others possessed: experience using desktop graphics computers. Campisi used Macintosh computers at the *Globe* to produce info-graphics, which were output to a Linotronic and pasted down on mechanicals. Campisi knew he'd be able to use the Mac as a "multiplier," helping him go toe-to-toe with larger studios without committing himself to their overhead. He bought a Mac II and hung out his shingle.

SQ: SERVICE QUOTIENT

At the *Globe*, Campisi had garnered a national reputation for publication design, and he planned to exploit that, concentrating on graphics for newspapers, magazines, books, and annual reports. Although the primary work is design, because Campisi does prototypes, the studio has to produce a lot of composites. It has to do them quickly to meet the often truncated schedules of publishers, with revisions and fresh starts just everyday hurdles in the road to approval. The Macs, Campisi said, have allowed him to provide a higher

---

> ### SNAPSHOT: RONN CAMPISI DESIGN
>
> Ronn Campisi Design
> 118 Newbury Street, Boston, MA 02116
> TEL: (617) 236-1339
> FAX: (617) 236-0458
>
> **Equipment:** (1) Macintosh II with 4 mb RAM, (1) Macintosh IIx with 5 mb RAM, (1) Macintosh IIcx with 8 mb RAM, (1) 90 mb hard disk, (1) 80 mb hard disk, (1) 40 mb hard disk, (3) 19-inch SuperMac color monitors, LaserWriter IINTX, Microtek grayscale scanner, 2400-baud modem.
>
> **Staff:** (3) designers.
>
> **Typical clients:** Newspaper and magazine publishers who are designing or redesigning periodicals, and corporations who require a sophisticated look for newsletters, in-house publications, and annual reports.

---

level of service at minimal cost: "There are three of us working here at the moment. If it weren't for the Macs, I'd need six—maybe eight—board artists to keep up with the volume.

"In addition to being able to work more quickly, all of the time we bill can be for design rather than for production. We do our projects on a flat rate basis, but it still comes down to an hourly rate. Since the designers produce their own comps, that rate can be higher and it makes each project more profitable."

DESIGN ON DEMAND?

While he credits the Mac with giving him the punch of a studio with a big bullpen, Campisi also has a wry appreciation for the other edge of the sword.

"We can show a client a lot of variations on a publication logo very quickly," he explained. "The downside is that now they've almost come to expect a logo-a-minute or something. The machines could crank it out, but we can't. Clients expect everything faster just because we have graphic computers. I tend to work fast because I was at a newspaper for ten years, but I find it hard to keep up the pace sometimes. Design needs some breathing time, but since we aren't doing much work by hand, we don't have a chance to take a mental break while doing mechanicals."

THE TELEPHONIC EDGE

Campisi said he thinks technology is shrinking the time available to designers.

"We used to be able to tell clients we'd send a piece they were waiting for by overnight express; then at least we could work on it until the late deadline for express packages. Now they want it sent by fax immediately," he said. "That hasn't changed the way I design, but it's definitely raised the stress level."

What one machine takes away, another can give back. To help meet client demands for instantaneous service, Campisi enlisted the help of AT&T and his modem. When things get tight, he knows he can have a "camera-ready" file on the client's desktop in a matter of minutes, even though his customers are scattered all over the United States.

"A lot of the work we do is for trade publishers, and many of them are already using Macintosh for desktop production," he said. "Their timetables are always tight, and there are a lot of small details that crop up as the deadline for the first issue approaches. They may make a content change, or they may suddenly get an idea of how to make something work better. We have to take their ideas and give them back usable artwork. If they're not in Boston, that could be a problem.

"*Macintosh News* was one of our clients in New York. We worked through the basic design and provided them with templates for their pages, including an Encapsulated PostScript File of their logo. The week they were to go on press, they decided to change the tagline under the logo. We worked it out and flashed them a revised logo file by modem. The day before they were sending their type to the service bureau for output, they called and said they'd noticed that one of the letters in the new tagline wasn't kerned perfectly."

A year ago, most publishers would have just pressed ahead and revised the tagline on issue number two. Not now.

"I got a call at eleven in the morning saying they were sending their cover to type and they wanted the tagline fixed," Campisi chuckled. "We opened our file, respaced the letters, and were ready to dial their modem an hour later. They had the revised logo in their file before lunch."

REACH OUT AND TOUCH SOMEONE

Ultimately, Campisi believes using high-speed telephone links will let designers get closer to their clients: "I think it will translate into being able to work better with the client. When there's a question about a piece of a publication, instead of waiting for a batch of pages to be finished, then faxing them over and waiting for a response, we can send our file to the client by modem. Then both of us can look at it on the screen in real time. We can use Timbuktu® [by Farallon Computing] or a similar utility to control the client's screen from our computer. If a headline doesn't fit or lines aren't breaking right, we can solve the problem with one phone call instead of going back and forth; we can both look at the screen and figure it out. I don't think I'd want to try to invent something new—a logo or layout—while the client was watching the screen, but it's terrific for solving production questions."

PRODUCTION PLUS

There are other pluses for production, too. By providing Mac templates for his clients, Campisi can enhance the studio's control over the final product and cut the client's work load as well. Rather than having the studio's tissues translated into mechanicals by the publisher's staff, Campisi's templates ensure that the elements are positioned, specified, and pasted correctly. It's also given him a marketing edge: "As more publishers install desktop production systems, the ability to give them templates is a sales hook, too. We had a publisher in the other day who has six magazines, all done on Macs. The fact that we could give them templates ready for their people to pour in the content was a major plus."

Campisi's next step will almost allow the studio to function as an in-house production department. One of his clients is Lotus Development Corp., developer of Lotus 1-2-3® and other software for both IBM-PCs and the Macintosh. Campisi said he began submitting Lotus's quarterly magazine as color files with separations in place, ready to be run out as final film by a service bureau in late 1990: "We don't get to bill for the mechanicals anymore, but it frees us up to do more design work on the pages," he noted.

• • •

TIME MAGAZINE

Around the world in eighty minutes

Fast is not a word people associate with most design work. But in the rough and tumble of daily deadlines, speed *does* matter. The less time wasted waiting for things to arrive, the more time there is to think and work. Of course, for weekly newsmagazines, time is literally money. That's why we wanted to know how *Time* magazine is using computers to trim the fat off its deadlines.

Although the company has used computers of various kinds for many years, ironically, it is desktop graphics computers that are having the most profound effect on the creative and production departments. Both *Time* and its sister publication, *Sports Illustrated*, are produced on Macintosh systems.

That's not surprising. What is surprising is that the magazine's photographers are now transmitting color photographs over regular dial-up telephone lines to the New York headquarters for layout and separation. Right. Layout *and* separation. Besides the obvious proving ground this provides for desktop color technology, there is another important facet: *Time* has a long history of pioneering in photography and image-making. Photographers such as W. Eugene Smith were using 35mm cameras for *Life* photo-essays while their peers in the newspaper business were still lugging around ancient four-by-five inch Speed Graphics. Time and again, the equipment *Time* has adopted for expe-

dience has become the standard for photographers worldwide.

For *Time*, time isn't merely *of* the essence, it *is* the essence of the publication. The faster it can get images processed and into print, the better it fulfills the expectations of its readers. But news doesn't always happen in places that are congenial to magazine deadlines. Trouble tends to occur in places that aren't well-served by commercial air routes. Until this year, the fastest, best way to get images from the field to New York was to put undeveloped 35mm film on an airliner or chartered jet and wait. But the magazine has been keeping its eye on developments in electronic imaging and in 1990, it all clicked. Now the fastest, best way to send photos from anywhere in the world is by telephone.

"We worked with National Digital Instruments to develop a system that would allow our photographers to scan their photos in the field, then transmit them to us," explained Kevin McVea, operations manager for the picture department at *Time*. "Their solution was to mate one of their laptop portable computers to a [Kodak] Eikonix scanner. However, we weren't happy with the system until they agreed to switch from the Eikonix scanner to the Nikon LS-3500."

HOT SPOTS

The magazine bought four systems from National Digital. Two were placed permanently in bureau offices in Paris and Hong Kong. The other two are used wherever there's a hot story brewing.

In the field, the photographers use 35mm cameras and an E-6 color film (such as Kodak Ektachrome). After shooting, they develop their own film, choose the best shots, and place them in the LS-3500.

Scanning at a resolution of more than 6,000 pixels by 4,000 pixels, the LS-3500 actually has finer resolution than the E-6 film itself, thus picking up all the nuances and details present in the image. This produces a file of about 20 mb, uncomfortably large for

---

SNAPSHOT: TIME MAGAZINE

Time/Warner Inc.
Time & Life Building, Rockefeller Center
1700 Broadway, New York, NY 10020
TEL: (212) 522-1212

Equipment: (35) Macintosh II-family workstations with 24-bit displays, (4) Nikon LS-3500 scanners with National Digital Instruments laptop computers, Scitex SmartScan color scanners.

Staff: (35) computer production artists.

Typical clients: Produce *Time* magazine (U.S. and foreign editions) each week.

transmission over a standard dial-up telephone line. Using a National Digital file compression utility, the images are squeezed to just under a megabyte each. Then the photographer dials the magazine's modem in New York and sends the files. Depending on how noise-free the telephone line is, the files can be transmitted at up to 19,200 bits per second (or 144 kb per minute). At that rate, it would take about seven minutes to transmit each photo, but the lines are seldom clear enough for the modem to work at its top speed. More commonly, McVea said, transmission takes ten to thirty minutes per photo. In less than than an hour and a half, the magazine can get images for last-minute updates from all four of its mobile units.

Twenty minutes seems like a lifetime when you're sitting at a keyboard waiting for an image to arrive. But, McVea said, despite the relatively slow transmission time, "it still beats the alternative. We used to have to charter a jet to get the film to New York in time to make our deadline; then when it got here we still had to process it and fit it into a layout. Occasionally, when things were happening in the Middle East or Eastern Europe, we would fly the film to a separation house in Italy that had a Crossfield system. They'd scan the film, then modem us the color separation file and we'd integrate it into a page layout." The portable system cuts out everyone except the photographer and the photo editor.

PRINT IT

Getting a photo is one thing. Getting a photo that's usable is another.

"We'd always rather have the original in New York if we can," McVea admitted, "but we've had no problems with the quality of the images coming over the telephone. In 1990 we made a two-page spread using a photo from Saudi Arabia and another two-page spread from the Helsinki Summit. I know *Newsweek* uses the same system we have, and they've done a cover using

an image that came in over a modem. We'll probably do that before the end of 1991.

"The system works well and the photographers like it. Basically, you just put the slide in and push a few buttons; there's very little manipulation of the image involved," McVea noted. "The National Data system doesn't allow us to do a lot with the data once it arrives, but we expect that to change. We should be able to manipulate the images on our Macs here shortly. We had to have a system that would fit into the overhead compartment in an airliner, and at the time we bought them, these systems were the only ones that were compact enough."

McVea said National Digital released an even more compact version at the end of 1990, one with a keyboard and monitor built into the scanner housing.

FUTURE PHOTOS

Time is aggressively experimenting with all kinds of digital imaging, including still video.

"We've tried the Sony Mavica system, but the quality's not quite there for us yet," he explained. "As long as you don't use the photos too big, in a high-pressure deadline system, they're acceptable. But it's not as good as what we get from the portable scanner."

For that reason, *Time* has taken a pass on video for the time being, preferring to wait for the next generation of cameras. The current crop, including the Canon and Sony products, record their images as analog signals on disk. They then have to be converted to digital form before they can be transmitted or used by a computer. However, McVea said, Kodak has shown a fully digital video system that may set a new standard for fast—and usable—color. Kodak's product is a back that will replace the back on a standard Nikon F3, a 35mm camera used by many professional photographers. McVea said the quality looks very promising. And for those of us for whom time does indeed fly, that's good news.

· · ·

CHAPTER 10

DESIGNER/TECHNOLOGISTS

Getting good results by getting technical

There's a myth that art and technology don't mix well, that artists are (or should be) too busy with their private vision to think much about science. But mastering one's art has always demanded mastery of the technical details, too. Many sculptors would feel right at home swapping tips at a metallurgist's convention. Photographers are conspicuously conversant with physics and chemistry. The best print designers have a firm grasp of lithography, and we can assume that Michelangelo was not altogether unacquainted with the mechanics of the scaffold. Bronze, photographic film, and printing presses are all tools of the trade, to be used, not feared. Why should graphics computers be any different?

For one thing, being so new, they're less familiar. Also, it's possible to use a graphics computer for basic tasks—and some advanced ones—without knowing too much about it. Graphics computers and software are complex, but they're no harder to master than the ability to judge film exposures without a light meter or to paint a smooth color blend with an airbrush. Which is to say that, like other kinds of art tools, some people have a knack for computers and others don't. Some people can draw, some can't. Some people can look at a piece of complicated software and figure out how it works and some can't.

Many studios skate along quite nicely without getting entangled in the technical details. But the studios making the most advanced uses of computers invariably have at least one person who supervises the graphics computers. Sometimes it's the studio's owner. Usually, it's someone with a background in design and strong personal interest in technology. Only rarely do they have a title that describes their job. They're important, but we don't know what to call them yet.

WHAT'S IN A NAME?

Among other things, titles tell us what we're supposed to do: art directors direct art; illustrators illustrate; production artists produce. What does a design technologist do? Or a technology manager?

What they do is keep the studio from being hogtied by its graphics computers. They recommend or reject hardware and software. They work the bugs out of new (and old) processes. They teach their colleagues how to use the gear better and more effectively. They experiment. In studios that have networks, they're the network administrator. Often, they provide special computer services or create special effects —animation or advanced color work—for the other designers. That's a lot of territory to cover in one or two words. Whatever they're called, these designer/technologists are vital.

Production managers have traditionally been the main liaison between studios and their vendors. They traffic type, choose suppliers, and evaluate separations.

Graphics computers compress the production process on both ends. The chain that begins with the designer and ends with mechanical art has fewer steps, and people are involved. The chain that begins with mechanicals and ends with the printing press also has fewer steps and fewer people involved. In some cases, the chain now begins and ends with the designer, who creates a file ready for final film without any intermediate steps. This shifts responsibility for the final product onto the designer and the studio.

It's not reasonable to expect that all designers will be equally adept this. Especially when color files are involved, it requires solid knowledge of and experience with PostScript imagesetters.

The need is for someone who understands the printing press, the computer, and the designer's intentions. Designers themselves seem to be taking on more and more of the technical burden. If it continues, this may reduce the need for production artists. It probably won't drastically cut the need for designer/technologists, however. As the cost of hardware drops and its capability increases, it seems likely that more produc-

tion functions will wind up in the studio. Ergo, the continuing need for someone expert in systems design, digital color reproduction, electronic imaging, telecommunications, and teaching technology.

TALKING TECHIES

How do technologists keep their repertoire of tricks and techniques at a marketable peak?

Reading is fundamental: You aren't the only one who doesn't have time to sit at a desk reviewing technical publications. But successful technologists make time to keep up with at least two major computer journals such as *MacWeek, MacWorld, MacUser, Publish!, Step-By-Step Electronic Design,* and *Desktop.*

Test drive before you buy: The technologists we spoke with try everything they can think of and persevere, working it through to a solution. When a new piece of gear or program is announced, they try to see it as soon as possible, and try it out if possible. If you hear of something you think will help you, they suggest calling manufacturers. You may find they'll come

to your shop to demonstrate their wares, or they may be able to refer you to a nearby dealer or design studio that already has the equipment.

Hit the road, Jack: To the extent they can, successful technologists attend industry trade shows such as MacWorld Expo, the Seybold Conference, and the various Graph/Expo and Grafix shows in the United States. This wasn't as important when Apple, Adobe, and Allied/Linotronic were the only major players in graphics computers. It will become increasingly important as the number of small, third-party suppliers of software and hardware increases.

Heard it through the grapevine: Most technologists are part of an informal network. They trade information and techniques with their opposite numbers at other studios, with freelancers, and with the folks at their service bureau.

BEING THERE

This is starting to sound like a pretty good job; some reading, a few hours of playing at the keyboard, chatting with friends on the telephone, and a few nights on the road checking out spiffy new electronic gizmos.

The reality, of course, is nowhere near as glamorous. On a wilderness trip, breaking trail—finding and clearing a path—is usually left to the most adventurous. It requires a sure foot and a high tolerance for frustration and pain. Breaking trail technologically isn't physically treacherous, but it can dish up plenty of frustration.

Patience is important. It will be needed in order to remain pleasant while explaining the Illustrator blend function to a colleague for the seventy-second time. It will also be needed to deal with the "can you just..." syndrome: designers who'd rather interrupt someone else than learn how to do even the simple things—like saving a page layout as an encapsulated PostScript file—for themselves.

The successful technologist will be a diplomat. If an organization is installing graphics computers for the first time, the technologist can become a scapegoat for the glitches that will inevitably crop up. Designer/technologists may not be seen as whiz kids on the cutting edge, but as eggheads more concerned with fancy circuit boards than with cash flow or compassion. In large organizations that already have a data-processing department, the designer/technologist may be a target for DP managers who are afraid their turf is being invaded. In smaller studios, colleagues may see the technologist as a hatchet man bent on replacing designers with CPUs .

No one has a simple formula for defusing these landmines. They come with the territory. Management can help by showing consistent support for the technologist. If there are to be classes, everyone, including management, should attend. Managers should make it clear that the use of the computers is not a topic for debate. The sooner everyone in the studio is behind the program, the sooner the sniping will stop and the focus will shift to finding ways to work more efficiently

with the computers. Also, it's probably not a good idea to begin shoving people out the door the minute a workstation or two are operational. That only tends to confirm whatever fears are already present.

BUSINESS OPPORTUNITIES

There are real opportunities for designers who have a special affinity for graphics computers. There are jobs not only in studios, but in corporate art departments, in service bureaus, and as freelance consultants as well.

The 1990 rate for freelance technologists was sixty-five to seventy-five dollars an hour in the major metropolitan markets—comparable to what a senior designer might charge. That's a pretty rosy financial picture, but there are costs, too. For example, there are the non-billable hours spent fiddling with the system, finding new techniques and refining old ones. And everyone we spoke to was emphatic that, if you want to get involved with the technology seriously, you must have your own system; just experimenting at work in your free time won't cut it.

Freelancers in particular take a big hit from the cost of the technology they're consulting on. They need an advanced system to keep ahead of their clients. That means buying new gear soon after its release, when it's most expensive. It may also mean buying equipment or software they can't justify in terms of the direct revenue it produces.

As a consultant to large design firms, such as Landor Associates, San Francisco-based designer Mark Crumpacker found that he needed a lot of gear to keep his competitive edge. His personal workstation eventually expanded to include a color scanner, full 24-bit color display system, and a film recorder. The upside is that Crumpacker parlayed his expertise into a staff position at Landor Associates. Crumpacker has plenty of design experience, but it is his skill with computers that's opening doors to bigger, more interesting—and more lucrative—assignments.

124 . . .

MICHAEL SHEETS

Sometimes, the best-laid plans...

Point man is what the Army calls the guy who walks ahead of the others on a patrol. He's the guy who gets to see what's out there first. He's also the guy most likely to find the ambushes and landmines. Ask Michael Sheets. He can tell you what it's like being the point man for graphics technology.

After ten years as an art director for Batelle National Laboratories at the Hanford Nuclear Reservation in Washington state, Sheets took on the responsibility of maneuvering a large-scale Macintosh graphics installation through the corporate maze. Today, the Macs are there, but Sheets isn't. The rigors of fighting off DOS-happy data managers and high-level bureaucrats left their scars, and Sheets eventually felt he would be happier elsewhere. But the struggle also gave him valuable experience that he now markets—along with electronic design and multimedia services—to businesses in the Seattle area. His passage from corporate art director to freelance technologist fairly summarizes the unexpected joys and terrors of trying to do the right thing in the corporate arena.

BACKGROUND CHECK

Hanford Nuclear Reservation is one of those semi-secret government installations run by private contractors. Hanford was run by five companies—including Rockwell, Boeing, Kaiser Engineering, and Batelle—for the Department of Energy.

Sheets joined Batelle in 1975 as art director for a graphics group that numbered thirty-five artists. Most of the group worked on charts and graphs needed for Batelle's reports while Sheets and a select contingent handled corporate identity and marketing work. Given the volume of their output, by the mid-1980s, Batelle needed graphics computers. As art director, the task of finding, specifying, convincing the necessary committees of the need for, and installing the computers fell to Sheets.

"I bought my own Radio Shack TRS Model III in 1979. Later I looked at the Apple Lisa®. The operating system impressed me, but there was no way to get quality output," Sheets recalled. "That changed when the LaserWriter was introduced. However, when the decision was made to look for design computers, the sentiment at Batelle was to buy IBMs."

Sheets recommended the Macintosh and wrote up the appropriate purchase orders. Two months later he found the purchase order had been discreetly "filed" in the purchasing department. They'd been told by someone in the data processing department that the request for a Macintosh would never be approved.

"What broke it loose was a scientist from Batelle's main office in Columbus, Ohio, who was very impressed with the Mac," Sheets said. "He was a real dynamo, kept five secretaries busy non-stop, and was bringing in a lot of very big contracts. He came out to Hanford and I got a chance to talk to him about our needs. He suggested to the right people that we get the Macs we'd asked for."

Shortly after that, the purchase order was approved for two Mac Pluses and a LaserWriter.

"Unfortunately, they only approved the Mac for use as a design tool. I had to lay out the pages in the

Mac, print them on the laser, then take them across the hall to the typesetting department where they were rekeyed. Then the production artists used my laser printout as a dummy," Sheets said.

Though he had a Macintosh, Sheets said he felt boxed in. The limits of how far he could go became clear right away. Facing an extremely short deadline, Sheets decided to use laser output instead of typeset galleys for one of Batelle's publications. Accustomed to seeing nothing but repro-grade type from the in-house typesetting equipment, managers around the company were outraged.

It didn't appear the company was interested in compromising quality for expediency. And in fact, printing from the laser output may have set back the effort to win acceptance for the Macintosh. Sheets also suspects it may have spooked some of Batelle's data managers concerned about their own job security.

In some large organizations with existing data managers there is the possibility of encountering resistance from the "technical priesthood." These are people who guard the mainframes and support microcomputer users. Because the Mac needs so little support, it makes support people very nervous.

"The support group at Batelle felt the Macintosh was a threat," Sheets recounted. "When the first two Macs arrived, the data management people sent two network installers over to network them. They scheduled two days and, of course, it took them about fifteen minutes to plug the AppleTalk cables in. They hung around all day to 'make sure everything was running right' but they didn't come back the next day. The technical people got a little worried. If installing Macs was so easy, how secure were their jobs?"

Sheets spent "hundreds" of hours of his own time working with the Mac, pushing the envelope, trying to make it do new and more useful things. In the first three months, he documented labor savings of sixty percent over conventional methods. The technical

priesthood wasn't impressed. They were scared.

"We wanted to get PageMaker, but they started throwing this site-licensing argument at us, said we couldn't get a site license. We didn't need a site license because we only wanted one copy for one machine," Sheets mused.

People who work in organizations that have a lot of IBM machines frequently face this kind of single-mindedness from data managers. In general, they're not dumping on Macintosh because they don't like you in particular, they do it because the machines are foreign to them. If they have to accept microcomputers, they'll grudgingly allow IBM's to be tied into their network because at least they're made by a company the data managers trust.

Despite these obstacles, Sheets pressed ahead, lobbying for full computerization of his department. The next hurdle was a major one: The Department of Energy reorganized Hanford. Rockwell was replaced by Westinghouse as the prime contractor, and the various corporate graphics groups on the Reservation were consolidated under the management of Boeing Corporation's computer services division.

HARD SELL

Boeing's data department was heavily oriented to number crunching, word processing, and to IBM hardware. They put on a full-court press to convince Sheets that IBMs could do anything a Mac could. They sent him to Comdex, the annual mega-computer show. He was put on a variety of committees studying electronic publishing and document processing at Hanford. He was asked to write endless reports and recommendations. He was involved with a small electronic publishing group using IBM-compatible machines and Ventura Publisher®.

After these experiences, Sheets was more convinced than ever that the Macintosh was the right machine for the job.

"Finally, they sent me to MacWorld Expo 1988 with a group of IBM-oriented people," Sheets said. "They were totally amazed at what they saw. One of the people on the trip was the technical equipment director for Boeing. He and I decided to write a joint report on what we had seen."

The report recommended that Boeing convert its entire graphics department to computers—Macintosh computers. It asked for thirty-five SEs and a handful of Mac IIs. This time, Sheets had the right ammunition.

In the corporate world, gut conviction is rarely enough to carry the day, especially against entrenched opposition. When data managers with decades of experience are against you, you better offer something a little more objective than your own feelings.

"We found that the way to convince Boeing was using numbers," Sheets said. "Someone at Batelle slipped us a copy of a study that had been done by the Westinghouse corporate data management group. It showed that not only was the Mac the best computer for graphics, but for all types of computer tasks. It showed that the average IBM user was using three software programs while the average Mac user was using twelve programs. The time for training someone to median proficiency on a word processing program was about twenty hours on the Mac versus 120 hours for an IBM. We got information from other design groups who were already using Macs that showed some of them had reduced costs by as much as 60 percent. Also, because Boeing wasn't buying clones, the IBM machines weren't any cheaper than the Mac stations."

The report, endorsed by Boeing's own equipment specialist, did the trick. The equipment was ordered, including a high-end desktop publishing station with a RasterOps 24-bit color monitor, color scanner, and a full complement of software.

After two years of skirmishing, the artists finally had their Macs, but Sheets was about to find out that getting the equipment was only half the battle.

"The purchasing people came in and said we were on our own, that they wouldn't support us. That didn't stop them from billing us an additional 25 percent for their 'services' on everything we bought," he said.

The Hanford computer store refused to order PhoneNet® instead of AppleTalk because it was too much trouble to add another item to their inventory tracking system.

While Sheets made sure his colleagues got a copy of every piece of software he could lay his hands on, other graphics managers issued just one program, MacDraw II®. After Sheets conducted a series of one-day orientations demonstrating a variety of graphics software, these artists asked their managers why they hadn't been given more programs.

"Basically, they were told they got McDraw II so they wouldn't be 'confused' by the other programs," Sheets said.

As a result, Sheets said, the group lost nine key employees over a two year period. They weren't computer shy—all of them had graphics computers at home. They were frustrated by not having the best tools available for their jobs.

SCHOOL'S OUT

Eventually, Sheets too had had enough and left. But he took with him a kit full of unique experiences.

"If you're trying to work with a bureaucracy to get graphics computers installed, don't expect too much cooperation," Sheets advised. "You have to be persistent. You have to be a self-starter, willing to learn about the technology on your own. When it comes down to comparing systems, you need to know more about the capabilities of the computers than anyone else. It's important to be articulate, to be able to express exactly what you want to say. A lot of artists aren't verbally oriented. In the end, it wasn't the quality of the Macintosh system that impressed the people at Boeing, it was the bottom-line numbers."

It doesn't hurt to be a little political, either. "Some of the managers probably thought I pushed too hard," Sheets admitted. "Some people got their backs up and weren't going to cooperate no matter what. They felt their expertise was being passed over in favor of the recommendations of people who didn't know computers. I tried to put myself in their shoes and realize that they did feel a little threatened."

Sheets said he found it helps to have an eye for the people who are likely to improve tremendously when given a computer.

"You never really know how a particular person is going to take to a computer," he cautioned. "There are some people who are gadget freaks, who really like computers. They aren't necessarily the right folks to start your program with. They tend to get lost in the technical details, although their interest in technology does tell me they have a desire to learn."

THE AFTERLIFE

Sheets is now back at ARO Designs, a company he has operated with his wife, also an artist, for the past two decades. He's capitalizing on his hard-won experience, even selling it back to his former colleagues at Batelle.

In the past two years, the Hanford Nuclear Reservation has gotten a lot of bad press over its environmental record. Recently, ARO completed a multimedia exhibit highlighting changes in the facility's environmental policies. A Macintosh IIcx with a color monitor was placed in a pedestal. The monitor was equipped with a MicroTouch® touch screen. Color photographs and color animation created in MacroMind Director were integrated with original music sequenced for MIDI on the Macintosh and voice-over narration recorded using a Farallon MacRecorder®.

"The centerpiece of the display was a four foot by six foot plexiglass map of the Reservation. It had hundreds of LED lights that were hooked up to the Mac.

When a viewer pressed a button on the computer screen, animation and photos relating to environmental monitoring would appear. Narration and music would play back, and the LEDs lit up to show where on the Reservation this particular kind of monitoring was taking place.

"I think this project used every piece of software and every technique I've ever picked up," Sheets quipped. "It was a big job, but we were able to bill about $35,000."

ARO's mainstays are publications and illustrations, but Sheets says the company is moving toward video and creating final film for printers. "I want to keep more of what comes in instead of giving it to the service bureau or the production house," he said.

Sheets has also found himself in high demand as a technical consultant.

"Beginning the last year I was at Hanford, people call me from all over the country asking questions. I have no idea how they get my number, but they do," Sheets said. "I charge the same rate for consulting as I do for graphics services, forty dollars an hour. I know that wouldn't be much in some metropolitan areas, but it's pretty competitive with what the better design studios here charge."

Sheets is unafraid of giving away the store, however: "One of our longtime clients is a medical lab. I went over last week because they were having some problems with their Macintosh. They're the perfect example of why the technicians at Boeing were wrong to keep people in the dark about the computers. Instead of hiding information, we told our client everything we could. We helped them install their first Macintosh system. They now do some things we used to do for them in house. But they've also grown and become more successful. So, instead of losing revenue, we now get more projects from them than we ever have, and the work we're now getting is more interesting and more challenging."

TOM HARPER

Falling back from proprietary pre-press to PostScript—and getting ahead

Digital production is nothing new for Peterson & Blyth. The studio, well-known for its high-profile packaging clients, has had at least one Macintosh since the machine's inception. In the early years, when the Mac was limited in its output capabilities, font availability, and quality, it wasn't quite enough. Still, partners Ron Peterson and John Blyth were believers; so much so that they brought in a Context® design console. The Context, a proprietary pre-press and design station, allowed them to design and produce their packaging digitally, right through to final film.

But there were some major drawbacks. For one, the Context cost upwards of $300,000, making it unrealistic to buy multiple workstations. Second, its design software wasn't very fluid. Third, the operator needed a formal training course to learn the system. And fourth, because there was just one console and one operator, designers had to look over his shoulder to make changes to a file. Forget real-time design. Make that really time-consuming design.

In 1988, the partners felt the Macintosh had advanced enough to make a full-bore stab at digitizing the studio. The Context disappeared. Macs appeared on every desk. A technologist, familiar with computers and networks, was hired to make the Macs talk to each other and smooth the transition. The machines were installed and they did work, but file transfers were agonizingly slow. And the computer meister's experience with business software—spreadsheets, databases, word processing—wasn't terribly helpful in training designers to use graphics programs.

In 1989, Tom Harper made a visit to Peterson & Blyth. A freelance art director, typographer, and Mac enthusiast, Harper hoped to sell a few services to the studio. His experience with the Macs piqued their interest, and the occasional call to come in and digitize a logo soon turned into a full-time job. His mission: Get the systems, and the designers, working more efficiently.

WHEN YOU'RE SICK, CALL A DOCTOR

"It's almost too easy to set up a system and then call yourself a consultant. It may be running, but you may have font conflicts, spooling problems, whatever. The partners originally thought they needed someone whose background was hardware and programming," Harper recalled. "They had one. He was a whiz with databases, but he knew nothing about why fonts act the way they do. I started working with Macs in 1986 and I've worked with Freehand since its release. I worked in a type house where we had eight Macs, so I was familiar with all of the problems you have in moving files between machines, training new operators, managing fonts, running things to an imagesetter. I've experimented a lot, and I've made a lot of mistakes."

Harper's experience on both sides of the art table—as a designer and in production shops—allowed him to zero in on the rough spots and begin smoothing them: "They were training in Quark XPress, which is a terrific program for doing publications, but not so terrific for packaging. You can't draw in Xpress, for example, and at that time you couldn't flip type up on its side. They were also using Illustrator, but the masking and blending were giving some of the design-

---

SNAPSHOT: PETERSON & BLYTH

Peterson & Blyth Associates
216 E. 45th Street, New York, NY 10017
TEL: (212) 557-5566
FAX: (212) 818-0627

Equipment: (14) Macintosh II-family workstations with 24-bit displays, (1) SE/30 file server, EtherTalk Network, (1) Apple scanner, (1) La Cie color scanner, (1) QMS color printer, (1) Apple LaserWriter NTX.

Staff: (12) designers, (1) designer/technologist.

Typical clients: Packaging for major corporations such as Quaker Oats, Johnson & Johnson, and 3M Corp.

ers trouble. I moved them over to Freehand, which I was very familiar with, and which also handles type quite nicely. Freehand is slower than Illustrator, but it seemed to be an environment that the designers were comfortable with."

PRINT BUFFER

Harper views his job as that of a buffer, keeping the designers and studio management from having to deal with the details of the technology.

"The designers aren't computer mavens yet, and I'm not sure they should have to be," Harper said. "If you tell them to 'open up the Font DA mover and create a new font file,' you may get a blank look. I'm the buffer that makes it all nice and friendly and keeps headaches to a minimum."

Harper also works directly with partners Ron Peterson and John Blyth, updating them on the state of the technology and advising them on purchases. He reads—constantly—and goes to trade shows.

"I do a lot of wait-and-see," he cautioned. "It's easy to see a demo at a trade show and get excited. Three years ago, I saw a demo that really impressed me. I came back to the shop where I was working and told them it was hot; it integrated text and graphics in color. After I bought the thing I found out this software is the most miserable program known to the Macintosh world. When you're reading, you have to know that the 'official' shipping dates aren't necessarily going to be the real shipping dates. After a while you get to know which companies keep their word about features and ship dates.

"Also, I'm on the telephone constantly with software developers. They want to hear about what doesn't work in their programs, they want suggestions on how to make them better."

Harper said his job is to take the hardware and software and "break it," to find out how much demand can be reliably placed on it. It keeps him one step ahead of the questions the studio designers are likely to ask and gives him an opportunity to work with the manufacturers on a solution before it becomes a problem for the studio.

This constant experimentation gives Harper an edge that most designers are unlikely to have to time to acquire. "At MacWorld Expo this year, I went to the Aldus booth to ask a question and began fooling around with one of their machines," he recalled. "Pretty soon, I was giving demos. People were asking me how to do rotations, special fills, and so on. I use the program so much, I knew more about it than the official Aldus demonstrators."

Harper's approach to sharing this knowledge with Peterson & Blyth's designers has been informal and low-key. Aside from a monthly mini-user's group meeting, he advises the designers to work their way through the tutorials that come with most programs. Then, as they encounter difficulties, he works with them one-on-one. Everybody learns at a different rate, he said, and that makes group exercises difficult. They may go at too fast a pace for some while others feel they're crawling through the material.

NETWORK NEWS

One of Harper's first tasks at Peterson & Blyth was to sort out the studio's network. The first consultant had linked the machines using LocalTalk®, definitely the slow boat to China. (For more on networks and network terminology, *see* Chapter Twelve: Networking).

"LocalTalk would have been fine if we were doing word processing, but I knew it was going to become a nightmare as soon as everyone was proficient with the machines," Harper said. "LocalTalk just doesn't move data fast enough for you to deal effectively with color files and scanned images."

A Macintosh SE/30 was set up as the network server. Harper put an EtherTalk® board in each computer, then linked them with a Farallon star controller.

Having a high-speed network allows Harper to organize the fonts logically on the server, and helps prevent font conflicts when files are moved from one machine to another. It also gives him, as the network's manager, a bit of control. That makes it easier to keep the studio's massive font library up to date and ensure that everyone is using the same version of the various programs.

"The idea of this network is to keep from restricting the designers in any way, so we have about 400 typefaces," Harper noted. "When you have that many fonts, keeping them on a big hard drive on the server is the only way to make it work." To that end, the server is equipped with a Northern Telecom 700 mb drive with a 2 gigabyte tape backup.

"We really ask a lot of our network, because the fonts are stored on the server instead of on each machine," Harper pointed out. "When a designer prints, Type Manager® has to come out of the system folder on their workstation, go to the font library on the server, get the printer font information, then take it back to the workstation, which routes it to the printer. That has to happen times twelve, the number of workstations on the network."

The EtherTalk boards cost the studio around $500 each and the star controller cost around $2,000. In addition, new cables had to be dropped into the offices. Each EtherTalk channel runs over a single pair of wires, but there weren't enough pairs in the walls to accommodate all of the workstations.

BACKING UP ISN'T HARD TO DO

This arrangement is ideally suited to keeping everyone's work safe, as well. The backup software does an auto-backup each day.

Each designer has a folder on their desktop called "Active." At the end of the day, the server goes out across the network and looks onto each hard drive. It then copies the contents of each "Active" folder onto the tape. The tape goes out of the building every night, just in case, say, a meteorite falls on the studio.

THE MISSING LINK

Peterson & Blyth started in digital production with the Context pre-press system, then abandoned that for a non-production Macintosh network. That path may now have come full circle; Harper has begun transferring Macintosh files to a Context for film output.

Peterson & Blyth can now offer the convenience of electronic mechanicals combined with the color quality of a high-end pre-press system.

"Other than the usual font conflicts you get when moving between systems, it's actually worked pretty well," Harper said.

"At present, we haven't used any color scans done in-house for finished work," Harper pointed out. "We don't have a Nikon slide scanner, for example, because we don't really need one. We have La Cie flatbed color scanner that can give us for-position color images. We then print those to our QMS color laser for a quick comp. We hope to push encapsulated PostScript files from PhotoShop through the Context, though we haven't done it yet. The advantage to the client is that we won't lose any quality by printing paper mechanicals and then shooting negatives; everything stays digital and the composite color film is actually first-generation material."

While desktop graphics computers continue to become easier to use, Harper has no fear that his role as a technologist will become obsolete: "We're in for a real turning point in 1991," he predicted, citing the release of PhotoShop, Illustrator 3, and Quark 3.0. These programs, he said, bring the promise of color production straight from the desktop, but at the price of increased complexity. That's probably as good a piece of job security as Harper could ask for: Reducing complex software to the simplest and friendliest level possible is what he does best.

• • •

BRIAN BLACKWELDER

PostScript smarts—not just for designers anymore

Brian Blackwelder seems an unlikely immigrant to the art community. A business major in college, he has nonetheless developed a near-fanatic following among designers in the San Francisco Bay Area. His specialty isn't illustration, airbrush, or marker comps. It's PostScript. What Blackwelder does with PostScript is to make it behave when it's sent to an output device, whether a color printer or an imagesetter. For designers with deadlines to make, he offers both a friendly face and a steady hand on the keyboard. Designers will literally change prep houses when Blackwelder changes shops. Like a lawyer with a loyal clientele, that kind of devotion is money in the bank.

Blackwelder doesn't consider himself a four-star designer, but his business instincts set off alarm bells when he realized he had achieved such status. He formed a joint venture with a trade typographer and is now converting his PostScript smarts into profits. His long suit is providing a buffer between designers and the sometimes grim realities of pre-press work. For smaller studios without an in-house technologist, and for larger studios who don't have an interest in getting bogged down in the pre-press process, Blackwelder provides advice, expertise, and, when needed, solace.

"We see a lot of designers just muddling through with the Macintosh," he said. "They're good designers, but they haven't taken the time to learn this new production tool. As fast as things are changing, they should think about continuing education classes. Doctors and lawyers have to take CE classes to keep up with new developments; why not designers?

"Even though our clients tend to be large design firms, it's surprising to me how little some of their young designers just out of college know about preparing artwork for a printer. Many art schools don't seem to be teaching production skills. Unfortunately, they aren't learning computer techniques, either."

Especially for young designers, Blackwelder believes the payoff of computer literacy will be job security: "In San Francisco, it's common for artists to be asked *which* software they know, rather than whether or not they know how to use a graphics computer. That's taken for granted. If they have no computer experience at all, they don't get the job. There will always be places where things are done traditionally, but especially for younger designers, anywhere they would *want* to work will require computer skills."

REVERSING FIELD

The job market for designers with computer skills obviously includes those who do what Blackwelder does. For most, the path to that kind of job has been one of happenstance. Most of the designer/technologists we've talked to simply gravitated to the field because they liked it and could do it. While that may change over time, the dearth of computer-trained designers has created openings for some, like Blackwelder, without formal art training to move into the graphic arts. Blackwelder isn't sure that's been terribly helpful.

"Initially, it's given rise to a lot of second-rate design that has given anything done on a computer a bad name," he pointed out, "things that aren't exam-

---

SNAPSHOT: RAPID LASERGRAPHICS

Rapid Lasergraphics
1045 Sansome Street, #122, San Francisco, CA 94105
TEL: (415) 291-8166
FAX: (415) 291-8566

Equipment: (8) Macintosh II-family workstations with 24-bit RasterOps displays, 4 mb RAM; (1) QMS thermal color printer; (1) LaserWriter; (1) Canon CLC-500 color copier; (1) Barneyscan 4520 multi-format scanner; removable storage; (1) Linotronic L-330 imagesetter; (1) wide-measure L-530 imagesetter.

Staff: (7) computer production artists, (1) production manager.

Typical clients: Design studios, corporate art departments, and publishers with a need for four-color comps and composite separation film at competitive prices.

---

ples of good writing, good art direction, or good production. In some cases, people who specialize in marketing have had to design ads because their boss put a computer on their desk and gave them Quark."

That might seem to dilute the value of computer design skills: If any marketing assistant with a Mac can be an in-house agency, why pay for design smarts?

"Designers should know what good work looks like," he said. "They can take some of this poorly produced stuff and some examples of good design and show them to a marketing manager. Even someone who isn't trained as a designer can tell the difference, if it's pointed out to them. They may not know that the type is poorly kerned, but if they're shown a comparative piece with good typography, that's the first step in educating them that they need professional help.

"We like telling people they need professional help," Blackwelder chortled.

A MAN'S GOT TO KNOW HIS LIMITATIONS

Giving a full range of professional help, especially to designers, is what Rapid Lasergraphics is all about. The company scans transparencies using its Barneyscan 4520, which accepts both 35mm and four-by-five inch transparencies. With its workstations, software, and wide-measure L-530 imagesetter, Rapid is able to offer virtual one-stop shopping for commercial-grade electronic pre-press.

But Blackwelder also knows his limitations and feels that designers, too, have to redefine their own boundaries in this new digital age.

"We're primarily an output bureau," he explained. "An art director came in recently and asked if she could watch while we retouched a transparency she had. We're not set up to to do that kind of work. There is a studio down the street that does (*see* Chapter Three, Imaging & Pre-Press, page 22). We tried to send her there, but she resisted because she said she had a Mac and PhotoShop in her own studio. That's

true, she did. But what she didn't have was the experience to efficiently produce a color image suitable for printing.

"This art director ended up taking the job to a Scitex house. Ultimately, she paid a lot more for that than she would have going to an imaging specialist with a serious desktop system. There's a perception among some clients that desktop means cheap. They have a hard time justifying a large bill from a retoucher who uses desktop gear when they have some of the same kinds of gear in their own studio. My advice is that, if you have some real work with a real deadline, then go to someone who can help you get some real work done."

One area of difficulty Blackwelder sees is designers who work without considering how an effect they've created in the computer will be produced. A company's logo with a smooth gradated tint behind it might look great on letterhead, but if it has to be extruded into plastic—say on the front panel of the company's products—they may be limited to a fifteen line-per-inch screen.

"It's up to the designer to know how to build a file so that it can be reproduced effectively," he said. "Some of the larger studios in San Francisco have had unpleasant experiences with visuals presented to a client that couldn't be reproduced cost-effectively. They've even given out written orders prohibiting designers from repeating the mistakes by building a file incorrectly.

"It's too easy to knock out some dazzling comps with the computer without thinking about how you're actually going to produce the piece. Then, when you show the comps to a pre-press shop they say, 'I hope you have a lot money because we have people who're going to be here all weekend stripping that up.'

"If your studio intends to do color production work you need someone who knows both computers and traditional production to keep you out of trouble."

· · ·
FINANCIAL CONTROL

Studio management—by the numbers

The Greeks called mathematics the mother of all arts. For them, music was an audible expression of addition (going up the scale), subtraction (down the scale), and multiplication (harmonies). And so it is today. Jazz musicians talk off-handedly about "fractional" chords —fifths, sevenths, ninths, fourteenths—and rhythms, as in three-four or five-eight. Designers are no exception. The visual proportions of the Golden Section are still taught in art schools, and anyone without an intuitive grasp of measurement shouldn't be allowed within shouting distance of an art table. So why is math so inimical to many artists? Math-phobia, widespread enough in the general population, is positively epidemic among visual artists.

That could be because math just doesn't seem to allow much room for creativity. Until you reach the theoretical stratosphere inhabited by geniuses from Cal Tech or MIT, there is only one right answer to each problem. There's a limit to how much of oneself can be expressed through long division.

That's a fine attitude as long as you're within the walls of your studio doing battle with the demons of inspiration and deadline. However, the world at large has interests other than whether you recycle a piece of an old design or invent something entirely new. They want to know if you have enough money left at the end of the month to pay the rent on your studio. The art store will be sure to bill you for the supplies, and the type house, while sympathetic, does expect to receive its checks on time.

Lacking a wealthy patron or the wherewithal to hire a full-time number-cruncher, where's a designer to turn? To the glowing video eye on your desk, of course. Too many studios have forged ahead, blazing trails toward the glowing horizon of electronic design but have left their bookkeeping behind in the Dark Ages. Mesmerized by the thrill of electronically cutting and pasting, they forget that the first—and still most prevalent—use of computers is to crunch numbers.

Keeping detailed records of expenses and income won't necessarily net you more income than relying on luck and good guessing, but that's the way to bet. Fortunately, using the computer, there are ways to do that without delving too deeply into the black art of accounting. It does take willpower to think out your rates, overhead, and income structure; what kinds of information you need to have in the computer; and how you will use that information to improve your bottom line.

KEEPING SCORE

All of the larger studios we spoke with have sophisticated accounting programs running on their in-house computers. Too many of the smaller ones keep bills in an envelope and time charges on slips of paper. This suggests that one difference between big, successful studios and small, growing ones is that the successful ones know where their money is coming from and where it's going.

Of course, larger studios can afford to hire an experienced accountant to keep track of the money. In this chapter, we'll concentrate on solutions for smaller studios. The problem has been that most accounting programs are written for accountants, not designers. And accountants are almost as good as lawyers at creating verbal smokescreens designed to keep the uninitiated off of their turf. Just getting to the point where you understand what you're supposed to key into the computer may require reading several thick manuals; never mind finding the time to input, manipulate, print out, and analyze the numbers.

"I have a lot of friends who bill jobs by the feel—they feel the client will pay $3,000 or whatever for this job, so that's what they make out the bill for," observed Steven Hawk of Hawk Designworks in suburban Chicago. "Generally, they make a living, but they're never sure how well they're doing until the end of the month comes."

SNAPSHOT: COUNTING THE HOURS

Not using your computer for
accounting can be costly...

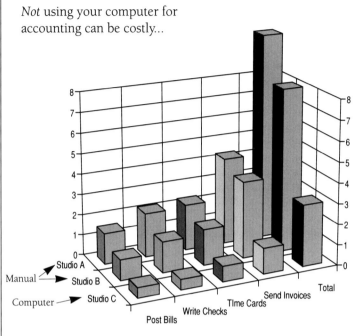

...taking nearly a full day out of your schedule each month.

Hawk said his business is simple enough to be run without a computer, though he wouldn't think of doing it that way. On the other hand, as a solo practitioner, he hardly has the time or patience to deal with the many bells and whistles of a full-featured accounting program.

Good news: There is something in between. A lot of things, in fact, ranging from homegrown tracking systems built around easy-to-use database software to solid off-the-shelf time-and-billing packages such as TimeSlips® and DesignSoft®.

LESS IS MORE

One reason that few designers, even those who have converted to electronic design, use their computers to handle finance is that good accounting software was late in coming to the Macintosh. The Mac is perfectly capable of handling numbers quickly and efficiently, but until 1990, software developers concentrated on graphics applications. As a result, few studios run finance and accounting on their Macs; many more

have mixed systems, with Macs in the studio and a couple of IBM-compatible machines in the front office to take care of the paperwork. Though it's simple enough to network IBMs and Macs together, none of the studios we spoke with—large or small—had found it necessary to do so. The designs are done on Macs and the numbers are crunched on IBMs.

Having dual systems is no longer necessary. With the release of programs such as atOnce!® and Managing Your Money®, the Mac now has the ability to keep books for companies with multiple operating divisions, hundreds of employees, and revenues into the low millions. Using Oracle® or a database such as 4-D® or Omnis®, it's possible to construct a finance and accounting program of almost any size. With years of data already on file on IBMs, it's unlikely that large studios will switch to Mac-based accounting systems anytime soon. If you have a Mac and haven't already committed your finances to disk, however, you have the opportunity to consolidate all of your data on one system. As you'll see, that can be a big advantage.

When it comes to accounting software, bigger isn't always better. Bigger can mean more complexity, more data to enter, more reports to pull. The majority of design businesses are small with simple structures. Until recently, IBM computers have had an advantage over the Mac, offering a wide variety of small-scale accounting and control programs. That's changed. There are now good, small-scale options for Mac studios as well. Steven Hawk has used DesignSoft, a time-and-billing program from Highgate, Cross & Cathey paired with OneWrite®, a check-register based accounting program on his IBM-compatible machines for five years. DesignSoft is now available for the Macintosh and the latest version even has an accounts payable/accounts receivable module that makes it a true accounting system. Our first accounting system was a very simple one we built using Reflex® database software by Borland.

KNOW THYSELF

Another thing the Greeks were big on was self-knowledge. If you own a design studio, the things you need to know about yourself are: How much it will cost to design and produce each job; how much time and money were spent on each job; who owes you money; and who you owe money to. It's also nice to be able to project your cash flow a month or two down the road, have the system show you all the outstanding invoices and when they were due, give you a reading of how much you'll owe in expenses for the next several months, and show how you're doing profit-wise for the year to date and the year ahead.

Oh yes, and taxes. Getting firm documentation on expenses (by category), income, and losses will make April 15 far less taxing. You can even do your own tax returns if you have the patience, but good record keeping makes it simple to hand over your year-end summaries to an accountant and have them fill out the forms: No rifling through presstype boxes full of receipts the night before. All of this is possible without abandoning art to become a full-time bookkeeper. It's a matter of making the commitment to knowing instead of guessing; reducing your business to a system; and getting a mental grip on what the studio does, how much of it, and how profitably. It's a lot less effort than it sounds, and after all, the computer is going to do all the arithmetic. All you have to do is to enter the data faithfully once a week or so.

BREAKING THE CODE

Whether you decide to use a simple accounting package, a complex one, or to roll your own, it helps to know a few accounting terms. We've yet to find a basic accounting book that was truly basic enough. Anything after the first chapter gives us the willies. To save you the trouble, here's a capsule of the most important terms:

Account: A series of related transactions, such as invoices, bills to be paid, equipment that is being depreciated, or the amount of equity each stockholder has in a corporation. Accounts keep track of things both individually—each invoice or bill is listed—and by category. That way you know at any time how much you've spent on typesetting for a particular job or for all jobs in the last week, month, or year.

Accounts receivable: This is what people owe you; invoices that you have sent but haven't yet collected.

Accounts payable: This what you owe other people. These are the bills from the typesetter, art store, free-lancers, and so on that haven't yet been paid.

Ledger: A listing in which each transaction that is made in an account—adding an unpaid bill or logging in a check—is *posted*. Posting an account simply means writing down the transactions for that account in the ledger.

Account code: A series of letters and/or numbers that identify, in shorthand, a specific account. Most accountants like to use four-digit numeric codes to identify accounts. Don't ask why, just use four digits; it's practical and your accountant will feel comfortable with it. For example, our code for shipping charges is 2000. Every time we ship something, the expense is listed under account code 2000. Actually, 2000 is just a summary of all shipping expenses incurred during the year. It's broken down further as follows: 2001 is for money paid to the U.S. Postal Service; 2002 is Federal Express; 2003 is United Parcel Service; 2004 is air express charges from other carriers; 2005 is messenger services. To make things simple, shipping is the only code that starts with 2000; the next account, promotional expenses, is 3000. Each invoice we receive or expenditure that is made is entered into our database and coded with the correct number. We can then ask the computer to print a list of all expenses coded 2000 through 2005. That list is our shipping expense for the year. Each individual entry is also coded with the client's name and a job code; so we can quickly retrieve all shipping charges related to a single client or a single job. Likewise, we can quickly retrieve a list of all expenses made on behalf of a client or for a particular job.

Chart of accounts: A listing of the account codes for a business showing the number of each account and its name. You'll need to assign an account code to every category of expense or income that you intend to track. It's simple enough to do yourself, but if you use an outside accountant to look over your books or do your taxes, it doesn't hurt to ask for their help.

P&L: The accounts receivable and accounts payable are the things you'll be most concerned with on a day-to-day basis. At some point, when you want to borrow money or file your taxes, you'll also need a profit and loss statement. Using the information contained in the various accounts, this short statement summarizes the financial condition of a business at any given time. It's a snapshot of the business' money matters. It lists all assets (equipment you own and money people owe you) and liabilities (money you owe other people, balances on loans) along with expenses and income. The infamous "bottom line" originally referred to the bottom line of a P&L statement, which shows net profit or loss.

HISTORY DOES REPEAT ITSELF

Chart of accounts? P&L? Ledgers? Sounds like a lot of work, right? For a small studio, one to three people, it shouldn't take more than an hour or two a week to actually keypunch the information you need. Aside from saving you the agony of plowing through a grocery bag full of receipts with a hand calculator each spring, keeping all that data will make you a much more accurate estimator. You'll become more profitable not only by seeing where you're overspending your budgets (express services or rush charges at the typesetter), but also by bidding jobs at their real costs. Steven Hawk said he now has more than three hundred completed jobs in his database and can estimate new jobs within 10 percent every time. It allows you to see which clients give you consistently profitable business and which ones take back your profits by asking for extra services or extended hand-holding.

Your initial foray into accounting needn't be overly complex. Start by capturing only the information that's most critical, see how you use it, then move on from there. A plan for building a basic estimating and tracking system is contained in the first case study. All you need are a spreadsheet program (such as Excel or Lotus 1-2-3) and a database, such as Reflex or Personal Filer®.

Building a basic accounting system and keeping up with the data entry can be frustrating, but it's far less frustrating than bidding a project by intuition and knowing that, if you're wrong, you will lose next year's vacation. Who knows? You may even find that with the computer doing the arithmetic, math can be something akin to fun.

BLOUNT & WALKER

KISS accounting

One of the bedrock truisms of business is the venerable KISS principle: Keep It Simple, Stupid. Not wanting to waste scarce brain cells on things like accounts payable, we developed two simple tools to help us run our studio. The first is a tracking system that tells us who we have to pay, when, and why. That takes care of the past. The second is an automated estimator that tells us what it's likely to cost to do a job based on what past jobs cost, how much we pay for office rent, what kind of salary we'd like to draw, and so on. The all-important notion of what the market will bear isn't discarded when pricing a job; instead we use the estimator to check what our real costs will be and measure them against what the client is likely to want to pay. We have turned down a number of jobs after discovering that projects were, on the whole, profitable but ate up too large a proportion of our time in too short a period or that the expenses were too high in relation to the overall fees—presenting an unacceptable business risk unless the expenses were prepaid.

In short, the estimator is a mathematical model of the project from which we can see at a glance what *kind* of a project it's going to be: heavy design, heavy production, lots of time talking to the printer or service bureau, how much time each week during its pro-

duction will be devoted to it alone, and so on. We can also see how many days it takes to produce how much profit, and measure that against how much we project to earn over the course of the year.

THE RATING GAME

Before you can set up an estimator and tracking system, you have to make some decisions. You need to know what you expect to make in the next year and how much your expenses will be.

Even though we bid most projects on a flat-fee basis, everything comes down to time. How many hours will we be able to sell and what rate will we have to charge to cover our overhead and pay ourselves a salary that matches our expectations? Setting rates is one of the trickiest parts of running a studio. On the one hand, pricing yourself in the upper tier of the market can make it more difficult to get jobs. But charging low fees is no guarantee you'll get work, either. As Samuel Johnson once said, "There is nothing a man can make that another can't make a little worse and sell a little more cheaply." No matter what you charge, you can bet that someone out there will do it for less.

We know you love your work, but you have to eat. And you deserve to be paid for what you do. To figure out what that ought to be, you need three numbers: your desired salary, your overhead—costs unrelated to any specific project, and the number of hours you can work in a year.

SIMPLE ADDITION

To figure your overhead, add up all the things you pay that you don't get to charge directly to clients. Our calculation includes employees' salaries, payroll taxes and benefits, office rent, utilities, telephone, equipment leases, office supplies (stationery, pencils), advertising budget, capital budget (for acquiring new equipment), loans payable, electronic communications services, health insurance, life insurance, equipment insurance,

---

SNAPSHOT: BLOUNT & WALKER

Blount & Walker Visual Communications, Inc.
136 Buckskin Way, Winter Springs, FL 32708
TEL: (407) 699-7444
FAX: (407) 699-1480

Equipment: (2) Macintosh II-family workstations with 24-bit displays, (1) Mac Plus, (1) LaserWriter Plus, (2) 100 mb hard drives, (1) 45 mb removable cartridge drive, (1) video scanner, (1) flatbed scanner.

Staff: (2) designers, (1) computer production artist.

Typical clients: Corporations and publishers with a need for concept-to-finished-product service for books, brochures, magazines, and other promotional or editorial materials.

liability insurance, automobile lease, non-project travel, subscriptions, professional development (memberships and books), and a small miscellaneous amount to cover unexpected expenses.

Now, how many hours can you work in a year? If you work five days a week, eight hours a day, you end up with 2,080 hours annually. But wait. Aren't you going to take Christmas, New Year's Day, and the Fourth of July off? And what about sick days? A vacation? Deducting two weeks for vacation, a week for holidays, and a week for sick days, you wind up with 240 workdays in a year, or 1,920 hours (if you work full eight hour days). Office workers are generally only at work seven hours a day (the extra hour goes to lunch and bathroom breaks). And anyone who's ever worked in an office knows that not everyone is working even when they're physically present. Deduct another hour a day for coffee breaks, walking to and from the copying machine, and time spent staring blankly off into space, and you come closer to the truth: maybe five and a half or six hours per day of work. Unless you're a very disciplined person or you work incredibly long hours, you probably don't do much better than that. Figure on 1,440 hours of worktime each year if you keep a normal schedule. Between holidays, the flu, and calls of nature, you've lost sixteen working weeks—four months!—before you've watched the last football game on New Year's Day. Now you know why you put in longer hours than your friends who work for someone else.

TEMPUS FUGIT

As the Roman proverb says, time flies. (Or, as Groucho Marx said, "Time flies like a bird; fruit flies like a banana.") Those of us who sell our time usually find that we have far less of it than we need. Of the 1,440 hours available each year, how many will you devote to administrative tasks like calling the copying machine repairman, fending off salesmen bent on giv-

ing you an unwanted quote for health insurance, invoicing clients, and writing checks? Is that a day (six hours) a week? If so, knock another 300 hours off your inventory. If you're the one selling the studio's work, how much time will you need to spend on marketing? Another day a week? Knock off another 300 hours. We're finally getting down to the nub of it. When all is said and done, even if you're creatively inspired every available moment, you aren't going to have more than 840 hours to actually do the work that brings in the money. That's about five out of the twelve months. (Of course, now you have to ask yourself why you're so tired when you're only working five months out of the year.)

How much do you think you're worth? How much do you aspire to make? Set a salary that will buy you the things you want. But wait, that's take-home pay. The tax man is going to want a bite. If you're self-employed and your gross salary will be less than $100,000 a year, your marginal tax rate (all taxes divided by total income) should be in the neighborhood of 20 percent. That is, while your actual Federal tax rate may be 28 percent (with another 15 percent bite for Social Security), after the standard deductions, equipment depreciation and the like, you will end up paying about a fifth of your income in taxes. To figure out what your gross pay must be to take home an amount that will make you happy, multiply your take-home by 1.25. (This number doesn't include state taxes, if any.)

Now, add in your overhead: Desired salary X 1.25 + Overhead = Minimum earnings required. To figure your hourly rate, divide the result by 840 (the number of hours available). *Voilà*. This is your minimum hourly rate. You may want to tack on 10 percent for profit and/or unexpected contingencies. To see how this works, let's take an example. If you want a take-home salary of $3,000 a month (with which to pay for rent, food, and that long-awaited trip to Italy), you'll need to earn $3,750 a month plus your overhead. If your overhead amounts to $1,000 a month, then you need to collect $4,750 a month on top of the expenses you'll bill to the client. On a yearly basis, that's $57,000, or $67.85 per billable hour:

$3,000	Take home pay
750	Taxes
1,000	Overhead
$4,750	Per month

	$4,750	
x	12	Months
	57,000	Annually

	$57,000	
÷	840	Available hours
	67.85	Per hour

In setting these rates, you're assuming that you'll be able to sell all 840 hours at the full rate and collect on the invoices. If your experience is that you have weeks when work is thin, or if you've had trouble collecting on invoices, deduct those non-billable hours from your inventory and add in an extra percentage to required revenues to cover the bad debts.

When calculating the hourly rate for a studio, don't forget to add in all the billable hours for your colleagues. They may produce more hours in a year, especially if they do less sales and administrative work. If you have people of different skill levels, you may want to have more than one rate and assign work on the basis of the skill required.

OUR ESTIMATION

Once you have your rate pegged, you can begin building an estimator. We use Microsoft Excel, a spreadsheet program. There's no one best way to build an estimator; because many of our projects are quite large

and complex, our estimator runs three full pages. Until you become familiar with how to "model" a project using a spreadsheet, stick to something simple like the example opposite.

Obviously, it would be easy enough to fill in the blanks by hand and add the amounts with a calculator. But the spreadsheet has two important advantages: speed and flexibility. The spreadsheet is a giant tic-tac-toe grid. Each "box"—the spot where the column headed "C' and the row marked "19" intersect for example—can contain either words, dates, or mathematical formulas. By pointing and clicking with the mouse, the spreadsheet can be directed to find any number of other boxes and then add, subtract, multiply, or divide their contents and display the results. In box C-19, we've entered the formula "=B19 * D10." This directs the program to find the amount in B19 (which is the estimated time needed to plan this job), and multiply it by the amount in D10 (which is the rate for planning, $70 per hour). The result, $140, is the amount that the client should be charged for this part of the process.

Again, you could do that with a hand calculator, but if the specifications change after you've done an estimate by hand, you have to redo the entire estimate. The spreadsheet will calculate amounts that depend on other amounts automatically. If one specification changes, the increases or decreases are reflected throughout the estimate.

For example, how much overhead should you charge against each job? If you take your yearly overhead and divide it by the number of days you expect to bill (the 840 hours divided by eight hours per day, or 105 days), that will give you the amount of overhead you have to charge off per day of studio time billed. The spreadsheet can make that calculation automatically by adding up the hours to be spent on the job, dividing by eight (to get the number of studio-days involved), then multiplying out the amount of

	A	B	C	D	E	F	G	H
1								
2	Client:		Bid Price:	$5,500		Net Revenue:	$3,917	
3	Job:		Cost:	$1,583		Studio Labor:	$2,251	
4	Date:		Materials:	$292		Overhead:	$715	
5	Date Due:		Outside Labor:	$1,084		Net Profit:	$952	
6			Mark-up:	15%		Profit %:	17%	
7	Specs:	8.5 x 11						
8	Product	Brochure				Studio Days:	6.22	
9	Pages	4						
10	No. of colors	2	Rate 1:	$70				
11	Photos	8	Rate 2:	$35				
12	Illustrations	2						
13								
14		Hours	Cost		Hours	Cost		Cost
15	Studio Labor	37.3	$2,251	Outside Labor:	16	$1,084	Materials:	$292
16								
17	Client Contact	7	490	Photography	12	804	Telephone	$0
18	Travel	2.5	87.5				Postage	$3
19	Planning	2	140				Express	$0
20							Messenger	$30
21	Design	3	210	Design			Research	$50
22	Scan	0.8	28	Scan			Stock Photos	$0
23	Illustrate	0	0	Illustrate	4	280	Photostats	$2
24	Layout	2	140	Layout			Art Materials	$33
25	Composite	6	210	Composite			Laser Suppls	$3
26							Travel/Enter	$0
27	Revisions	4	280	Revisions			Separations	$0
28	File Prep	2	140	File Prep			Svc Bureau	$96
29	Svc Bureau	1	35	Svc Bureau			Printing	$0
30							Binding	$0
31	Mark Color	1	70	Mark Color			Archive Disks	$2
32	Printer	2	140	Printer			Miscellaneous	$75
33	Color Proofs	4	280	Color Proofs				
34								

Each of these boxes contains a mathematical formula. The "Cost" box (D3) at the top of the sheet contains the formula "=(D4+D5) + ((D4+D5)*D6). This tells the program to add the boxes D4 and D5 (outside labor and materials costs) and then add a 15 percent markup ((D4+D5) * .15) and display the total. Changing the mark-up percentage or any of the labor costs will cause the program to automatically recalculate your total cost to perform the project, shown in box D3.

overhead. (If you have more than one person in the studio, remember to divide your overhead by the total billable hours available from all studio employees.)

Likewise, the cost of output from your service bureau will be determined by the number of pages required, whether you want film or paper output, and the number of colors for the job. The time needed to scan artwork will be determined by number of photos or illustrations in the job.

These items can be linked together in the estimator. In the example, the listing "Service Bureau" under the "Materials" category shows the expected bill for output. In this case, it's a two-color job that will be output in film. Each sheet of film costs $12. Four pages, two sheets per page adds up to eight pieces of film. Eight times twelve is ninety-six; the estimator shows the film cost at $96. If the specs were changed to four-color, the film cost would automatically double to account for two more sheets of film per page. Similarly, the time needed to design, layout, make composites, revise the files, prepare them for the service bureau, mark pages for the printer, and check color proofs are all linked to the job specifications. If the job specs are changed, the number of hours estimated for each of those functions will change, and the total costs shown at the top of the estimator will go up or down accordingly.

This allows you to play with the specs of a job to find a formula that fits both the client's budget and your financial needs. If the number of pages in a job is causing the price to balloon, you might suggest fewer pages with more colors or vice versa. Each change you make in the specs for the job will change the cost to the client and your profit. The spreadsheet allows you to quickly explore a number of alternatives until you find the *best* possible solution for you and the client.

Notice also that there are two rates listed in the center of the estimator. Each labor entry in the estimator is linked to one of these two rates, which can reflect different wage scales for employees or different charges for different types of work. You might charge clerical work at a lower rate, for example. You can enter as many different rates as needed to reflect the character of your studio and your colleagues.

The labor items work like this: Making a composite, for example, will take about one and a half hours per page. The box containing the time estimate for composites, B25, contains the formula "=B9 ∗ 1.5."

That tells the spreadsheet to multiply the number of pages for the job (which is listed in box B9) by the average time to complete one page of a composite.

You can quickly see where your labor will be spent. You may also find that some time-intensive tasks are better done by freelancers if they will work at a lower rate than you do. If you have a job with a great deal of scanning, for example, it may be worthwhile to pay someone on a piece-work basis to come in and scan the art. It relieves you of a burdensome task and lowers the cost to the client. Again, the spreadsheet can show you, by making one keyboard entry, the effect of such a change on the entire project

from the time needed for your studio to complete the job to your net profit.

DON'T KNOW MUCH ABOUT HISTORY

The key to making an estimator work is to know how long it actually takes you to do things. If you don't currently keep time slips, start doing so. You can use the spread sheet to keep your times, if you want, by simply setting up a grid in which each column represents time spent on a project, and the rows numbered one through thirty-one are the days of the month. Each day, enter the time you spend on the various projects. Remember to include a category for administrative time, new business, and any other non-project tasks you perform regularly. Leave a blank column to the right of each project column. In it, you can enter a note relating to the time spent on each project each day. By keeping these sheets, you can begin seeing how much time you need for different kinds of tasks. You'll be surprised how quickly patterns emerge.

We used to use spreadsheets to keep our times until StopWatch® came along. A desk accessory from DesignSoft, it puts a small stopwatch on your screen. The stopwatch allows you to track two tasks simultaneously and to write a short note about each one, such as "client contact, airline brochure." You just click once on the stopwatch to begin timing an event, then click once to stop. When you stop, the program writes the time and the note to a file. At the end of the week, you can go back and enter those times into a project log or a timesheet.

BOOKS REVIEW

With a firm handle on your past and your future, it's time to get a handle on the present: the state of your bank account. For smaller studios, it's not really necessary to have an elaborate, multi-user dedicated accounting package. It's probably more efficient to simply collect the data (who you owe and how much),

Payables — Vendor

Vendor	Charter Realty
Amount	550.75
EstimateAmnt	550.75
InvoiceNumber	0191
Date_of_Inv	1/1/91
Date_Due	1/1/91
Paid	YES
Date_Paid	1/1/91
Cash	
Check	YES
CheckNumber	1998
Project	OVERHEAD
Client	Studio
Bill_To_Client	
Paid_By_Clien	
Account_Code	1000
Notes	Office rent for January

Data Entry

All

Vendor	Amount	Account_Code
Federal Express	$25.25	4001
Charter Realty	$550.75	1000
Charter Realty	$550.75	1000
The Service Bureau	$128.15	2002
The Service Bureau	$627.67	2002
Photostat Plus	$57.56	2003
Photostats Plus	$76.87	2004
ColorWorks Press	$2527.65	2006
Federal Express	$15.25	4001
EGP Copier	$115.75	6003
EGP Copier	$115.75	6003

Total $4791.40

Report Display

The illustration at left, "payables," shows the data entry form and a sample record for a simple accounting system. Each bill received is entered into this form, enabling the database to keep track of all expenses. The expenses can be printed out in many different forms. The report above, "all," lists all expenses entered in the database.

write the checks as needed, then let a CPA handle your tax returns at the end of the year. They know the rules for depreciating equipment, how to balance partners' capital accounts, and a lot of other things that confuse the beejabbers out of the rest of us.

If you want a full-function accounting package, by all means, get one. But all you really need is a simple database and a series of reports.

A database is more or less an electronic filing cabinet. The difference between these files and paper files is that the computer can quickly scan all of the files in a database and extract pieces of the information, like invoices that are past due, bills that are thirty days old and haven't been paid, how much you spent on type in the last year, and so on. We use Reflex, a product of Borland International. It's not as powerful as Omnis or 4-D, two other popular Macintosh databases, but the program files are smaller and it's easier to learn. Reflex is also not as flexible as dBase®, the popular IBM-compatible database, but it's much simpler to use.

Each piece of information you enter into a database (say, a bill from the type house), is called a record. Each file (we have one called "payables," which contains all of the bills we've received since the beginning of the year) is a series of records. You enter the records one at a time, but after that, they can be sorted, printed out, and the numeric fields in them calculated in any combination you desire.

The illustrations above show a basic data entry window and report for a simple accounts payable ledger. Each item of information in the records (left) such as "vendor" and "date of invoice" is called a "field." While there are some restrictions on the number and size of fields you can have in a record, you're not likely to bump up against those limits in even the simplest of database programs. You determine what

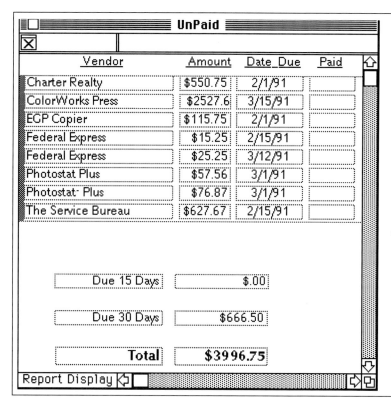

Vendor	Amount	Date Due	Paid
Charter Realty	$550.75	2/1/91	
ColorWorks Press	$2527.6	3/15/91	
EGP Copier	$115.75	2/1/91	
Federal Express	$15.25	2/15/91	
Federal Express	$25.25	3/12/91	
Photostat Plus	$57.56	3/1/91	
Photostat Plus	$76.87	3/1/91	
The Service Bureau	$627.67	2/15/91	

Due 15 Days	$.00
Due 30 Days	$666.50
Total	$3996.75

Report Display

This is a sample report from the database called "payables." It shows several kinds of key information. First, it lists all bills that have been entered into the database and have not yet been marked as paid. Using this list and the "date due" column, you can print out the information you need to write checks once a week or once a month. The totals show the value of all unpaid invoices and how soon the monies are due, allowing you to project how much cash will have to be laid out over the next month. The time periods are arbitrary; you can forecast expenses for the next quarter or next year, if you like. Notice that the "paid" field, which contains the date each invoice is paid, has been included. If you've made a mistake in your search and a bill which is actually paid is listed, this field would contain a date. You would then know that something was amiss. When building reports, include enough fields to verify whether the report is accurate.

information you want to collect, designing the entry form using point-and-click options and dialog boxes. Each time you're ready to enter new records (say when bills arrive), the database displays a blank entry form. You fill in the blanks for each new record. The records can be displayed, sorted, and printed easily.

INFORMATION PLEASE!

Using this simple set of records, you can quickly retrieve a great deal of useful information: bills due; bills that will become due in the next week, month, or quarter; how much expense was incurred for each project; estimated expenses for each project; and—whenever you're curious or tax time rolls around—you can see exactly how much you spent on any category of expense, from typesetting to supplies.

The database can be asked to find and display records based on a series of search commands, such as

"AND, OR, NOT, INCLUDES, STARTS WITH, EQUALS, GREATER THAN, LESS THAN, GREATER THAN OR EQUAL TO, and LESS THAN OR EQUAL TO." Using these commands you can direct the database to find all unpaid bills, as has been done in the illustration above. To create this report, we clicked on the menu item "new report," and, through a series of dialog boxes, told the database to display the vendor, amount, date due, and status of all records in the payables database for which paid does not equal yes. Unfortunately, most databases don't understand plain English. If you had to type out the query (a search command) instead of building it by picking menu items, it would read, "FIND (Vendor, Amount, Date Due, Paid) FROM Payables WHERE "Paid" DOES NOT EQUAL Yes." By stringing together these commands, you can perform complex searches, such as finding all unpaid bills for type and materials for a spe-

Salty_Tees_Catalog_Expns

Amount	Vendor	Estimate	Bill	Paid
$2527.65	ColorWorks Press	2505.5	YES	NO
$25.25	Federal Express	0	YES	NO
$76.87	Photostats Plus	75.15	YES	NO
$627.67	The Service Bureau	550.25	YES	NO

Estimated Expense $3130.90

Actual Expense $3257.44

Report Display

Account2000

Vendor	Amount	Date Paid	Account Code
ColorWorks Press	$2527.6		2006
Photostat Plus	$57.56		2003
Photostats Plus	$76.87		2004
The Service Bureau	$128.15	2/1/91	2002
The Service Bureau	$627.67		2002

Total $3417.90

Report Display

The expenses related to a specific project can be pulled into a report (left) and totaled very easily. In this case, dialog boxes and menu choices were used to create a report showing the amount owed, the vendor, the estimate, whether the expense should be billed to the client or not, and whether the client has paid for the expense or not. This is valuable as it lets you see how much expense you're floating for clients at any given time. If you wanted to know how much expense you hadn't collected on for all of your clients, another report could be built asking the database to list all payables for which "Bill To Client" equals "yes" and "Paid By Client" equals "no." You could also quickly find out how much you owe a specific vendor. To find out how much you owe a printer (such as ColorWorks Press, above) you would ask for a report listing all invoices for which "Paid" equals "no" and "Vendor" includes "ColorW...." The program would then display all open invoices due this vendor. The window "Account2000" is a list of all expenses charged against account code 2000, which in this case includes typesetting, photostats, color keys, and so on. This allows you to view your expenditures by category and to quickly total them in order to complete your tax returns.

cific client on a specific date, or adding all expenses paid to one vendor for a project or time period.

Two useful reports are illustrated above. The left-hand report, "Salty Tees Catalog Expns" shows all of the expenses incurred for a specific project along with a total of the estimate of expenses given to the client. The other, "Account2000," lists expenses incurred to date that fall under account code 2000, which in this case includes typesetting, stats, and other materials. At the end of the quarter or the year, it's simple to print out a list of expenses for each account code and hand them to an accountant to complete your taxes.

The account code in each record (*see illustration on page 143*) identifies the nature of the expense. If you wish, you can set up account codes to identify and collect information on the status of a partnership's capital accounts, equipment that is to be depreciated, and the other details needed to file returns for your studio.

A receivables database and employee database can be built on the same model as the "payables" example shown here. Fields from each database can be "linked" together so that an expense invoice entered in the "payables" file will automatically be posted to the client's invoice records, for example.

A database is a very flexible way to keep your records. You're in control through a series of simple menus and dialog boxes. Because the database handles words, numbers—even pictures—with equal facility, you can track literally anything.

Any accounting system is only as good as your record keeping. The computer can't tell you to pay a bill or invoice a client you haven't entered in the database. Using it, however, will give you not only a firm grip on your finances, but the confidence that comes from actually knowing the condition of your studio instead of merely guessing.

. . .

HAWK DESIGNWORKS

A five-year history helps Hawk hit estimates with exacting precision

Since the most common use for IBM-compatible computers in design studios is for number-crunching, it's fitting that the only all-IBM studio we interviewed should fall in the finance chapter. Steven Hawk of Hawk Designworks has been using IBM-compatible machines for production and financial reporting for more than five years.

A former art director for several Chicago-area ad agencies, when Hawk decided to fly solo, he knew he'd need a computer to keep his books and do correspondence. At that time, 1985, the Mac was a fledgling product with no link to high-resolution output devices such as Linotronic imagesetters. That severely limited its utility as a production device. Also, given the lack of good business software for the Mac at that time, Hawk settled on an IBM-compatible machine. Although he said he's since come to envy colleagues who've stocked their art tables with Macs, he did get a head start in one critical area of studio management: Computerized accounting.

"I had a manual system for tracking expenses I'd developed during my time at the agencies," Hawk recalled. "I found a time-and-billing package called DesignSoft. I called them and asked for a demonstration copy of their software. At that point, I hadn't

bought my computer yet so I took the demo to a computer dealer and ran them on one of his machines. The program worked like I thought it should; in fact, it worked a lot like my own manual system, so I bought it. Also, the developer, Highgate & Cathey, is in Wheaton, which is about fifteen minutes from my studio. I figured if I needed help, they were close enough for me to just drop by."

Over the years, Hawk has developed a close relationship with Highgate & Cathey, serving as a combination sounding board and beta test site; he even occasionally suggests new features or improvements.

Although not suggested by Hawk, one of the "improvements" made by the developer has been a Macintosh version and new modules that turn DesignSoft into a full-featured accounting program.

TIME TIME TIME

The basis of any studio accounting system is a way to track the time spent on each client's work. For Hawk, that's a daybook.

"I have a week-at-a-glance calendar. Every day I write down my hours for each job. Once a week, I take a few minutes to enter those hours into DesignSoft," Hawk explained. He writes down everything, from five-minute phone calls to sending sales letters to prospective clients. Combined with entries for outside expenses—photo shoots, type, stats, materials—the information provides a complete view of every job in progress.

"I can sit down for ten minutes and review the state of the business in as much detail as I need, current as of the last time I entered hours and expenses," he said. "All of the data is in one place. I rely on it so heavily, in fact, that I panicked last spring when my hard disk crashed. I realized then that I couldn't do a thing without it."

For each job, Hawk is able to review how many hours have been expended to date, how many hours

---

SNAPSHOT: HAWK DESIGNWORKS

Hawk Designworks.
352 N. Craig Place, Lombard, IL 60148
TEL: (708) 495-4778
FAX: (708) 620-7203

Equipment: AST 80386 IBM-compatible cpu with EGA color monitor and 8 mb RAM, MS-Windows 3 windowing software, PCPageMaker, (2) 40 mb hard disk drives, (1) 100 mb tape backup unit, (1) laser printer with PostScript interpreter, (1) modem.

Staff: (1) designer.

Typical clients: Manufacturers who need well-produced catalogs and collateral materials for industrial products.

```
┌─────────────────────────────────────────────────────────────┐
│                    ▓ AIR01 Summary ▓                        │
├─────────────────────────────────────────────────────────────┤
│  Client Code:   AIR                │ Fees to Date:    150.00 │
│  Job Number:    AIR01              │ Expen to Date:   182.40 │
│  Client Name:   AIRLINE            │ Total to Date    332.40 │
│  Description:   New AL8601 Series Aircraft Brochure          │
│  Project Code:  broc               │ Fee Balance:      50.00 │
│                                    │ Expen Balance:  5417.60 │
│  Contact:       Chuck              │ Total Balance:  5467.60 │
│  Client P.O.:   PO-198512          │                         │
│  Client Ref:    AL8601             │ Actual Expense:  152.00 │
│                                    │ Mark-Up:          30.40 │
│  Start Date:    01/19/88           │ Gross Profit:    180.40 │
│  Due Date:      02/05/90           │ Total Hours:       3.00 │
│                                    │ Invoiced:          0.00 │
│  Other:        [I        ]         │ Tax to Date:       0.00 │
│  Other:                            │ Surplus:        -120.00 │
│  Other:                            │                         │
│                                    │ Fee Ratio          0.45 │
│  Fee Quote:      200.00            │ Exp Ratio          0.55 │
│  Expense Quote: 5600.00            │                         │
│  Total Quote:   5800.00            │                         │
│                                                              │
└─────────────────────────────────────────────────────────────┘
```

The job summary window in DesignSoft shows at a glance the status of any active job. The fields marked "other" can be defined by the user for special coding or additional information. The quotes and expenses on the left side of the window show the estimate given to the client. The numbers on the right side reflect what has actually happened, in terms of time and expense.

have been invoiced, how much has been billed in fees and expenses, how much in fees and expenses remain based on the estimate given the client, the ratio of time spent to date to the estimated total time required, and the ratio of total expenses incurred to date to total expenses in the estimate.

These last two figures, Hawk said, are indispensable. They allow him to know immediately when a job is going over budget. If the project isn't to the type house yet and DesignSoft shows he's already spent nine-tenths of the time estimated for the job, something is wrong.

STELLAR COLLECTIONS

"Invoicing jobs is real direct using this program," Hawk said. "You just go to the menu and choose 'bill invoices.'"

DesignSoft gives a list of all jobs for which

amounts haven't been billed. Clicking on one of these and choosing "summary" from the menu will show a summary of all charges, billed and unbilled, for that project. To bill them, you simply tell the program to print an invoice.

DesignSoft even allows you to design your own invoice format, pulling information from any of the fields in its database and placing it in almost any position on the page. Unfortunately, at this time you have to design the form from a dialog box while watching a small thumbnail view of the form itself instead of moving actual type around with a mouse in a full-size view.

DesignSoft does share information fully between its various modules. Invoices sent to clients show up in the list of accounts receivable until you mark them as paid, for example.

When we spoke with Hawk, the accounting module was in beta test, and he hadn't yet switched his

The billing module of DesignSoft is "very direct" according to Steven Hawk. To invoice a job or portion of a job, you work from this simple dialog box. Clicking on one of the jobs listed in the scroll window at lower right queues it for invoicing. You choose the invoice format, the date, and how many days the client has to pay, and DesignSoft does the rest, printing a completed invoice.

receivables over from OneWrite, a small-business accounting package, to DesignSoft.

"When I started using DesignSoft, there was no way to track payables and write checks automatically," he explained. "Using OneWrite, I tell it which bills I want to pay and the checks are printed automatically on my laser printer. At the same time, the program automatically marks the bills as 'paid' in the database." DesignSoft's accounting modules now do the same thing, except you can't print checks.

MODERN HISTORY

The program really shines in estimating, Hawk said. All of the hours and materials costs for every job he's done since 1985 are archived and available on his hard disk. While it requires certain standard fields, such as "client" and "address" to be filled in for each record, DesignSoft also leaves room for several fields that can

be defined by the user. Hawk uses one of these fields to categorize each job according to its printing specifications. A four-page, four-color brochure for example is listed as 4P4C. A four-page, two-color job would be coded as 4P2C. Using the DesignSoft report feature, Hawk can have the program average the number of design hours spent and expenses required on every four-page, four-color job he's completed in the last five years and print a report.

"Each job is a little unique, but over time, you'd be surprised how similar they become in terms of the number of hours and amount of expenses required," he noted. "By averaging previous jobs and factoring in any unusual wrinkles, I'm usually able to come within 10 percent of the actual time and expense for any job I do on the first try. I don't have to call one client in twenty to tell them we're over budget. And I can do the estimates very quickly."

```
▦▦▦▦▦▦▦▦ Open Invoices ▦▦▦▦▦▦▦▦
Client:        AIRLINE                                    ⬆
               Invoice:    Sent:     Paid:    Age:   Amount:
               148         01/07/91  02/06/91  0     332.40
                                              Total:  332.40

          Current  30-44 Days  45-59 Days  60-89 Days  90 or more
          -------  ----------  ----------  ----------  ----------
          332.40     0.00        0.00        0.00        0.00
```

```
Invoice:  [            ]
Sent:     [01/07/91]   Due:   [01/07/91]
Code:     [      ]     Name:  [          ]
Amount:   [0.00]       Note:  [          ]
Job:      [          ]

                    [ Delete ] [ Cancel ] [  OK  ]

Paid Date: [01/07/91]                        [ Pay ]
```

```
▦▦▦▦ Paid Payables ▦▦▦▦
St Invoice:   Sent:     Paid:     Code Vendor:        Amount:   NoteAge:
0             01/07/91  01/07/91                        0.00    0
```

```
Invoice:  [148         ]
Sent:     [01/07/91]   Due:   [02/06/91]
Code:     [AIR]        Name:  [AIRLINE]
Amount:   [332.40]     Note:  [          ]
Job:      [AIR01]

                    [ Delete ] [ Cancel ] [  OK  ]

Paid Date: [01/07/91]                        [ Pay ]
```

```
▦▦▦▦ Open Invoices ▦▦▦▦
St Invoice:   Sent:     Due:      Code Client:        Amount:   NoteAge:
0  148        01/07/91  02/06/91  AIR  AIRLINE         332.40   0
```

Other views of the data collected by DesignSoft show open invoices (upper left), paid bills (upper right), and receivables (lower left). These windows are part of the new accounting module, which turns the program it into a fairly full-featured accounting system, though it still lacks a few niceties such as automatic check printing and multiple companies or divisions. None of these shortcomings, however, is likely to affect it's value for a studio with fewer than ten designers. Our experience with accounting software has been that the simpler it is, the easier it is to use and the more likely we are to update it faithfully.

To pin down those "wrinkles," Hawk keeps a hard copy printout of every detail of every job he's done. This gives him a quick way to find out, for example, how many hours he spent designing a tricky die-cut or doing overlays for a six-color job. When a new job comes up with similar specs, he has a record to fall back on in estimating the time needed.

This history has helped Hawk with other financial details, as well. "When I bought a house, the bank asked for detailed financials on the studio. Using the information I'd transferred from DesignSoft to OneWrite, I was able to print them a profit and loss statement in a matter of minutes," he chuckled. "My banker really appreciates getting information from me in a form he's familiar with. Now when I want to extend my credit line, all I do is mail him a current P&L and then call him on the telephone."

Hawk said DesignSoft and OneWrite together have kept him from getting bogged down in the details of keeping track of the business while giving him a concise and accurate overview. The confidence he gets from knowing precisely where he stands with each job and each client at any point in the year lets him keep his concentration on the work, where it belongs.

"Having all of the business records in the computer and being able to get answers quickly frees me from having to scramble for information. I never have to worry about whether I'm doing what I need to be doing," he explained. "For example, the first job I set up each year is called 'new business development.' I budget the amount of time I want to spend on getting new clients that year, then, at any time, I can quickly get a report on how I'm doing. If I budget two hundred hours and, by July, I only have twenty-five hours logged, I know I need to start hustling and send out some promos."

· · ·

CHAPTER 12

NETWORKING

The final frontier

In the IBM/DOS world, if you're not networked, you're not. (Or, as Descartes might have said, "I'm connected, therefore I am.") It seems ironic that a machine (the IBM and its clones) that is not supplied with a built-in network capability is more often networked than a machine (the Mac) that comes from the manufacturer ready to plug in to the rest of the world. To be clear about it, connecting a couple of Macs with a laser printer using AppleTalk cables does technically constitute a network. But it is *trés* crude. Humble though it may be, this crude arrangement seems to fill the networking needs of the vast majority of design studios.

While some of the studios we interviewed have upgraded from plain AppleTalk to Ethernet, few have installed the kind of integrated networking system—file server, electronic mail, high-speed file transfer, automated data back-up—that is common in even small DOS-based offices.

ALL YOU NEED IS....

There are some good reasons why networking hasn't become a hot topic for design shops. First, they tend to be relatively small, informal organizations with a minimum of hierarchy. There isn't a lot of passing of instructions and documents up and down a chain of command. Second, while more than one person may work on a project, the work tends to be sequential rather than simultaneous. Take a group of accounting workers, for example. Even a small business may have three or four people who spend each day entering financial transactions into a central database file. They have to be networked; if each of them works with a separate copy of the main file, at the end of the day they'd have four copies of the main file, each with different information in it. In a design studio, projects tend to be broken into discrete steps, with one person handling each step. There's little simultaneous work going on. The exception would be projects requiring a lot of production; a magazine or book, for example,

with a large number of pages. But here again, studios tend to assign a range of pages to each person. If editors will be working on the pages while they are being produced, a network could help by making the files available to all workers at all times, but the work itself can still be done sequentially rather than simultaneously. Last, but hardly least, the kind of communication that takes place between designers is a lot more effective when done face-to-face rather than through a disembodied electronic mail system. The things they need to communicate tend to be qualitative rather than quantitative; you can't get much of a feeling for voice inflection or body English from an E-mail message.

One other important reason for the slow growth of networks in studios is that the electronic files that get passed around are quite large: graphics files are commonly several megabytes rather than the few kilobytes sufficient for most word processing and spreadsheet files. Even relatively fast (and expensive) networks choke when they're asked to move color scans from workstation to workstation. Instead, most studios use "sneaker-net" and the pervasive 45 mb removable cartridge drives: when you need to move a big file, you write it onto a 45 mb cartridge and walk it over to your colleague. It's quick, it works, and it's pretty cheap, especially when compared to the cost of buying a dedicated file server and/or Ethernet boards for a large group of machines.

Cost-effective as it is, sneaker-net just isn't up to effectively sharing slow (and expensive) printers such as QMS color lasers and high-resolution imagesetters. When three designers are sitting at their keyboards waiting impatiently for jobs to print on a single QMS, you know you're in trouble. What to do? First ask what you *can* do.

DEFINITION PLEASE

Though it hardly seems possible, network terminology is even more obtuse than regular computer jargon.

SNAPSHOT: HOW MUCH IS YOUR TIME WORTH?

The time needed to download a 5 mb file from a network using popular hardware/software combinations is plotted against the cost, per machine, of the network equipment.

Cost per node for
5-node network

```
$1,500 ─
 1,400 ─      TOPS over
 1,300 ─    Ethernet with an
              SE/30 server
 1,200 ─
 1,100 ─      TOPS over
 1,000 ─    Ethernet with Mac
              Classic server
   900 ─
   800 ─                    TOPS over
   700 ─                 LocalTalk with
                           SE/30 server
   600 ─
   500 ─                    TOPS over
   400 ─                LocalTalk with Mac
                           Classic server
   300 ─
   200 ─                 TOPS over LocalTalk
   100 ─                    without server

            1    2    3    4    5    6    7    8    9    10

        Time to download 5 mb file, in minutes ──────────▶
```

Networks aren't cheap. We compared the price and performance of network hardware and software for a network of five Macs. LocalTalk is the system that is supplied with the Macintosh. Ethernet requires an add-in card for each machine. TOPS is one of the most popular network software packages. The costs shown do not include the cost of the basic workstations; they are the costs, per machine, for the network gear alone. The chart assumes you already have the wiring in place to carry the network signal.

TOPS alone costs about $180 per copy, and you'll need one copy for each machine on the network.

The SE/30, while a good file server, adds little to network speed; a Mac Classic will work almost as well for networks up to ten nodes. The SE/30 is about 20 percent faster than the Classic for other network functions, however, such as reading a large database from the file server. The best price/performance ratio is gotten by running TOPS over Ethernet using a Mac Classic as a server.

AppleTalk? Ethernet? TOPS®? Novell®? Star-LAN®? Token rings? We're going to stick to the basics here, but before you go talk to the local Apple dealer about a network or begin checking off blanks on a mail-order form, it may be helpful to have a few facts and figures in hand.

It may seem logical that, since all computers can talk to printers, they should be able to talk to each other. Not true. Especially not true of IBM machines and their clones. It's possible to connect the serial ports of two DOS computers and transfer information between them (this is called "hardwiring" or using a "null-modem" cable), but there's no facility for adding a printer to the circuit or including three, four, or twenty other computers to the party. They would all talk at once, perhaps even in different languages (depending on the software being used), resulting in a veritable digital Tower of Babel.

To network these computers, you have to add some hardware and software. First, a circuit board plugs into an expansion slot inside the computer. The board is a network card that provides a two-way port for incoming and outgoing data. A plug on the back allows connection of the necessary wires. Second, a control program that tells the computer how to act is needed so that all the machines on the network can understand each other. The software contains the network "protocol," which governs which machines can talk and when. Depending on the type of network, a file server—a machine dedicated to controlling traffic on the network—or a controller, a box that does more or less the same thing, may be needed.

Perhaps because it has always been second-banana saleswise, Apple was smart enough to know it ought to provide an easy way to connect the Macintosh to other Macintoshes and to other brands of computers. That was done by implementing a simple but functional networking capability right in the Mac's operating system. When you open the Chooser from the Apple menu and select a printer, you're using that network, which is called AppleTalk. On the Mac, the printer port is actually a network port. Just as the Mac can send data to a printer through AppleTalk, it can send data to other computers as well. It just doesn't do it very fast. AppleTalk defines the networking capabilities of the Macintosh. The network hardware supplied with the Mac is a chip (the "transmitter"), located on the main logic board, that transmits and receives data using a system called LocalTalk. LocalTalk can run over regular twisted-pair wiring (like a telephone wire), coaxial cable (such as the AppleTalk cables supplied with the LaserWriter), or fiber optic cables. (More on wires later.) Regardless of the kind of wiring involved, LocalTalk always operates at the same speed.

HOW FAST IS FAST?

Although data moves around inside your Mac at an almost blinding speed, once it's put into a LocalTalk mode to go to a printer or another computer, the data goes into slow motion. The electrons fairly crawl through the wires, moving at a rate of 230,400 bits per second. Granted, that's almost ten times as fast as a 2,400 bps modem. And it sounds pretty quick until you consider that a 25 mb color scan is going to take about half an hour to get from one place to another. Even a 2.5 mb page layout file will take three or four minutes to arrive. Multiply that by four or five designers on the network and you can see why sneaker-net is so popular.

There are alternatives. Ethernet is the most popular network upgrade for the Macintosh. It allows data to move between machines over the same kinds of wires used for LocalTalk at speeds up to 10 megabits (or roughly 1.25 megabytes) per second. Our hypothetical color scan can now migrate from desktop to desktop in under thirty seconds. Terrific, right?

Well, almost. First, the chip that enables the Mac to send data via LocalTalk doesn't speak Ethernet. Just like the poor benighted IBM user, you now need an Ethernet card for each machine (or "node") that will use Ethernet, costing from $400 to $600 per card at 1990 prices. It's possible to mix Ethernet and LocalTalk nodes on the same network. Theoretically, if you had heavy traffic between two machines, you could put them on an Ethernet branch and connect them to the main LocalTalk network using a hardware or software "bridge." In actuality, the electrical signals don't move through the wires any faster because of Ethernet; the Ethernet transmitter simply sends out the data in bigger batches (called "packets") and it sends them more frequently than a LocalTalk transmitter does. The result is greater throughput.

A middle ground is the FlashBox, a small hardware device placed between a Mac's printer port and the LocalTalk wiring. It moves data at 770,000 bits per second. If LocalTalk is just a bit too slow and Ethernet is too pricey, it's an alternative.

The second difficulty with Ethernet, one which it shares with LocalTalk, is that all of the machines are allowed to talk simultaneously. In essence, it's like a highway system with no traffic lights. If two machines dump data into the network at the same time, they collide somewhere on the network. This is called "contention." When that happens, both machines have to re-send the block of data (or packet) that was destroyed. This slows down all the data moving on the network. If you have enough machines talking often enough, the network just chokes and dies. There is a solution. It's called a "token ring" network. In this scheme, an electronic "token" is passed sequentially from machine to machine. Only the machine that possesses the token can speak. Think of it as a group of schoolchildren seated in a circle. The teacher hands one of them an eraser, which is passed around the circle. Only the child with the eraser can talk. The others have to listen. Presto. No more contention problems.

YOU GOT TO SERVE SOMEBODY

The basic AppleTalk instructions that come with your Mac allow it to be connected to other Macs, but it can't really talk to them directly. There's no facility for sending or receiving files to anything other than a printer. You do this by installing a software program such as AppleShare® or TOPS. AppleShare and TOPS allow you to send and receive files to other machines using LocalTalk or Ethernet transmitters.

TOPS can be run in either "distributed" or "dedicated" mode. In the distributed mode, every machine can be both a server (sending files to others) and a receiver (or "client" in network-speak). If you need to send a file to another machine, you can send it directly there without having to go through the server. The advantage is that you don't have an expensive machine just sitting there serving the other workstations.

If you run AppleShare, on the other hand, you have to dedicate a computer to AppleShare. It becomes what's known as a "dedicated" file server. From that machine, you have access to desk accessories, but that's about it; you can't use it for word processing, scanning, or layout. All network traffic takes place between a single node and the server. To get a file from one node to another, the sender has to copy the file to the server. Then the recipient has to copy the file from the server to his own disk.

Despite the cost, a dedicated file server *will* speed up the network. It can act as a sort of traffic cop and central filing cabinet simultaneously. Under TOPS, to allow other workstations access to your files, you use options in a dialog box to "publish" your files—making selected files, groups of folders, or the entire hard disk available to others. When using TOPS in distributed mode, your work will be interrupted every time someone on the network has to access one of your files. If those are big Illustrator or scan files and you're on LocalTalk, the inconvenience can be considerable. It's possible to make one of your working Macs a dedicated TOPS server by running TOPS in the background under Multifinder, but don't expect to spin any logos on it. The demands of traffic on the network will seriously degrade the server's performance.

The cost of a server can be ameliorated in several ways. First, it isn't necessary to have a state-of-the art Mac working as a server. If you have a Plus laying around unused, it will work just fine as a server, especially if you have less than five nodes. Somewhere above five nodes, the difference in network speed between a Plus and an SE/30 (a very popular network server) will be about 10 percent. Another common money-saving strategy is to run a Mac II-family machine "headless," without a keyboard and monitor. When you need to access the server directly, it can be done from another machine on the network using Timbuktu or a similar remote-access utility. Jasmine sells a machine configured for just this purpose.

It's also possible to use an MS-DOS machine as an AppleShare or TOPS server, though folks who tried this early on (in late 1989) reported a lot of network crashes and molasses-like performance. Things have gotten better since then, but if you want to mix Macs and IBM-compatibles on a network, you'll get the fastest and most consistent performance using a Mac as the server.

HOT WIRED

With "network" messages being carried by Nikes in the average design studio, it may seem a bit premature to talk about what kinds of network wiring you should install. Not really. The reason is as simple as dollars and cents. Whether you're installing network cables in a new office or working them into and around the fixtures in an existing office, labor—physically stringing the cables—is a large proportion, maybe two-thirds, of the overall cost. If you're going to drop cable in the walls, it makes sense to put in enough to take care of your needs for the next decade or so.

With the rapid changes occurring in the field, figuring out what those changes are likely to be is a tall order. But you can make some guesses. Two years ago we used to talk about "big" hard drives being 80 mb to 100 mb. If you're manipulating color in any significant way, you now need 100 mb of *free working space* on your disk, not to mention room for applications and storage. "Big" hard drives are now measured in gigabytes. The applications and files that are stored on these drives have grown, too. If you think your future includes graphics files ricocheting from workstation to workstation through your studio, think big: big hard drives, and big network capacity.

The current speed king is Ethernet, but in the past it has required bulky, expensive coaxial cables (like the ones used for cable television). This year, the hot ticket among network types is 10BASE-T, a protocol that puts Ethernet onto simple twisted-pair wiring, such as telephone wires (just like LocalTalk!). It appears likely that 10BASE-T is going to be the protocol of choice in the early 1990s, speeding communications while allowing the huge base of business users who already have twisted-pair wiring installed to avoid an expensive retrofit.

A little further down the road is fiber optic cable, strands of glass or plastic that carry flashes of light instead of electrical pulses. Yep, just like the stuff US Sprint says it sends your telephone calls over. We're talking huge bandwidths. Bandwidth is to a signal-carrying device (such as a wire) what the number of freight cars is to a freight train. The greater the bandwidth, the more information can be carried simultaneously. Haruo Yamaguchi, the chairman of NTT (the Japanese equivalent of AT&T), has predicted that, within this decade, fiber optic cables will be capable of carrying ten million telephone channels simultaneously on a single fiber. The barrier is not the capacity of the fiber optic material, but rather the transmitters and receivers attached to it. To date, that barrier stands at 44 megabits per second, or roughly 5.5 megabytes per second. That's the bandwidth for a T-3 data line operated by a telephone company.

The rate at which you can transfer data between microcomputers, however, is limited by the speed of their transceivers, which work much slower than these high-speed data lines. Ethernet (144 kbps) doesn't run any faster on fiber optic cable than it does on twisted-pair telephone wire. It may run better —fiber optics are less affected by electrical fields such those as generated by office equipment—but it won't run faster.

While network specialists don't advise most businesses to buy into fiber optic cable just yet, most businesses don't envision zipping 32-bit color images around from desk to desk in real time. If you intend to make large color graphics part of your work, Ethernet is the best solution available until faster transmitters become available. And, you can run it just as fast on twisted-pair wiring as you can on fiber optics. But if you're going to pay someone to bury cable in the walls, think seriously about putting in fiber optics so you won't have to do it all over again in a few years.

Having fiber optics links inside the studio may become a big advantage when ISDN links are more widely available. ISDN stands for Integrated Services Digital Network. It's a telephone network standard that allows all kinds of signals—computer data, voice, video—to move over the same wires in digital (rather than the standard analog) form. Because their signals don't have to be changed from digital to analog and back again using a modem, computers benefit tremendously from ISDN connections. The current ISDN standards allow a number of channels to run simultaneously on one set of cables, with each channel operating at 64,000 bps. (A T-3 data line, therefore, handles more than 650 channels—each carrying 64 kbps—simultaneously). These lines are already available for lease from telephone companies in parts of the United States and Europe. Being able to connect a high-speed internal network to a high-speed telephone network will make communicating with your service bureau a lot easier.

154 · · ·

Currently, Hornall Anderson Design Works has a 9,600 bps Shiva NetModem® connected to its internal network. This allows the studio to send files directly to its service bureau by modem, saving time and courier charges. However, with color graphics, that's not always the fastest route. Because of the long transmission times required, large color files are sent to the bureau on 45 mb removable cartridges.

"It's kind of hard to explain our procedure when Jack Anderson asks me how a taxi driving through heavy traffic can get our files to the bureau faster than electrons, which move at the speed of light," joked designer/network administrator Brian O'Neill. "But we can't have a machine tied up for an hour transmitting one page of a file."

The answer, of course, is that the taxi's total bandwidth is much greater than a telephone link. Operating at 9,600 bps, a modem can transmit roughly 45 mb in an hour. While the taxi may take an hour to go twenty miles to the service bureau, you could get several *hundred* 45 mb cartridges in the back seat with room left over for a case of CD-ROMs *and* a woman on her way to the airport.

ISDN may be the answer to today's frustrations. Of course, by the time it's widely available, there will likely be a whole new set of frustrations waiting to take their place. When it comes to testing human patience, computer technology abhors a vacuum.

THE NAME OF THE GAME

So far we've focused on stuff—hardware and software. But there's a whole other side to networking that has to be addressed. It's called humanware, the people who use the network.

The hip name for a bunch of people using networked workstations is a "workgroup." This has given rise to such non pareil expressions as "netware" (software designed to run on a network) and "groupware" (software designed so that more than one person can work effectively on the same data).

Some strides have been made in writing programs that allow notes to be made in the margins of documents (design notes on an electronic rough, for example) and so on.

Still missing, however, is the true workgroup page layout package that would "hot link" all the elements of a document so that it would be updated automatically as pieces were refined by various people. Ideally, if you have a group of people working on one project, the software should know from whence each piece of the project came. And the workers should be able to keep working on the pieces even after the final document has been assembled in rough form. Whenever the master file is opened, the software should automatically pick up the latest version of all elements of the file from machines throughout the network and display them without the operator having to manually update layouts, refill picture boxes with updated art, get the latest version of the text, and so on.

This kind of automation is already available for single users on a single machine in programs such as MicroSoft Works®. A word processing document that includes a graph can maintain a "hot link" to the spreadsheet used to create the graph. If the spreadsheet is changed, the graph is automatically updated in the word processing file.

Apple seems to be moving in this direction with rumored improvements to System 7.0 that will allow applications to control each other and maintain dynamic links. A Quark file will know where it got a piece of scanned art, for example, and will automatically find, retrieve, and display the latest version of the file each time the Quark document is opened. How this will work across a network is unknown, however.

Until that time comes, keeping versions straight and documents updated will be left to the fastest, most intelligent, and most flexible element of the computer network: the human operator.

WICKHAM ASSOCIATES

Got those old mixed-platform graphics network blues

Many studios would like to have Wickham Associates' problems—too much work going from too many machines to too many printer choices.

The bulk of the studio's work is print design —business presentations, annual reports, collateral material—as well as a lot of magazine work, both design and production. Color illustrations and photo-illustrations are part of the mix. Graphics computers give the studio the ability to offer more complex, high-intensity design without overstretching client budgets. They've also complicated daily operations.

Not all of the work is done on Macs; especially for magazine work, in which the page formats are often repetitive, it's more efficient for the designers to work on tissues, passing them to production artists for lay-out. Still, there are ten Macs, plus two Sun 386i SPARCstations, a laser printer, a high-resolution color scanner, and two Agfa imagesetters running every day.

WHO'S TALKING TO WHOM?

Though there is an Ethernet link between the SPARCstations and one Macintosh, so far, the studio has gotten by using AppleTalk, sending small files over the wires and moving big files around on 45 mb

removable cartridges. File interchanges between the Macintosh network and the SPARCstations is done by moving the file to be transferred to the 45 mb drive on the Macintosh that has Ethernet and then sending it to the Sun machines.

Networking the imagesetters has posed the biggest difficulties.

"We can run negative materials on these setters," said Tom Jones, the studio's creative director and de facto technology chief. That gives the studio a big time advantage when working on publications. "The problem is in sending something to one of the imagesetters and then waiting for the RIP to process it. People end up sitting around while the RIP chews on a file."

Hoping to solve the problem, Jones recently bought a dedicated 80286 IBM-compatible machine with a 200 mb hard drive and a software package called PServe® to help liberate the Macs from the lumbering imagesetters. The server acts as a central spooler and as a central repository for the studio's fonts.

"We had the fonts on each individual Mac, and it was killing our network," Jones explained. "Some of the magazines we do have a large number of fonts in them." Font calls, where the printer asks the machine that originated the document being printed to send it the printer font outlines, are the bane of slow networks, like AppleTalk. "PServe will also run on a Mac, but I didn't think it was worth the extra money; the 80286 machine cost us about $1,500. Also, I felt it would frustrate the designers if they saw a Mac sitting there with no one using it."

The studio brought another high volume node son line in spring of 1991: an Agfa PIX color imaging and pre-press station. Wickham has been a test site for Agfa's high-end imaging products.

The Agfa pre-press system runs on a Sun SPARCstation and gives the studio high-quality photographic scanning, retouching, and film output for process color separations.

SNAPSHOT: WICKHAM ASSOCIATES, INC.

Wickham Associates, Inc.
1211 Connecticut Ave, Washington, DC 20015
TEL: (202) 296-4860
FAX: (202) 331-1025

Equipment: (10) Macintosh workstations including Plus, SE, SE/30, and Macintosh II-family CPUs; (2) 386i Sun SPARCstations; (4) IBM-compatible CPUs for support services; (1) 80286-based file server; (1) 9000-series Agfa/Compugraphic imagesetter; (1) 400-series Agfa/Compugraphic imagesetter; (1) Agfa ACS-100 color scanner; 45 mb removable-cartridge drives.

Staff: (4) designers, (6) computer production artists, (3) support staff.

Typical clients: Corporate clients, and publishers with a need for four-color print materials.

"The color station is going to remain separate from the rest of the network, I think," Jones postulated. "Moving color photo files around the network is a bear, and something we don't really need to be doing."

WISH LIST

One does get the sense from Jones, as from most designers who've thought about it, that moving big color files around his workgroup in real time is something that he might *like* to do, if it were feasible.

Certainly, there are solutions around: Ethernet, 10BASE-T, fiber optic cabling. But Jones isn't quite ready to invest the studio's resources.

"Sometimes things sound wonderful in theory but they're dubious in application," he explained. "I've been bitten a couple of times and like to be sure of myself before committing. That's why we have the 45 mb cartridge dives; we're assured that everyone can remain productive. At this point, anything other than AppleTalk would be very expensive. Buying Ethernet cards for every machine on the network would speed things up tremendously. But I'm not sure I'd want to put out that kind of money to increase the throughput of a Plus. I'm not sure it makes sense financially."

HUMANWARE SOLUTIONS

Despite challenges on the technical front, Wickham has managed to evolve very effective procedures for tracking its work. This extends from the simplest details—such as naming conventions—to outputting the right version and archiving the files.

Naming conventions may seem mundane and DOS-like, but they really are a help. They simply spell out the way in which files should be named. In the bad old days, when DOS was the only choice, everyone was limited to file names that were no more than eight characters long. Some "shell" programs—which insulate users from having to deal directly with the operating system—allow longer filenames, but most

everyone has played along, trying to squeeze as much information as possible into those eight characters. This helped popularize file naming conventions. Someone would sit down and actually think up a logical way to name files so that everyone who knew the system would have a pretty good idea what was in a file just by looking at the name.

This greatly simplifies things when a worker is away from their desk and someone else needs to access a specific file. Naming parts of a job "Bob" or "Fred" isn't very helpful. A date, job code, client name, and version number are helpful. Think of yourself looking for the latest version of an illustration for, say, a Flying Carpet Airlines brochure. You go to a colleague's hard drive and begin scrolling through files: "Dingbat 1," "More of the same," "Not This Again," "For Al," "Take Five." Your only option is to open all the files. If, however, those files were named "1/21/91 FC Broch Ill.1," "1/23/91 FC Broch Ill.2," and "1/25/91 FC Broch Ill.3," it would be clear instantly which file you needed.

Backing up client work is another oft-neglected task. Wickham has a production group with a designated administrator who ensures it gets done.

"For our magazines, one designer is usually in charge, so they're responsible for keeping records of their work up to the time it goes to the production group," Jones explained. "After that, the administrator makes sure that, at the end of each day, all work in progress is backed up on 45 mb cartridges.

Wickham keeps client data on file for a year. After that, if the client still wants to keep it on file, the studio sells them the cartridge. So far, Jones said, the studio hasn't gone so far as to take the cartridges out of the office every night for safekeeping: "We haven't gotten that crazy about it. Of course, now that I've mentioned it, it will probably come back to haunt us."

Yep. And that, as you'll doubtless recognize, is all part of the fun of running a big-time computer graphics network.

APPENDIX

· · ·

Here are names and addresses for service bureaus, suppliers and software companies mentioned in this book:

ASSOCIATIONS

BMUG (Berkeley Macintosh Users Group), 1442 A Walnut St., #62, Berkeley, CA 94709 (415) 849-9114

Boston Computer Society, 48 Grove St., Somerville, MA 02144 (617) 625-7080

International Design By Electronics Association, c/o Frankfurt Gips Balkind, 244 E. 58th St., New York, NY 10022 (212) 421-5888

National Association of Desktop Publishers, P.O. Box 508, Kenmore Station, Boston, MA 02215 (617) 437-6472

SERVICE BUREAUS

Advanced Laser Graphics, 1850 K St., Metro Level NW, Washington, DC 20006 (202) 835-0100

Digital PrePress Inc., 1201 Folsom St., San Francisco, CA 94103 (415) 882-9961 Contact: Sanjay Sakhuja

Graphic Connexions, 10 Abeel Rd., Cranbury, NJ 08546 (609) 655-8970 Contact: Derek White

Photo Lab Inc., 1026 Redna Terr., Cincinnati, OH 45215 (800) 733-3124 Contact: David Rahe

Prototype Services, Inc., 1660 N. Besley Ct., Chicago, IL 60622 (312) 772-9200 Contact: Jim Bednar

Quad Text, W224 N3322 Duplaineville Rd., Pewaukee, WI 53072 (414) 246-9200 Contact: Alan Darling

Rapid Lasergraphics, 1045 Sansome St., # 122, San Francisco, CA 94105 (415) 291-8166 Contact: Brian Blackwelder

SprintOut, 50 Clifford St., Providence, RI 02903 (401) 421-2264 Contact: Jay Higgins

SUPPLIERS

Abaton Technology, 48431 Milmont Dr., Fremont, CA 94538 (800) 444-5321

Adobe Systems, P.O. Box 7900, Mountain View, CA 94309 (415) 961-4400

Agfa Corp., Agfa/Compugraphic Division, 200 Ballardvale St., Wilmington, MA 01887 (508) 658-5600

Aldus Corp., 411 First Avenue S., Seattle, WA 98104 (206) 622-5500

Asanté Technologies, 405 Tasman Drive, Sunnyvale, CA 94089 (800) 662-9686

Bitstream, Athenaeum House, 215 First St., Cambridge, MA 01242 (617) 497-6222

Borland International, 4585 Scotts Valley Dr., Scotts Valley, CA 95066 (800) 543-7543

Canon USA, Inc., One Canon Plaza, Lake Success, NY 11042 (516) 488-6700 Contact: Graphic Systems Division

Casady & Greene, P.O. Box 223779, Carmel, CA 93922 (408) 624-8716

Claris, 5201 Patrick Henry Dr., Santa Clara, CA 95052 (800) 729-2292

Data Translation, 100 Locke Dr., Marlboro, MA 01752 (508) 481-3700

Deneba (Canvas), 3305 N.W. 74th Ave., Miami, FL 33122 (305) 594-6965

DesignSoft, Highgate Cross & Cathey, 130 West Liberty Dr., Wheaton, IL 60187 (800) 426-0265

Digidesign, 1360 Willow Rd., Suite 101, Menlo Park, CA 94025 (415) 688-0600

DuPont Electronics, 515 Fishing Creek Rd., New Cumberland, PA 17070 (800) 237-2374

Eastman Kodak, 343 State St., Rochester, NY 14650 (800) 233-1650

Electronic Arts, 1820 Gateway Dr., San Mateo, CA 94404 (415) 571-7171

Farallon Computing, 2000 Powell St., Suite 600, Emeryville, CA 94608 (415) 596-9100

Hayes Microcomputer Producters, P.O. Box 105203, Atlanta, GA (800) 635-1225

Jasmine Technologies, 1225 Elko Dr., Sunnyvale, CA 94089 (800) 347-3228

La Cie, 19552 SW 90th Ct., Tualatin, OR 97062 (800) 999-0143

Letraset USA, 40 Eisenhower Drive, Paramus, NJ 07653 (201) 845-6100

Linotype, 425 Oser Ave., Hauppague, NY 11788 (516) 434-2000

MacroMind, 410 Townsend, #408, San Francisco, CA 94107 (415) 442-0200

Microsoft, One Microsoft Way, Redmond, WA 98052 (206) 882-8088

Microtek Lab Inc., 680 Knox St., Torrance, CA 90502 (213) 321-2121, Contact: Michelle Hammond

Nikon Inc., 1300 Walt Whitman Rd., Melville, NY 11747, (516) 547-4352 Contact: Doug Howe

Novell, 1157 San Antonio Rd., Mountain View, CA 94043 (415) 969-1999

Paracomp, 1725 Montgomery St., 2nd Floor, San Francisco, CA 94111 (415) 956-4091

Pixar, 1001 W. Cutting Blvd., Suite 200, Richmond, CA 94804 (415) 236-4000

QMS, P.O. Box 81250, Mobile, AL 36689 (800) 523-2696

Quark, 300 S. Jackson St., #100, Denver, CO 80209 (800) 356-9693

RasterOps, 2500 Walsh Ave., Santa Clara, CA 95051 (800) 468-7600

Sharp Electronics, Sharp Plaza, Mahwah, NJ 07430 (201) 529-8731

Shiva, One Cambridge Center, Cambridge, MA 02141 (800) 458-3550

Silicon Beach, 9770 Carroll Center Rd., San Diego, CA 92126 (619) 695-6956

Sitka (TOPS), 950 Marina Village Parkway, Alameda, CA 94501 (800) 445-8677

SuperMac Technology, 485 Potrero Ave., Sunnyvale, CA 94086 (800) 624-8999

Sony USA, 2256 S. Delaware St., Denver, CO 80223 (800) 222-7669

Strata, Inc., 2 West St. George Blvd., Ancestor Square, St. George, UT 84770 (801) 628-5218

The Voyager Company, 1351 Pacific Coast Highway, Santa Monica, CA 90401 (213) 451-1383

Time Arts Inc., 1425 Corporate Center Parkway, Santa Rosa, CA 95407 (707) 576-7722

Timeslips, 239 Western Ave., Essex, MA 01929 (800) 338-5314

Treacyfaces, Inc., 111 Sibley Ave., Ardmore, PA 19003 (215) 896-0860

Truevision, 7340 Shadeland Station, Indianapolis, IN 46256 (800) 858-8783

Verbum (magazine), P.O. Box 15439, San Diego, CA 92115

INDEX